A FRAMEWORK FOR TEACHING BASIC ECONOMIC CONCEPTS

with
SCOPE AND SEQUENCE GUIDELINES
K-12

Editors: Phillip Saunders • June Gilliard

OVER **45** YEARS
National Council on Economic Education
SINCE 1949

Economics America

National Council on
Economic Education

A partnership of education,
business, and labor

EDITORS

Phillip Saunders is professor of economics and director of the Center for Economic Education at Indiana University in Bloomington.

June V. Gilliard is the former director of curriculum for the National Council on Economic Education and president of JG Consultant Services.

ACKNOWLEDGMENTS

The following people were authors of the original *Framework:* Phillip Saunders, G. L. Bach, James D. Calderwood, W. Lee Hansen, and Herbert Stein. Authors of the original *Scope and Sequence* were: June V. Gilliard, Jean Caldwell, Bruce R. Dalgaard, Robert J. Highsmith, Robert Reinke, and Michael Watts.

ISBN 1-56183-487-4
5   4   3   2

Contents

Chapter VI. Guidelines, 5-8

Chapter VII. Guidelines, 9-12

Foreword

This publication is an updated and edited merger of two previous National Council on Economic Education documents: *A Framework for Teaching the Basic Concepts* and *Economics: What and When*. The combined publication is designed to aid those who construct curricula or who provide economics instruction in the nation's elementary and secondary schools. This new publication and much of the work of the National Council on Economic Education have their roots in the 1961 *Report of the National Task Force on Economic Education*. The task force *Report* was the first systematic effort by distinguished economists and teachers to give direction and shape to economic education in grades K-12. The *Report* pointed to the need for more and improved economic instruction in elementary and secondary schools, stressed the importance of taking a more systematic, reasoned approach to the study of economic problems, outlined what constitutes the economic understanding one needs for responsible citizenship, and offered a series of recommendations for putting the *Report's* conclusions into effect.

The first edition of the *Framework* was published in 1977 with a major revision in 1984. *Economics: What and When* was originally published in 1989. The change in the name of the Joint Council on Economic Education to the National Council on Economic Education and the launching of a broad based **Economics**America program in 1993 led to a slightly updated reprinting of the *Framework*, but subsequent experience indicated a need to update and combine the *Framework* and *Economics: What and When* into a single integrated document. The chapters that follow first present a brief explanation of the economic concepts selected for emphasis and then make recommendations for sequencing these concepts within the curriculum. These recommendations reflect the commitment of the National Council on Economic Education and its network of affiliated state councils and centers to developmental education—that is, the systematic introduction and development of concepts in simple forms at the lower grade levels, followed by increasingly sophisticated expositions of the same concepts as students mature intellectually.

Support for this project was provided by the National Science Foundation.

Joan Sullivan Baranski
Publisher

Chapter 1

Introduction

This publication is an updated and edited merger of two previous National Council on Economic Education documents: *A Framework for Teaching the Basic Concepts* and *Economics: What and When.* The combined publication is designed to aid those who construct curricula or who provide economics instruction in the nation's elementary and secondary schools. Our purpose is to present a concisely stated set of basic concepts for teaching economics below the college level and a set of guidelines to enable schools to develop a systematic program of studies from kindergarten through twelfth grade. Today's students will face an increasing variety of important economic decisions in their personal lives and as citizens in a democratic society. Our goal is to enable students, by the time they graduate from high school, to understand enough economics to make reasoned judgements about both personal economic questions and broader questions of economic policy in a complex and changing world. Specifically, we want to assist schools in developing economic education programs in which students can acquire the knowledge and skills they need to become:

- Productive members of the work force
- Responsible citizens
- Knowledgeable consumers
- Prudent savers and investors
- Effective participants in a global economy
- Competent decision makers throughout their lives

A Brief History

This publication and much of the work of the National Council on Economic Education have their roots in the 1961 *Report of the National Task Force on Economic Education.* The task force *Report* was the first systematic effort by distinguished economists and teachers to give direction and shape to economic education in grades K-12. The *Report* pointed to the need for more and improved economic instruction in elementary and secondary schools, stressed the importance of taking a more systematic, reasoned approach to the study of economic problems, outlined what constitutes the economic understanding one needs for responsible citizenship, and offered a series of recommendations for putting the report's conclusions into effect.

Publication of the Task Force Report led the then Joint Council on Economic Education (JCEE) to develop a process called the Developmental Economic Education Program (DEEP). The process is still in action and much expanded. Through it, the affiliated state council and center staff members, using the **Economics**America programs, work with school systems to develop curricula for teaching basic economic understandings every high school graduate should have, determine how this understanding can best be taught to students, and designate at which grade levels specific economic materials can best be used in the curriculum.

During the 1960s, economic educators and teachers—in and out of DEEP—continued to develop curriculum materials in economics and to upgrade the capability of teachers to work with them. By the mid-1970s, persistent efforts of economists, specialists in economic education (economic educators), and teachers to clarify which economic concepts should be taught and how to teach them most effectively, produced a consensus about what could be accomplished and how it should be done. This consensus embraces the following points:

1. An understanding of basic economic concepts is more important than a heavy dose of factual knowledge.
2. Instructional efforts should concentrate on aiding students to achieve a fundamental understanding of a limited set of economic concepts and their interrelationships.
3. Students should be given a conceptual framework to help them organize their understanding of economics, and they should be exposed to a manner of thinking that emphasized systematic, objective analysis.
4. The real personal and social advantages of economic understanding become apparent as individuals achieve competence in applying their knowledge to a wide range of economic issues they confront.

This consensus led to the publication of the first edition of the *Framework* in 1977 and a major revision in 1984. *Economics: What and When* was originally published in 1989. The change in the name of the Joint Council on Economic Education to the National Council on Economic Education and the launching of a broad-based **Economics**America program in 1993 led to a slightly updated reprinting of the *Framework*, but subsequent experience indicated a need to update and combine the *Framework* and *Economics: What and When* into a single integrated document. In the chapters that follow, we first present a brief explanation of the economic concepts selected for emphasis and then make recommendations for sequencing these concepts within the curriculum. These recommendations reflect the commitment of the National Council on Economic Education and its network of affiliated state councils and centers to developmental education—that is, the systematic introduction and development of concepts in simple forms at the lower grade levels, followed by increasingly sophisticated expositions of the same concepts as students mature intellectually. Recommendations pertaining to the grade placement of economic concepts and content are based on a consideration of

- the structure of the discipline of economics;
- cognitive development theories and research;
- current school practices.

A Reasoned Approach

If the goal of economic education is to prepare students for effective decision making and responsible citizenship, individuals must be helped to become intelligent readers of newspaper and news magazines, perceptive watchers of television, careful listeners to radio, and critical observers of the political process. Effective economic decisions are more likely to be reached if, in addition to a mastery of basic concepts and an appreciation of how the concepts relate to each other, individuals have an understanding of the broad social goals that are most often used to evaluate economic performance and policies and an orderly, reasoned approach to economic decision making. We have included a statement on broad social goals in our explanation of basic economic concepts in Chapter II. Here we want to emphasize that the most important step toward understanding in economics—as in other branches of knowledge—is the replacement of emotional judgment by objective, reasoned analysis.

An orderly and reasoned approach to economic decision making involves the following steps:

1. *State the problem or issue.* What are the important facts? What questions of choice are raised? What is the heart of the problem?
2. *Determine the personal or broad social goals to be attained.* Assign some rough order or priority for achieving them.
3. *Consider the principal alternative means of achieving these goals.* Take account of the limits on available resources and other restrictions that limit freedom of action.
4. *Select the economic concepts needed to understand the problem and use them to appraise the merits of each alternative.* Which concepts are most useful in grasping the essentials of the problem? Which concepts are most useful in exploring the effect of each alternative solution?
5. *Decide which alternative best leads to the attainment of the most goals or the most important goals.* Which of the solutions seem to be most feasible? Which are the most desirable? What are the trade-offs among the different goals, that is, how much of one goal must be given up in order to achieve more of another?

The importance of an orderly and reasoned approach lies in the systematic set of procedures it establishes to help students organize their thinking about issues—whether in economics or in other subjects. Although the approach may not come naturally to everyone, its application comes more easily, even routinely, the more it is practiced.

In advancing the reasoned approach as an essential element for solving economic problems effectively, teachers should observe several cautions: (1) The phrase "alternative means of achieving these goals" in the third step does not mean students should consider only new and different ways of doing things. Frequently, no change, or merely a slight modification in the existing ways of doing things, is superior to some untried proposal. (2) Not every question or new problem in economics should be forced into the pattern proposed above; only those steps applicable to a particular problem—or to the state of the student's knowledge and ability—should be carried out. (3) The application of an orderly and reasoned approach should not be permitted to become a mechanical exercise.

Decision-making Grids

In many cases, use of a formal decision-making grid facilitates the application of the reasoned approach. Exhibit 1 illustrates such a grid: the alternative courses of action (including doing nothing) are listed in the first column on the left, and the goals or criteria for evaluating alternatives are listed across the top row. The intersection of the rows and columns in a decision-making grid creates boxes or "cells" which match up

EXHIBIT 1
Sample Decision-making Grid for Systematic Evaluation of Each Alternative with Respect to Each Goal or Criterion

ALTERNATIVES	GOALS OR CRITERIA			
	Goal or Criterion 1	Goal or Criterion 2	Goal or Criterion 3	Goal or Criterion 4
Alternative 1				
Alternative 2				
Alternative 3				
Alternative 4				

each goal or criterion with each alternative. The evaluation marks placed in the cells of the grid can take various forms. For example, each alternative can receive a numerical ranking denoting its ability to achieve a goal or criterion (say, 1, 2, 3,4, 5, with 1 denoting lowest ability). The numbers are written in the appropriate cells; adding the rankings row by row provides a rough measure of the overall desirability or feasibility of each alternative. Another technique is to place a plus sign (+) in a cell to show that an alternative helps meet a goal or criterion, a minus sign (-) to show that an alternative hinders meeting a goal or criterion, a zero (0) to show that an alternative neither helps nor hinders, and a question mark (?) if the effect of the alternative is unclear. In cases where alternatives differ in the extent of their ability to help or hinder, multiple pluses and minuses can be used.

A decision-making problem usually arises because a "do nothing-leave things as they are" policy has not led to the achievement of some desired goal. Before choosing the "best" alternative policy, it is often wise to check to make sure all the major alternatives and all of the relevant goals have been considered. Advocates of particular alternatives often point out only the advantages of their proposals. They frequently fail to mention other attractive alternatives or the possible costs of their own proposals. Use of a formal decision-making grid forces the weighing of alternatives against all the relevant goals and criteria. Although the systematic evaluation of alternatives does not assure unanimity when goals conflict or evaluations differ, the technique usually helps to clarify where the differences lie and the relative costs of alternatives in terms of different criteria.

Not all decisions involve public policy issues; many decisions involve personal consumption or production situations. Use of the reasoned approach and a decision-making grid is appropriate in any situation—public or personal—requiring choice-making. For example, in the lesson "Malcolm Decides," which appears in *Trade-offs* (an audiovisual series the National Council on Economic Education participated in producing), a boy who delivers newspapers receives a $15 gift certificate. He can use the certificate to purchase one of several recreational items: a model airplane, a bow and arrow set, a hockey game, a soccer ball, or a portable radio. Since each of these alternatives meets the criterion of costing no more than $15, additional criteria are necessary: Will the item break easily or will it last? (durability). Will his parents approve of the item and let him use it? (parental consent). Are there any additional costs? (no other costs)—e.g., batteries must be purchased for the hockey game but are included in the price of the radio. Will he be able to use it any time he chooses? (full-time use).

Exhibit 2 shows the completed decision-making grid that Malcolm uses to choose the radio. By placing a plus sign (+) in each cell where an alternative meets a criterion and a minus sign (-) in each cell where an alternative does not meet a criterion, Malcolm sees

EXHIBIT 2
Sample Decision-making Grid for Using a $15 Gift Certificate

ALTERNATIVES	CRITERIA				
	Costs $15 or Less	Durability	Parental Consent	No Other Costs	Full-Time Use
Airplane	+	−	+	+	+
Bow & arrow	+	+	−	+	−
Hockey game	+	+	+	−	+
Soccer ball	+	+	+	+	−
Radio	+	+	+	+	+

that only the radio has five pluses. Each of the other alternatives has at least one minus.

Often one alternative does not meet all the goals or criteria, or all criteria are not regarded as equally important. But, even in such instances, a decision-making grid can help clarify the issues and make the decision a more reasoned one.

By highlighting the costs, benefits, and trade-offs of different choices, the "economic way of thinking," equips students to evaluate alternative courses of action or inaction in personal economic situations involving their roles as consumers, workers, savers, and investors, and in social situations involving their roles as citizens and voters.

Some Barriers to Effective Teaching of Economics

We are aware of the hurdles that must be overcome in raising the level of economic understanding—particularly through improved education in the schools. The time allocated to economics in school curricula has always been limited. It may become even more limited as efforts are made to improve the teaching and learning of traditional basic subjects. As a result, a large part of the knowledge economics students acquire comes and will come through the introduction of economics into other subjects such as social studies, history, home economics, and business education. Sometimes misunderstood controversies within the economics profession itself may also pose a barrier to increased emphasis on economic education in the schools.

Recent experiences make it clear that economists do not have all the answers to the many and varied economic issues and questions we confront both personally and as members of the larger socioeconomic system. For example, although economists believe they now have the knowledge and tools to prevent massive economic depressions such as the one that occurred in the 1930's, much remains to be learned about how to moderate inflation while still holding down the rate of unemployment.

There are several reasons that answers are not always found to the problems economists confront. Economic systems are complex and defy easy comprehension. Moreover, our ability to know exactly how effectively the economy and its components function is often limited by the difficulty of obtaining accurate and timely measurements of economic activity. Finally, a variety of unanticipated political and social events affects economic activity and makes accurate predictions of the results of economic decisions very difficult. Unlike the situation in the physical sciences, carefully controlled experiments are difficult to undertake in economics.

Even if our understanding of the economy and economic decision making were further improved, not all disagreements among economists would vanish. Certainly, some disagreements will be resolved as our understanding increases. Many will persist, however, because of differences in judgments about the actual or predicted effects of specific decisions; still others will endure because individual economists, like most other individuals, hold differing sets of values.

A failure to distinguish between analysis (what *is* happening) and value judgments (what *ought to be* happening) is the source of much confusion in many discussions of economic problems. The first approach, often called "positive economics," aims to understand how the economy works. In principle, disputes about positive economic statements can be settled by facts and evidence. The second approach, often called "normative economics," deals with the way the economy, or some part of it, ought to work. Normative economic statements cannot be called true or false by referring to objective data. Positive economics can do much to help resolve economic disputes. However, many questions that concern economic policy involve reconciling differences in normative values. On normative questions, people must apply their capacity to make reasoned decisions based on their own values.

We believe that the study of economics can give students a richer understanding of the world in which they live, study, and work, as well as provide them with a conceptual framework for making some of the more significant decisions of their lives.

Chapter II

Basic Concepts

Economic concepts are the bases of economic understanding and reasoned decision making. Economic concepts provide the analytical tools needed to understand and make reasoned decisions about economic issues—both personal and social. These concepts also constitute the basic vocabulary of economics.

The list of concepts discussed below focuses on what many economists consider the most basic among the many concepts in economics. Some measurement concepts and methods that are helpful in understanding and explaining economic performance are included, and the broad social goals most often used to evaluate economic performance and policies are also discussed. Exhibit 3, on the next page, lists the basic concepts discussed in this chapter. (The table of contents, at the beginning of this book, also lists subsidiary concepts that fall under the basic concepts.)

Although the concepts listed in Exhibit 3 are basic to the attainment of economic understanding, they cannot all be treated alike in the K-12 curriculum. Some are easier to learn because teachers can find a greater variety of concrete examples to illustrate them. Some concepts are easier to understand because their definitions do not require prior knowledge of other concepts. Consequently, these concepts can be taught—with varying complexity as well as late in the K-12 curriculum. The reverse is also true. Certain concepts are complex and therefore cannot be taught with all their ramifications at all grade levels. Some are relatively difficult to learn because they involve grasping relationships among several concepts. For these reasons, statements on the suitable grade placement of the concepts are included in chapters V, VI, and VII.

Fundamental Economic Concepts

The basic economic problem confronting individuals, groups of individuals, and entire societies is that productive resources are limited relative to people's wants. Thus arises the basic condition of scarcity. Scarcity requires people to make choices about how to utilize available resources most effectively in order to satisfy their wants. Since most major economic problems arise from the fact of scarcity, an understanding of this concept is the starting point for an understanding of economics.

1. SCARCITY AND CHOICE

Scarcity is the condition that results from the imbalance between relatively unlimited wants and the relatively limited resources available for satisfying those wants. No society has ever had enough resources to produce the full amount and variety of goods and services its members wanted.

EXHIBIT 3
Basic Concepts

FUNDAMENTAL ECONOMIC CONCEPTS

1. Scarcity and Choice
2. Opportunity Cost and Trade-offs
3. Productivity
4. Economic Systems
5. Economic Institutions and Incentives
6. Exchange, Money, and Interdependence

MICROECONOMIC CONCEPTS

7. Markets and Prices
8. Supply and Demand
9. Competition and Market Structure
10. Income Distribution
11. Market Failures
12. The Role of Government

MACROECONOMIC CONCEPTS

13. Gross Domestic Product
14. Aggregate Supply and Aggregate Demand
15. Unemployment
16. Inflation and Deflation
17. Monetary Policy
18. Fiscal Policy

INTERNATIONAL ECONOMIC CONCEPTS

19. Absolute and Comparative Advantage and Barriers to Trade
20. Exchange Rates and the Balance of Payments
21. International Aspects of Growth and Stability

MEASUREMENT CONCEPTS AND METHODS

Tables
Charts and Graphs
Ratios and Percentages
Percentage Changes
Index Numbers
Real vs. Nominal Values
Averages and Distributions Around the Average

BROAD SOCIAL GOALS

Economic Freedom
Economic Efficiency
Economic Equity
Economic Security
Full Employment
Price Stability
Economic Growth
Other Goals

Scarcity necessitates **choice**. If we can't have everything we would like, we must choose those things we want most. Thus, both individuals and societies must continuously make choices about how to use the scarce resources available to them. The concept of scarcity can be understood more clearly by examining the sub-concepts of economic wants and productive resources.

Economic Wants

In modern societies, people have a wide variety of wants. Some, such as those for love and affection, cannot easily be classified as economic in nature. Others, such as food, clothing, shelter, medical care, entertainment, and even leisure time, are wants with major economic implications. Some wants are individual, whereas others, such as a family's desire for a home or a club's desire for a recreation center, are group wants. Many wants—such as the foregoing—are private, but others are public—such as society's wants for highways, education, and national defense.

For simplicity, we can say that **economic wants** are those that can be satisfied by the consumption of a good or service. We include the desire for leisure as an economic want because consumers need leisure time in which to enjoy the consumption of certain goods and services. **Goods** are physically tangible things such as food, shoes, cars, and houses. **Services** are physically intangible things such as medical care, haircuts, and education. One fact that emerges clearly in the study of economics: people's wants for goods and services exceed society's capacity to produce them.

Productive Resources

Productive resources (sometimes called factors of production) consist of what is required to produce the goods and services that people want. There are three basic categories of productive resources.

Human Resources—The health, strength, education, and skills of people. The number of people available for work and the hours they work constitute only one dimension of human resources. Another dimension is the level of ability of people and their motivation. The quality of human resources reflects past efforts to improve skills, knowledge, and motivation through education and training. The ability of some people to organize economic activity by taking the risks associated with starting a new business or introducing a new good or service into the market-place in hopes of earning a profit is given a special name, "entrepreneurship," which comes from a French word meaning "to undertake."

Natural Resources—The gifts of nature that are used to produce goods and services. They include land, timber, fish, oil and mineral deposits, the fertility of the soil, climatic conditions suitable for growing crops, and so on. Some of these resources are used up in the process of production, others renew themselves, while still others can be renewed through the conscious efforts of people.

Capital Goods—The buildings, equipment, machinery, ports, roads, dams, and other manufactured and constructed things needed to produce or provide access to other goods and to supply services. The variety of capital goods available and the ways they are used reflect the state of technology, which in turn reflects existing scientific and technical knowledge and the resources devoted to developing such knowledge.

A list of 17 content statements dealing with the concept of *Scarcity and Choice*, suggested for inclusion in the K-12 curriculum, is in Chapter IV. Chapters V, VI, and VII indicate placement in grades K-4, 5-8, and 9-12.

2. OPPORTUNITY COST AND TRADE-OFFS

Opportunity cost is the forgone benefit of the next best alternative when scarce resources are used for one purpose rather than another. If we use some of our limited resources for one purpose, we must give up the opportunity to use these resources for other purposes. Thus, the term "opportunity cost" refers to the most desirable of the alternatives not chosen. If, for example, a piece of land could be used for an office building, a sports stadium, a department store, or a parking garage, the opportunity cost of using the land for a department store is the loss of only the most desirable of the forgone alternatives. It is either the loss of the office building or of the sports stadium or of the parking garage—not all three; which of these is the most desirable can be determined only by more careful investigation. If a young college graduate chooses to become an accountant rather than a lawyer or an architect or an engineer, opportunity cost refers only to the loss of the most important of the forgone alternatives.

Trade-offs involve accepting or choosing less of one thing to get more of something else. Individuals who choose one good or service instead of another, or more of one thing and less of another, are making a trade-off. Society also makes trade-offs, e.g., between its need for more energy and its desire to preserve the environment. Evaluating trade-offs, when done carefully and systematically, involves comparing the costs and benefits of each of the available alternatives. Trade-offs made by society also require determining how the costs and benefits of decisions affect different groups within the economy, e.g., the rich vis-à-vis the poor, city residents vis-à-vis rural residents, etc.

Most choices and trade-offs are not all-or-nothing propositions; instead, they typically involve small changes *at the margin*—a little more of this for a little less of that. Decisions about small changes at the margin are made more often than decisions about big changes, and the former are usually easier to assess than the latter. Consumers continuously practice **marginalism** as they consider whether to buy one unit more or one unit less of a good or service in an effort to obtain the mix of goods and services that will provide them with the greatest satisfaction for their available buying power. Similarly, producers must decide whether to produce one unit less of output or to hire or lay off an additional worker in order to make the best use of their resources.

A list of five content statements dealing with the concept of *Opportunity Cost and Trade-offs*, suggested for inclusion in the K-12 curriculum, is in Chapter IV. Chapters V, VI, and VII indicate placement in grades K-4, 5-8, and 9-12.

3. PRODUCTIVITY

Productivity is the amount of output (goods and services) produced per unit of input (productive resources) used. An increase in productivity means producing more goods and services with the same amount of resources, producing the same amount of goods and services with fewer resources, or a combination of these two possibilities. A dramatic example of increased productivity occurred in U.S. agriculture in the half century between 1939 and 1980, when output doubled while the number of persons working directly in agriculture dropped from 12 million to 3 million.

While productivity is often measured or referred to only in terms of the productivity of labor, a proper view of the sources of productivity incorporates the effects of all inputs to production. The three principal means of increasing productivity are: (1) specialization and the division of labor; (2) investment in capital goods; and (3) investment in human capital. All three of these means often involve a process of technological change that leads to more efficient production techniques and the creation of more goods and services. Sometimes productivity can be increased by other means, such as reorganizing the work process or relocating the production site.

Increases in productivity help reduce scarcity, but do not eliminate it entirely. Moreover, productivity increases themselves entail opportunity costs since the resources used to enhance productivity in one endeavor cannot be employed in another. Thus, there are both costs and benefits when productivity is increased.

Specialization and the Division of Labor

Specialization occurs when an economic unit produces a narrower range of goods and services than it consumes. Specialization can be practiced by individuals, business firms, cities, regions, or countries. Regions of countries, for example, normally specialize in the production of those goods and services they are best fitted to produce, given their particular endowment of productive resources. They then sell most of what they produce to people living elsewhere, and buy whatever else they need from other regions. What they buy may include the raw materials needed to produce the goods and services in which they specialize. Specialization is the basis of trade and exchange among individuals, businesses, cities, regions, and countries. Within the United States, for example, consumers in its various regions buy and use products originating in other regions—Idaho potatoes, Florida orange juice, Iowa corn, California vegetables. Hartford insurance, etc.,—plus products originating abroad such as coffee, bananas, tea, clothing, and cameras. Industries do the same for the raw materials, components, and certain finished products they need.

The concept of **division of labor** is closely related to specialization, but usually refers to the process whereby workers perform only a single or a very few steps of a major production task, as when working on an assembly line. As applied to labor, the concept of specialization usually refers to a person's occupation and the special training it requires, e.g., carpenter, electrician, computer programmer, mathematics teacher, landscape architect, eye surgeon.

On the one hand, specialization in all of its forms and the division of labor usually increase productivity. On the other hand, they also reduce self-sufficiency and increase economic interdependence, thereby creating a greater need for the exchange of goods and services. The concepts of interdependence and exchange are discussed in more detail later.

Investment in capital goods

Investment in capital goods occurs when savings are used to increase the economy's productive capacity by financing the construction of new factories, machines, means of communication, and the like. **Saving** occurs when individuals, businesses, and the economy as a whole do not consume all of current income (or output). From an individual standpoint, saving represents income not spent. Much unspent income may be placed in financial institutions such as banks and saving and loan associations, which in turn make loans to those who wish to buy capital goods or other resources. Individuals may also place their savings more directly, by purchasing newly issued shares of corporate stock, bonds, and similar financial instruments or by buying instruments already issued from others, who may use the funds they receive to buy new issues. Individuals may also contribute to pension funds or purchase mutual funds and the like. Such funds also typically buy financial instruments.

To a large extent, the process of saving and investment represents a diversion of productive resources from the output of goods and services for current consumption to the creation of up-to-date, technologically advanced capital goods that can expand production and increase the productivity of human an natural resources. Workers using modern logging and transportation equipment, for example, can cut more trees and deliver more lumber than they can produce with hand saws and horse-drawn wagons. An office worker using a word processor can produce more letters than one using a typewriter, who in turn, can produce more than someone using a quill pen. A pilot can fly more passengers more miles faster with a jet plane than with a propeller-driven aircraft, and so on.

Capital goods often cost a great deal of money and last for a long time. Investing in capital goods, therefore, carries the opportunity cost of other uses to which the money could be put, and it also usually involves taking a risk. For example, if still newer technology emerges quickly or if market conditions change, a machine may become obsolete before it has generated enough income to pay back those who invested in it. Businesses that invest in capital goods, therefore, must anticipate that they will receive enough income to make it worth while to accept the possible risks.

Investment in Human Capital

Investment in human capital occurs when the health, education, and training of the population are increased through the efforts of individuals, businesses, or governments. Good health, education, and relevant training all contribute to workers' productivity. However, investment in human capital, like investment in capital goods, also involves an element of risk. Individuals who invest time or money in more education and training usually become more productive, get better jobs, increase their incomes, and find greater satisfaction in their work and leisure, but these benefits are not guaranteed. Investing in education and training also carries opportunity costs because it employs resources that could be put to other uses. The cost of a college education, for example, includes not only direct payments for tuition, books, and fees, but is also the loss of the output and income that could have become available if the student had been working full time instead of going to school.

Technological Change

Technological change can be defined as the incorporation into production of new knowledge and processes that result in (1) a different organization of the production process, (2) improvements or the introduction of innovation is capital goods, or (3) modifications of the goods and services currently being produced or the invention and introduction of new goods and services. The computer, the jet plane, and the fax machine are but a few relatively recent and striking examples of technological change. Such improvements depend heavily on basic and applied research, assessments of the probable success of a new technology, gifted and knowledgeable experimenters and inventors, and the amount of savings available to underwrite the costs of developing and introducing new technology.

Effects of Government

In addition to the effects on productivity of individual and business decisions about saving and investing, government actions and policies also play a role. Historically, governments have encouraged increases in productivity by actions such as providing transportation facilities, providing education, and underwriting or performing agricultural research. Governments also establish a framework of law and political stability that makes long-term private commitments feasible and profitable. However, governments can hamper productivity increases if their laws or regulations serve particular groups rather than the general welfare, if their tax policies adversely affect saving and investment, or if they enact price regulations and trade restrictions that prevent resources form moving to their most productive uses. The role of government in the U.S. economy is discussed in more detail later.

A list of 13 content statements dealing with the concept of *Productivity*, suggested for inclusion in the K-12 curriculum, is in Chapter IV. Chapters V, VI, and VII indicate placement in grades K-4, 5-8, and 9-12.

4. ECONOMIC SYSTEMS

People and societies organize economic life to deal with the basic problems raised by scarcity and opportunity costs through economic systems. An economic system can be described as the collection of institutions, laws, activities, controlling values, and human motivations that collectively provide a framework for economic decision-making.

In a world of scarcity and opportunity cost, all societies must make the basic economic decisions of what goods and services to produce, which ones to forgo or postpone, and when and how to transfer productive resources from one use to another. Decisions must also be made about how much effort to devote to increasing total output as well as how to divide the total output of society among its members—that is, how to distribute the total real income* an economic system generates. These decisions all hinge on how economic resources are allocated.

There are three basic approaches to economic decisions about resource allocation. One is based on **tradition**—that is, people generally repeat the decisions made at an earlier time or by an earlier generation. A second is based on **command**—that is, decisions are made largely by an authority such as a feudal lord or a government planning agency. Authority in a command economy can be exercised in a democratic fashion or it can be imposed from above by people whose power is not subject to the outcome of free elections. The third is based on **market prices**.**

---

* See section on Real vs. Nominal Values on p.43 for a fuller discussion of "real income."

** We chose not to use the terms such as "feudalism," "socialism," "communism," or capitalism" to describe economic systems because they mean different things to different people, and they carry emotional overtones in the minds of many.

A market economy is a system of decentralized decision making in which individuals and business firms, in their various capacities as consumers, producers, workers, savers, and investors, participate in the market through decisions that are reflected in the supply and demand for various good and services. The market "adds up" these millions of decisions about supply and demand and forges out of them an interrelated network of market prices that reflect the preferences of all the participants. Market prices—and the changes in them—act as signals to producers, telling them what buyers want. Market prices also act as rationing devices by allocating productive resources and finished goods and services among members of society according to what buyers are willing and able to pay.

No recent real-world economy is or has been a pure form of a traditional, a command, or a decentralized market economy. Every existing economy uses a different "mix" of allocating mechanisms to respond to the basic economic decisions, and each has somewhat different institutions, controlling values, and motivating forces at work that affect the operation of the economy. And many real-world economic systems have been undergoing fundamental changes during the last decades of the twentieth century. The element of tradition has been, for example, most evident in the rural areas of the developing countries of Asia and Africa, yet even those rural areas have participated in elements of a market economy and/or a command economy. The element of command had been most evident in the former Soviet Union until that country collapsed and was replaced by fifteen independent countries. China, which describes itself as a command economy, has many elements of traditional and market-price economies. Decentralized or market decision making has been most evident in the United States, Australia, Canada, and most countries of the European Community, but even among these countries considerable diversity continues to exist in the proportions of government planning and in the variety of economic institutions.

Understanding how economic decisions are made in a particular economy requires careful attention to questions such as the following:

- What is the actual "mix" of allocating mechanisms? That is, how many economic decisions are tradition oriented? How many are made by central command? How many are left to decentralized market forces?
- What are the most important economic institutions of the society and what role do they play in shaping economic decisions?
- What are the controlling values and motivating forces that condition economic behavior in the society?
- What, if any, significant changes appear to be taking place in the economic system?

Finally, it should be noted that people of all societies, regardless of the type of economic system, engage in certain basic economic activities. These include **producing, exchanging,** and **consuming** goods and services, as well as **saving** and **investing** so that capital goods and human capital can be accumulated to increase output and productivity. The distinguishing characteristics of an economic system thus are not the economic activities that are carried on, but the kinds of economic institutions that exist and the way they influence decision making.

A list of nine content statements dealing with the concept of *Economic Systems*, suggested for inclusion in the K-12 curriculum, is in Chapter IV. Chapters V, VI, and VII indicate placement in grades K-4, 5-8, and 9-12.

5. ECONOMIC INSTITUTIONS AND INCENTIVES

Economic institutions are of several kinds. In addition to households and families, there are formal organizations, such as corporations, government agencies, banks, labor unions, and cooperatives. There are also customary ways of doing things, such as the use of money, collective bargaining, the dominance of men or women in certain occupations, and the observance of various holidays. There are also different controlling values and beliefs that pervade different economic systems. (Some beliefs may be common to most systems.)

In the United States, the household is the typical unit of consumption. Households differ in size, composition, and the manner in which members make decisions. The private firm (which can take various legal forms, such as an individual proprietorship, partnership, or corporation) is the typical unit of production. These firms may participate in trade associations or employer organizations in seeking to promote their own industry interests and to influence legislatures and government administrative agencies. Workers may organize into labor unions to further their interests through collective bargaining and political action. Government agencies play an important regulatory role in the economy, and some governmental enterprises (such as the Tennessee Valley Authority, the federal mint, and municipal bus lines) produce goods or provide services directly. Other economic systems use different institutions. China, for example, carries on agricultural production through collective farms. In Sweden and Finland, cooperatives are more important than in most other European countries. By law, worker representatives serve on the boards of directors of large German corporations. Banks exist in almost every country, and virtually all societies us some form of money as a medium of exchange and a measure of value.

All societies have some system of property ownership. In the United States, for example, private ownership of property is emphasized. In others, such as China, government ownership is the rule except for some small enterprises and personal or household goods. Government planning had been highly centralized and comprehensive in the former Soviet Union, more decentralized in Hungary, and suggestive—"indicative"—in France. Some institutions exist only in certain types of economic systems, for example, collective bargaining about wages and working conditions takes place only in democratic industrial countries.

Cultural traditions of societies also influence the pattern of economic behavior. Examples range from the much-discussed "work ethic" of the Japanese, to the non-materialistic philosophy of certain Buddhist countries, and to the seasonal patterns of retail sales that are evident in most countries due to the occurrence of religious or secular holidays.

Incentives are factors that motivate and influence human behavior. Economic incentives work by offering larger or smaller claims to goods and services in order to influence people's behavior, usually through financial rewards and penalties. Not all human behavior is motivated by economic incentives. Sometimes people turn down higher-paying jobs because of unwillingness to move to a different geographic area. In some countries women leave the labor force for considerable periods of time in order to raise children despite the financial sacrifices involved. Because people want to preserve existing arrangements, or perhaps do someone a favor, business and government contracts are not always awarded to the lowest bidder. The most productive job applicants are not always hired because employers may want either to preserve or to change customary employment patterns. But when all is said and done, economic incentives, the desire to achieve financial or material gain and to avoid financial or material loss, are powerful motivating forces.

The pursuit of economic self-interest is the main motivating force in market economies. Consumers seek to allocate their incomes to obtain the greatest amount of satisfaction. Producers seek to maximize their profits, and this objective impels them to use the most efficient combinations of productive resources to produce the goods and services that consumers want to buy. Workers seek to sell their labor for the best return in money wages and working conditions. Savers seek high interest rates to earn the greatest income on their funds. In all these instances, economic self-interest is the motivation.

Profits are a particularly important incentive in a market economy. Profit is what remains after all costs of production have been deducted from the revenue derived from the sale of goods or services. It is the desire for profit that persuades entrepreneurs to establish new businesses, expand existing ones, and change the kinds of goods and services produced (e.g. from big automobiles to small ones or vice versa). The profit motive stimulates owners and managers to make businesses more efficient, to introduce cost-cutting technologies in production, and to compete more vigorously with other businesses for consumers' dollars. Previously earned profits provide an important source of funds for new investment and thereby stimulate economic growth. Similarly, losses (negative profits) are a signal to move resources elsewhere. Thus, in a competitive market economy, profits and losses spur efficiency, growth, and change. In situations where competition is lacking, however, the profit motive can lead to restrictions of output. (See the discussion of market failures—concept 11.)

In other economic systems, nonmarket incentives or forces are sometimes more evident. In command economies, for example, the authorities emphasize the contribution individuals and groups can make to the welfare of the state rather than to their own personal interests. In some earlier societies, a major motivation was to glorify the ruler (e.g., building pyramids in Pharaoh's Egypt) or a superior being (e.g., building cathedrals in medieval Europe). More recently, in Hitler's Germany and the Republic of South Africa, "race" determined the extent to which individuals could participate in the economy. Whatever the major incentives or force may be, they influence the structure of an economic system and how it functions.

Because economic institutions and economic incentives play such a central role in every economic system, an understanding of how they work is essential to understanding the U.S. economy. Not all economic decisions in that economy are left to individuals. As we have indicated, individuals and businesses form themselves into organized self-interest groups and use group pressure, both in the market and through political processes, to achieve their goals. Since some economic units or groups possess greater power than others, they can have greater influence on changes in the institutional framework within which economic activity occurs.

A list of 14 content statements dealing with the concept of *Economic Institutions and Incentives*, suggested for inclusion in the K-12 curriculum, is in Chapter IV. Chapters V, VI, and VII indicate placement in grades K-4, 5-8, and 9-12.

6. EXCHANGE, MONEY, AND INTERDEPENDENCE

As indicated above, individuals, groups, regions, and countries often specialize in the production of particular goods and in the performance of particular services. This leads to the output of more goods or services than the producers themselves wish to consume. In such situations, producers **exchange** their surpluses for other goods and services produced by people located elsewhere, and everyone is better off as a result. Indeed, the principle of voluntary exchange is based on the fact that *both* sides expect to gain from trade. If they did not, they would not trade.

The simplest form of exchange is **barter**, or the direct trading of goods or services between people. Since barter is usually inconvenient, **money** was developed to facilitate exchange. A wide variety of items has been used as money throughout history, and almost anything can serve as money so long as people are willing to accept it in exchange for goods and services. Money need *not* have any intrinsic value to serve as a medium of exchange. It is people's willingness to accept it in payment that gives money its value in the exchange process. In the United States today, people are willing to accept both currency (metal coins and paper bills) and checks in exchange for goods and services. Until recently, commercial banks were the only financial institutions permitted to establish checking accounts, and the standard definition of the money supply in the United States used to be that is consisted of currency in circulation and checking deposits at commercial banks. Money held in these forms did not earn interest, and it was convenient to separate "money" from other interest-paying assets such as savings accounts and other forms of so-called time deposits.

Our financial system is constantly evolving, however, and in the 1970s savings and loan associations, mutual savings banks, credit unions, and similar "thrift institutions" began offering accounts with names like "automatic transfer savings" (ATS), "negotiable orders of withdrawal" (NOW), and "share drafts," All these accounts consisted of interest-paying deposits against which the depositor could write checks. Beginning in 1982, U.S. banking regulations also allowed commercial banks to pay interest on checkable deposits. Indeed, so many changes have occurred in the U.S. financial system in recent years that several differently defined measures of the money supply are now published regularly by the Federal Reserve System, which is discussed in more detail later.

Specialization and exchange reduce self-sufficiency, and thus they increase interdependence. **Interdependence** means that decisions or events in one part of the world or in one sector of the economy affect decisions and events in other parts of the world and other sectors of the economy. Bad weather in Eastern Europe can affect sugar prices in the United States, and sugar prices can affect the sales of candy, soft drinks, and even the sales of machinery used to harvest sugar beets and sugar cane in various parts of the world. Wage increases in the steel industry can affect retail sales in Pittsburgh, the cost of producing automobiles in Detroit, and economic conditions in many other industries and places as well .

A list of 17 content statements dealing with the concept of *Exchange, Money, and Interdependence*, suggested for inclusion in the K-12 curriculum, is in Chapter IV. Chapters V, VI, and VII indicate placement in grades K-4, 5-8, and 9-12.

Microeconomic Concepts

Microeconomics is the study of the behavior of individual households, firms, and markets, of how prices and outputs are determined in those markets, and of how the price mechanism allocates resources and distributes income. To understand the kinds and amounts of goods and services an economy will produce requires that we know how the prices of goods and services are determined, how these prices determine the pattern of production, and how this pattern is influenced both by the structure of markets and by government actions.

7. MARKETS AND PRICES

Markets are institutional arrangements that enable buyers and sellers to exchange goods and services. A market does not need to have a single physical location. Some markets, such as the New York Stock Exchange or the Chicago Board of Trade, do have a physical location that people can see or visit. Other markets, such as the market for high school teachers or the market for new homes, however, do not have a specific location. Such markets function through advertisements, letters, telephone calls, computer networks, personal relationships, and face-to-face discussions in various places. A "market" can be said to exist so long as there are some arrangements that enable potential buyers and sellers to communicate about the exchange of goods and services.

Prices are the amounts of money that people pay in exchange for a unit of particular good or service, e.g., $2.00 per pound, $12.00 per hour, $0.50 per quart, $6.00 per dozen, etc. **Relative prices** refer to one price compared to another, that is, to the ratio between them. In an actual market, the collection of relative prices constitutes the **price structure** of that market. The collection of price relationships in an entire economy constitutes its total price structure.

Doubling all prices, or cutting all prices in half, for example would not change the price structure (or the relative price ratios) in a market. If the price of apples rises form $1.00 per dozen to $2,00 per dozen, and the price of oranges rises from $2.00 per dozen to $4.00 per dozen, the apple-to-orange price ratio is till 1 to 2 even though the **absolute prices** of both items have changed. A change in relative prices occurs only when the **exchange ratio** between items is altered. If the price of apples rises from $1.00 per dozen to $2.00 per dozen, and the price of oranges remains the same, there will be a change in the apple-to-orange price ratio, and this change in relative prices will lead people to want to buy fewer apples and more oranges than before these relative prices changed.

By comparing the relative prices of various products, consumers can determine which particular combination of goods and services would be most advantageous for them to buy. By comparing the relative prices of various resources as well as the relative prices of various goods and services, business firms can determine which combination of resources they can most advantageously employ to produce particular goods and services. By comparing relative prices in different markets, owners of resources can determine where they can most advantageously sell their resources or the services their resources can supply.

Relative prices and how they affect people's decisions are the means by which a market system provides answers to the basic economic questions: What goods and services will be produced? How will they be produced? Who will get them?

What to produce? The goods and services that are the most profitable.

How to produce them? At the lowest cost possible.

Who will get them? Whoever is willing and able to pay the market price.

It is important to understand how a system of interdependent market prices can, without central planning or direct control over the decisions of individual producers or consumers, enable countless goods and services to be produced and delivered in the quantities desired, at the desired places, and at the desired times. This occurs because relative prides perform three principal function in a market system. These are:(1) an **information** function, (2) an **incentive** function, and (3) a **rationing** function.

Information

Relative prices and the ratios among them provide the essential information consumers, producers, and resource owners in a market system need in order to decide whether, what, and how much to buy. To grasp fully the importance of the information function provided by prices, imagine shopping in a supermarket in which no prices are shown for the items on the shelves. Or imagine choosing between two job opportunities without knowing the salaries offered by each. Or imagine trying to decide whether to hire a painter to paint your house or to do it yourself when you lack information about how much painters charge or about the prices of paint, brushes, and other materials.

Incentives

Changes in relative price ratios create incentives for resources to move or be reallocated in a market economy. An increase in the price of soybeans relative to the price of corn encourages farmers to plant more soybeans and less corn. A decline in the salaries of lawyers relative to those of accountants is an incentive for fewer people to go into law and more into accounting. Increased profits attract resources in free markets, while increased losses produce opposite effects. Profits are the green lights of economic life; losses are the red lights. Just as a well-functioning traffic control system requires both green lights and red lights, so a well-functioning market system requires both profits and losses to help channel its scarce resources into their most valuable uses.

Rationing

The higher the price of anything, other things being equal, the less of it people will be willing and able to buy. Conversely, the lower the price, the more of it people will be willing and able to buy . Prices are the market's way of rationing limited resources, goods, and services to those most willing and able to pay for them. If the owner of a lot on a downtown street corner can receive a higher rent by leasing the land for an office building instead of for a parking garage or a warehouse, the land will be used for an office building, and the parking garage and the warehouse will be "rationed out" of this location. If 50,000 people would like to see a rock concert scheduled for a hall that can accommodate only 5,000 people, the price of tickets can be increased until only 5,000 are willing to pay that price; the other 45,000 people will be "rationed out" by the high price.

The Circular Flow of Resources, Goods, Services, and Money Payments

One way of illustrating the overall operation of a market economy is through a circular flow diagram such as the one in Exhibit 4. This exhibit presents a highly simplified overview of how a market economy operates. Owners of resources (families and individuals*) supply the services of their land, labor, and capital to business firms in exchange for money income payments in the form of wages, salaries, rents, interest, and profits. Owners of the resources in turn use these income payments to purchase the finished goods and services supplied by the business firms. Business firms then use the proceeds from these sales to pay the resource owners for the services the firms receive by employing the resources. This is how the circular flow of resources, goods and services, and money income payments is established and maintained.

Payments in the lower loop (sometimes called the factor market) appear as income to the resource owners who sell productive services, but these same payments appear as costs to the business firms that buy productive services. Likewise, payments in the upper loop (sometimes called the product market) appear as costs to the resource owners who buy goods and services, but these same payments appear as income to the business firms that sell goods and services.

An important point to emphasize is that all of the money payments shown in Exhibit 4 are determined by an interdependent set of market prices. In a system of interdependent market prices, every price depends to some extent on every other price. The prices resource owners are willing to pay for finished goods and services depend on the prices (income) they receive for the use of their resources. The prices of resources, in turn, depend on how much business firms are willing to pay for the services the resources provide. The amount that businesses are willing to pay for resources depends on the prices they receive for the finished goods and services they sell, but the prices business firms receive depend on what resource owners are willing to pay for goods and services. And so, round and round, the process continues.

Both resource owners and business firms would like to receive higher prices for what they sell and to pay lower prices for what they buy, but these objectives are not easy to attain when the prices that buyers pay are also the prices the sellers receive. As explained in greater detail in the next section, a market system relies on the inter-

EXHIBIT 4
The Circular Flow of Resources, Goods, Services, and Money Payments

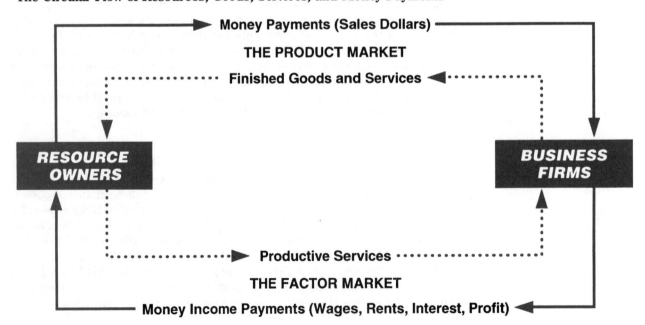

* corporations are also owners of resources, but the owners of a corporation—that is, its stockholders—are families and individuals or their representatives.

action between sellers (supply) and buyers (demand) to reconcile these conflicting objectives and to establish prices in particular markets. Competition among sellers give buyers a choice in deciding from whom (if anyone) to buy, and competition among buyers gives sellers a choice in deciding to whom (if anyone) to sell.

A list of seven content statements dealing with the concept of *Markets and Prices*, suggested for inclusion in the K-l2 curriculum, is in Chapter IV. Chapters V, VI, and VII indicate placement in grades K-4, 5-8, and 9-12.

8. SUPPLY AND DEMAND

Supply is a relationship between quantity and price. **Supply** is defined as the different quantities of a resource, good, or service that will be offered for sale at various possible prices during a specific time period. Generally, the higher the price of something, the more of it will be offered for sale—and vice versa.

Demand is, too, a relationship between quantity and price. **Demand** is defined as the different quantities of a resource, good, or service that will be purchased at various possible prices during a specific time period. Generally, the lower the price of something, the more of it will be purchased—and vice versa.

In competitive markets, supply and demand constitute the sum of many individual decisions to sell and to buy. The interaction of supply and demand determines the prices and the quantities that will "clear" competitive markets. This is illustrated in Exhibit 5, where hypothetical data are provided for a hypothetical product. The data in the exhibit are presented in tabular form as supply and demand "schedules." Columns 1 and 2 of the table constitute the supply schedule, while columns 2 and 3 constitute the demand schedule.

Exhibit 5 shows that the market-clearing price for this hypothetical product is $4.00 per unit. At any price below $4.00 per unit, the quantity demanded exceeds the quantity supplied, and competition among buyers will bid the price up to $4.00. At any price above $4.00 per unit, the quantity supplied exceeds the quantity demanded, and competition among sellers will cause the price to fall to $4.00. Only at a price of $4.00 a unit will the market "clear," with both the quantity supplied and the quantity demanded equal to each other at the same price.

EXHIBIT 5
Hypothetical Supply and Demand Schedules for a Hypothetical Product

(1) Quantity Supplied by Producers (millions of units)	(2) Price ($ per unit)	(3) Quantity Demanded by Consumers (millions of units)
70	$7.00	10
60	6.00	20
50	5.00	30
40	4.00	40
30	3.00	50
20	2.00	60
10	1.00	70

The schedules presented in Exhibit 5 can also be used to show that 40 million units is a market-clearing quantity. Only at a quantity of 40 million units will the market "clear," with both the price that sellers are willing to accept and the price that buyers are willing to pay equal to each other at the same quantity.

The market-clearing price of $4.00 and the market-clearing quantity of 40 million units shown in Exhibit 5 will persist so long as other things remain constant. If there is a change in supply, or if there is a change in demand—these changes are often described as "shifts" in supply or demand—there will be a change in the market-clearing price and the market-clearing quantity. An increase in supply, for example, would mean that sellers are willing to sell larger quantities at each and every price shown in Exhibit 5. This would result in a lower market-clearing price and a larger market-clearing quantity. A decrease in supply would have the opposite effect. Similarly, an increase in demand would mean that buyers are willing to buy larger quantities at each and every price shown in Exhibit 5. This would result in a higher market-clearing price and a larger market-clearing quantity. A decrease in demand would have the opposite effect. Furthermore, as mentioned earlier, changes in one market will affect relative price ratios and are thus likely to cause changes in other markets as well. A higher market-clearing price and a lower market-clearing quantity for coffee, for example, will tend to increase the demand for tea and to decrease the demand for the paper filters used in coffee makers.

The forces of supply and demand work most effectively in markets with large numbers of sellers and buyers, each with reasonably accurate information, who are competing to sell or buy a relatively homogeneous product. In markets that do not possess all of these characteristics, the forces of supply and demand are modified by the structures that prevail in those markets.

A list of 18 content statements dealing with the concept of *Supply and Demand*, suggested for inclusion in the K-12 curriculum, is in Chapter IV. Chapters V, VI, and VII indicate placement in grades K-4, 5-8, and 9-12.

9. COMPETITION AND MARKET STRUCTURE

The term **market structure** refers to the extent to which competition prevails in particular markets. The degree of competition is largely determined by the number of buyers and sellers participating in the market, the availability and accessibility of accurate information, the possibility of collusion among buyers and among sellers, the nature of the product, and the ease with which firms can enter and leave the market. The structure of markets may also be affected by various laws and government regulations, which are discussed later. In turn, market structure affects the level of prices, the amounts purchased, and the rate of profit earned by firms.

Some markets are highly competitive. They contain many producers or sellers, none of whom can independently dominate or affect the market price appreciably; the possibility of effective collusion is small; accurate information is easily accessible; the products sold by different producers are homogeneous or so similar that it is difficult to distinguish the product of one seller from that of another; and firms can enter the market without difficulty. Many farm products like wheat and corn are examples. Markets that are less competitive are dominated by a smaller number of producers or sellers; individual sellers may be able to affect and sometimes control prices; the possibility of effective collusion may exist; accurate information is less easily accessible; the product of one seller can more frequently be distinguished from that of another; and entry into the market is usually somewhat difficult. The U.S. auto industry is an example.

The spectrum of market structures runs from highly competitive markets to those that contain only a single seller (called a **monopoly**) or a single buyer (called a **monopsony**). Unregulated monopolies tend to sell at higher prices and to produce smaller quantities than would a set of competitive suppliers with the same cost structure. Unregulated monopsonies tend to buy at lower prices and to purchase smaller quantities than would a set of competitive buyers.

Economists distinguish still other types of market structures that are not highly competitive. Firms in a market structure with few sellers are called **oligopolies**. Firms in a market structure with few buyers are called **oligopsonies**. The term **monopolistic competition** is used to refer to a market structure that may have a good many firms selling similar products, but the products can be differentiated from each other by the use of brand names or advertising and marketing strategies or by making relatively minor variations in the product.

Collusion occurs when independent producers agree to coordinate their decisions in a manner that restricts competition. When collusion takes the form of an explicit agreement to fix prices and share markets among a group of producers that furnishes a large share of a particular product, the group is called a **cartel**.

We do not wish to encourage the memorization of terms for their own sake, nor do we think that it is necessary to introduce precollege students to the detailed analyses used by economists to distinguish between various market structures. The important thing for these students to realize is that the prices of goods and services as well as the quantities offered, which play such an important role in a market economy, are affected by the competitive structure of various markets. When confronted by particular market situations, students should be encouraged to try to identify the type of market structure that exists as reflected by characteristics such as the number of sellers (or buyers), possible barriers to entry into the industry, the accessibility of information, the possibility of collusive action, the degree of product differentiation, the role of government in the market, and the level of profits earned. An example of a modern cartel is OPEC, the Organization of Petroleum Exporting Countries.

A list of 14 content statements dealing with the concept of *Competition and Market Structure*, suggested for inclusion in the K-12 curriculum, is in Chapter IV. Chapters V, VI, and VII indicate placement in grades K-4, 5-8, and 9-12.

10. INCOME DISTRIBUTION

In a market economy, people's incomes depend largely on the value of goods or services (including labor) they are able to sell in the marketplace. People who own larger amounts of scarce resources or possess rare talents that are in great demand receive higher incomes than those without such resources or talents. As explained earlier, **wages** and **salaries** are payments for the services of labor; **rent** is payment for the use of someone's land or property; **interest** is payment for the use of borrowed money; and **profit** is the return to a business enterprise that results when the value of sales exceeds the cost of the goods or services sold.

The division of an economy's total income into wages and salaries, rent, interest, and profit is called the **functional distribution of income**, since it shows the breakdown of income received by the individuals and businesses based on the type of resources provided to the productive process. A functional distribution of income, of course, does not tell us how many people receive incomes from more than one source. For information on the **personal distribution of income**, we typically classify different population groups by the number of them receiving different amounts of income, including transfer payments.

Transfer payments, which have grown rapidly in recent years, consist mostly of payments by government for which the recipients do not currently perform productive services, although in some cases these payments are related to productive activity that was performed in the past. The most important transfer payments in the United States today are Social Security benefits, government employee retirement benefits, unemployment compensation, and public assistance such as aid to the elderly, aid to families with dependent children, veterans benefits, and food stamps.

Exhibit 6, on the following page, shows the distribution of personal income by function and by income level. Many forces shape the personal distribution of income. Various farm, business, labor and other groups such as the poor, veterans, and the elderly, continuously seek to expand their share of total income. Inherited wealth and practices and customs such as racial and gender discrimination also help to shape the distribution of income. There is controversy about the distribution of income and the extent, if any, to which it should be redistributed from its original recipients to others who are less well off. Decisions about income distribution are made through the political process as well as by the operations of the market economy.

A list of eight content statements dealing with the concept of *Income Distribution*, suggested for inclusion in the K-12 curriculum, is Chapter IV. Chapters V, VI, and VII indicate placement in grades K-4, 5-8, and 9-12.

EXHIBIT 6

Sources and Distribution of Personal Income in the United States

Sources of Personal Income (Functional Distribution), 1993		
Type of Income	*Amount of Income (billions of $)*	*Percent of Total Personal Income*
Wages, salaries, and other labor income less contributions for social insurance	$3,166.8	58.8%
Personal rental income	13.0	0.2
Personal interest income	695.8	12.9
Personal dividend income	158.3	2.9
Net income of unincorporated business (including farms)	442.1	8.2
Transfer payments	911.6	16.9
Total	$5,387.6	100.0%

Distribution of Personal Income, 1992				
Money Income Level	All families		Unrelated Individuals	
	Numbers in Millions	Percent of Total	Numbers in Millions	Percent of Total
Less than $5,000	2.3	3.4%	2.1	7.4%
$5,000–$9,999	3.8	5.6	5.9	20.9
10,000–14,999	4.9	7.2	4.2	14.9
15,000–24,999	10.6	15.5	5.7	20.2
25,000–34,999	10.2	15.0	4.1	14.5
35,000–49,999	13.2	19.4	3.2	11.3
50,000–74,999	13.5	19.8	2.0	7.1
75,000 and up	9.6	14.1	1.0	3.5
Total	68.1	100.0%	28.2	100.0%[a]

SOURCE: Figures for sources of personal income are from Council of Economic Advisers, Economic Indicators, February 1994, p. 5; those for distribution of personal income are from Bureau of the Census, Current Population Reports, Series P-60, No. 184, September 1993, p. 5. Personal dividend income excludes the parts of corporate profits paid as corporate income tax or retained for use in corporate business.

[a] Figures do not sum to 100.0 percent because of rounding.

11. MARKET FAILURES

Markets work best when they are reasonably competitive, when buyers and sellers have access to sufficient reliable information, when resources are relatively mobile and free to move from one use to another in response to changing conditions, and when market prices reflect the full costs and benefits incurred in producing and exchanging goods and services. Market "failures" occur when there are significant deviations from these conditions. The main forms of market failure are inadequate competition, lack of access to reliable information, resource immobility, externalities, and the need for public goods (i.e., goods or services the government provides because the market either does not supply them or supplies them in insufficient amounts). We discuss each of these market failures in turn.

Inadequate Competition

A market system relies on competition to give both buyers and sellers a choice in deciding with whom to exchange and on what terms to make such exchanges. Without competition there is no guarantee that scarce resources will be allocated to their most productive uses. Inadequate competition is, therefore, a serious problem in a market system. Yet maintaining competition is not always easy. In markets in which there are few buyers or few sellers, the buyers or the sellers may more easily collude to fix the prices at which they are willing to buy or sell. Even when a large number of sellers exists, a form of price fixing may occur, especially if the government helps, as it does in important segments of agriculture. Competition in some markets may be lessened through policies of price leadership exercised by one or a few firms or by "conscious parallelism" in price policy. In still other markets, in which it may not be efficient to have large numbers of producers of a particular good or service, we find **natural monopolies** such as various local water and gas companies.

Inadequate Information

Inadequate information about market conditions on the part of consumers, workers, and business managers can adversely affect the decisions they make and the efficiency with which the market mechanism allocates resources, goods, and services. Consumers, for example, may not be well-informed about the quality of product or of alternative products available. Unemployed workers may not know of job opportunities in unfamiliar labor markets. Business managers may not be aware of changing demographic patterns or changing economic conditions. Yet in many of these cases, it may be very difficult or extremely costly for individuals to seek out reliable information on their own. In such situations, public provision of information can lead to increased efficiency so long as the additional benefits to consumers, workers, or business managers exceed the government's additional costs or trouble of acquiring and disseminating the information.

Resource Immobility

Another condition that can impair the functioning of the market mechanism is resource immobility. Workers, for example, may not be able to move from declining to expanding industries because they lack the specialized skills required or the money needed to relocate themselves. Business firms may have investment funds tied up in obsolete equipment and machinery and be unable to take advantage of new investment opportunities until the old equipment is paid off.

Externalities

Externalities are the positive or negative side effects that result when the production or consumption of a good or service affects the welfare of people who are not the parties directly involved in a market exchange. A positive externality in consumption, for example, may result from the acquisition of additional education by an individual; when put to proper use, additional education increases the productivity of that individual, and society as a whole thereby benefits. A negative externality in consumption occurs, for example, when cigarette smoking by one individual has detrimental effects on nonsmokers. A positive externality in production occurs, for example, when a dam constructed to generate electric power provides flood control for downstream residents and/or creates an attractive lake for scenic and recreational purposes. A negative externality in production occurs, for example, when a factory discharges smoke or other pollutants into the air or into rivers and streams.

Positive externalities are sometimes called "third-party benefits," and negative externalities are sometimes called "third-party costs." Since external benefits and external cost are not reflected in the market prices paid by buyers and received by sellers, an unregulated market system underproduces goods and services that yield external benefits and overproduces goods and services that impose external costs.

Public Goods

Most goods and services produced and exchanged in the market are "private goods," which producers can withhold from would-be consumers who refuse to pay (that is, people who do not buy are excluded), and whose consumption by one person or family makes them unavailable to others (that is, consumption is not shared). **Public goods** are those the government supplies in situations involving nonexclusion and/or shared consumption.

A "pure" public good is a product or service producers cannot withhold from consumers who refuse to pay (**nonexclusion**), and the consumption of the product or service by one person does not reduce its usefulness to others (**shared consumption**). National defense, for example, cannot be provided exclusively to those who are willing to pay for it nor can it be withheld from those who are not able or not willing to pay. Likewise, in some situations, one person's use or consumption of a good or service does not prevent its concurrent use by others. The illumination that one person receives from a street light, for example, is not diminished by other's use of the same illumination.

Goods such as national defense, street lighting, and flood control are not adequately provided by the market system because private businesses will not produce things that people will not pay for and because individual consumers are reluctant to pay for goods and services that benefit nonpayers in the same way as those who pay.

Public Policy Responses to Market Failure

Governments have adopted various policies to deal with the several types of market failures described above. Antitrust laws and public regulatory agencies attempt to deal with inadequate competition. Public provision of information and statistical data when private provision would be prohibitively expensive can remedy inadequate knowledge; consumer protection laws can have a similar effect. Relocation allowances, favorable tax treatment, retraining programs, and the like, can lessen resource immobility. Taxation often discourages the production of goods and services that impose external costs, and subsidies often encourage the production of goods and services that provide external benefits.

Public policies aimed at correcting market failures do not always work out as intended, however, and under certain circumstances efforts to correct market failures can themselves become sources of inefficiency. When this happens, "Government Failures" may be said to occur. **Government Failures** can occur when special-interest groups exert undue influence on the political process and secure advantages for themselves that they cannot obtain in the marketplace. Government agencies often develop an internal dynamic of their own as they compete for additional staff and influence. Since they are not subject to the tests of monetary losses and bankruptcy that tend to eliminate inefficient operations in private-sector markets, inefficient government agencies may remain intact indefinitely. Managers in the public sector seldom gain from saving the taxpayers' money. If an agency fails to spend all of one year's appropriation, its case for a larger budget or even the same budget next year may be weakened. Finally, there is an element of compulsion in the public sector that does not exist in competitive markets. If the majority—either directly or through the legislative process—decides to pursue a particular policy, the minority must acquiesce and help pay for its costs, even if the minority strongly disagrees. In a democracy, however, the minority can reverse the policy if it is able to convince enough legislators or if the minority becomes the majority.

A list of nine content statements dealing with the concept of *Market Failures*, suggested for inclusion in the K-12 curriculum, is in Chapter IV. Chapters V, VI, and VII indicate placement in grades K-4, 5-8, and 9-12.

12. THE ROLE OF GOVERNMENT

All societies must establish some framework of law and order to safeguard their existence. A market economy could not function without some protection of property rights and enforcement of contracts. But, once this general point is made, there is room for debate about which laws and rules are necessary or desirable. In a market economy, business firms and resource owners are encouraged to compete vigorously in pursuit of their own self-interests. But what if they do not compete fairly? What if they agree to fix prices and restrict output? What if they lie or cheat? What if they sell spoiled meat or impure and therefore dangerous drugs without informing buyers?

Some argue that in the long run the market itself punishes such practices. The liars and cheaters will find it increasingly difficult to find customers. As their tactics are found out and this information gets around, fewer people will do business with them, and they will be punished in the currency of the marketplace—by monetary losses. While such punishment may eventually take care of those who violate the principles of fair competition, this does little to redress the harm done to the victims of those practices. Few people take comfort in learning that a particular drug which impaired their health is losing sales or that news of illness caused by spoiled meat contributes to the economic demise of an unscrupulous competitor.

All but the advocates of a completely unrestricted market system admit that some ground rules are necessary to keep competition within acceptable limits. Yet, when it comes to a specific issue, the matter becomes one of intense controversy. Should there be standards for weights and measures? Laws to forbid child labor? Health and safety regulations? Farm price supports? Zoning regulations? Minimum wage laws? Should the government enforce truth in advertising? Certify the purity of food and drugs?

Beyond establishing certain "rules of the game" in economic life, government activities in the U. S. economy today can be classified into several categories: preserving and fostering competition (antitrust laws), regulating natural monopolies, providing information and services to enable the market to work better, regulating externalities, providing certain public goods, offering some measure of economic security and income redistribution to individuals, assuring a sound monetary system, and promoting overall economic stability and growth. All of these activities involve some element of controversy; all entail at least some expenditures; and, as mentioned in the previous section, all contain potentials for government failures that somewhat parallel private-market failures.

Taxation

Goods and services provided by governments (federal, state, and local) are paid for by taxes or by borrowing from the public. **Taxes** are mandatory payments to government. **Proportional taxes** take the same percentage of income from people in all income groups. **Progressive taxes** take a larger percentage of income from people in higher-income groups than from people in lower-income ones; the federal income tax in the United States is an example of a progressive tax. **Regressive** taxes take a larger percentage of income from people in lower-income groups than from higher-income ones. Sales taxes and most excise taxes are examples of regressive taxes. Since low-income groups tend to spend a larger percentage of their income on taxed items than do high-income groups, the latter tend to save a larger proportion of their incomes.

Governments in the Circular Flow of Resources, Goods, Services, and Money Payments

Exhibit 7, on the following page, presents a more complete diagrammatic overview of the circular flow of resources, goods, services, and money payments in the United States today than Exhibit 4 presented earlier. Governments have been added to the circular flow shown in Exhibit 7. This exhibit indicates that resource owners sell the services of some of their labor and other resources to governments as well as to business firms and that business firms sell some of their finished goods and services to governments as well as to individual resource owners. Exhibit 7 also shows that governments collect money payments, including transfer payments (see concept 10, on income distribution), to both of these groups. Even Exhibit 7, however, is a simplified overview of how our economy operates. It does not show the saving and borrowing in financial markets by individuals, businesses, and governments, and it does not show trade with foreign nations.

A list of 11 content statements dealing with the concept of *The Role of Government,*

EXHIBIT 7
Governments in the Circular Flow of Resources, Goods, Services, and Money Payments

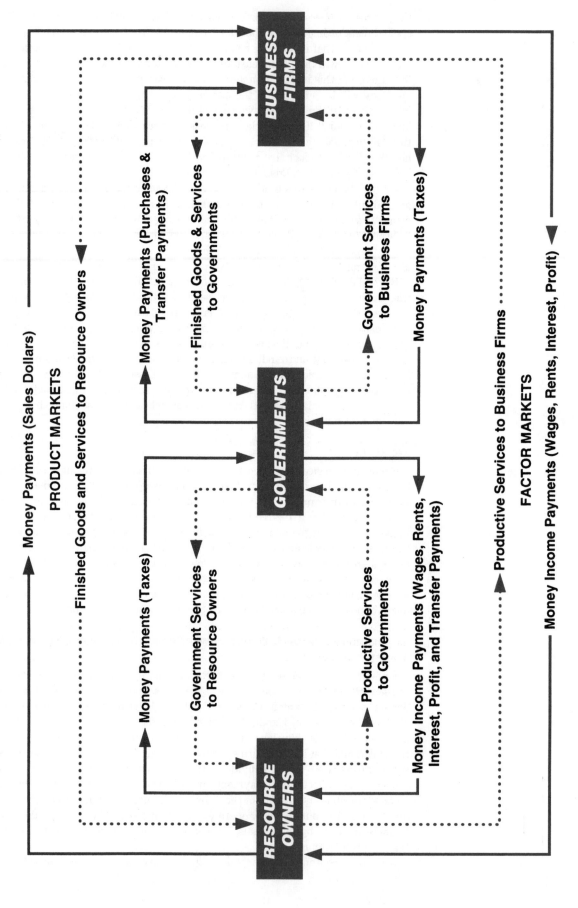

suggested for inclusion in the K-12 curriculum, is in Chapter IV. Chapters V, VI, and VII indicate placement in grades K-4, 5-8, and 9-12.

Macroeconomic Concepts

Macroeconomics is the study of the functioning of the economy as a whole, and it deals mainly with the total output and income of the economy, the total level of employment, and movements in the average level of all prices. The heart of macroeconomics consists of analyzing the determinants of aggregate supply (the total productive capacity of an economic system) and of aggregate demand (the total spending by economic units on the goods and services produced). In the short run, the main problem in macroeconomics is why aggregate demand sometimes exceeds aggregate supply, thereby bringing on inflation, and why aggregate demand sometimes falls short of aggregate supply, thereby bringing on unemployment and deflation—or at least less inflation. Over the long run, macroeconomics is concerned primarily with economic growth—increases in the productive capacity of the economy and in average real income per person.

13. GROSS DOMESTIC PRODUCT

Gross Domestic Product (GDP) is the most inclusive measure of an economy's output. GDP is defined as the market value of the total output of final goods and services produced in one year.* If periods shorter than a year are used to measure output, the results are usually converted to an annual rate. It is important to recognize that GDP measures the flow of output and not the stock of wealth. (The **stock of wealth** consists of the assets that are capable of producing output in the economy at any given time.) It is also important to know that GDP counts only final goods and services produced for the market. Most nonmarket production, such as the unpaid work of homemakers, is not counted in GDP. Intermediate sales of goods and services among different firms are excluded from GDP in order to avoid "double counting." If a farmer grows wheat and sells it to a miller, who grinds it into flour and sells the flour to a baker, who then bakes the flour into bread and sells the bread to a consumer, how much has the economy produced? It has produced one loaf of bread, which is all that is counted in GDP because the bread is the **final product** of the foregoing chain of economic activity. The wheat and the flour are **intermediate products**. It would be a mistake to count the wheat and the flour and the bread in GDP, since the value (price) of the bread already includes the value (price) of the flour and the value (price) of the wheat as well as the value of the farmer's and the miller's and the baker's services. When calculating GDP, the value of all goods and services purchased from other producers is subtracted from the sales figures of each producer, and thus only the **value added** at each stage of production is counted. The sum of the values added at each stage of production is equal to the price at which a unit of the final product is sold to its ultimate user.

"Nominal" or "money" GDP measures the output of goods and services in terms of the **current prices** paid to buy the output. "Real" GDP measures the output of goods and services in **constant prices**, that is, in the prices prevailing in a particular year. (See the discussion of real vs. nominal on p. 43). Comparing GDP in both constant and current prices enables us to distinguish between changes in nominal GDP that are caused by actual changes in output and changes in nominal GDP that are simply the result of changes in prices.

Real GDP is the most comprehensive measure of an economy's output of goods and services in one period compared to another period. **Economic growth** is usually defined as an increase in real GDP or, more meaningfully, in order to take account of population growth, as an increase in real GDP per capita, that is, in the amount of goods and services produced per person.

* The U.S. GDP includes profits earned by foreign-owned businesses and income earned by foreigners in the U.S., but it excludes profits earned by U.S. companies overseas and by U.S. residents working abroad.

A list of 12 content statements dealing with the concept of *Gross Domestic Product*, suggested for inclusion in the K-12 curriculum, is in Chapter IV. Chapters V, VI, and VII indicate placement in grades K-4, 5-8, and 9-12.

14. AGGREGATE SUPPLY AND AGGREGATE DEMAND

Aggregate supply is the total amount of goods and services (real GDP) produced by the economy during some stated period of time. The upper limit on aggregate supply is set by the productive capacity of the economy when all its resources are fully employed. While the economy's full-employment productive capacity is substantially fixed at any moment in time, past experience suggests that it normally grows as time goes on because of increases in the labor force, improved education and training of workers, more saving and capital investment, discovery of new resources, and technological advances.

Since the economy does not always operate at full employment, estimating its full-employment productive capacity is difficult. Some individuals have stronger attachments to the labor force than others, some machines can be operated profitably when their products command certain prices and not at lower ones, and individuals and businesses can change the number of hours they work in response to changing incentives. Some economists, therefore, have developed the concept of an aggregate supply "curve," which relates the total amount of goods and services produced to other variables in the economy such as the average price level or the actual or expected real incomes of suppliers of resources. Not all economists agree with this approach to aggregate supply, however, and much of the discussion and debate in macroeconomics at this writing is over the existence, shape, and behavior of an aggregate supply curve for the U.S. economy.

As indicated earlier, an increase in productive capacity often requires giving up some current consumption in exchange for future increases in output and income. This is true for individuals (who can postpone entering the labor force in order to obtain education, skill, and training that will make them more productive in the future); for businesses (which can retain part of their after-tax profits to buy new machinery rather than paying out all of their after-tax profit to their owners); and for governments (which can raise personal taxes to cut consumption and use the money to finance basic research and development projects, new highways, public training and retraining programs for individuals, etc., or can encourage the enhancement of productivity by granting tax reductions to business firms that buy new plants and equipment). A persistent question in macroeconomics is: How much of our resources should be devoted to increasing our productive capacity as opposed to how much should be spent on current consumption?

Aggregate demand is the total amount of spending on goods and services in the economy during some stated period of time. There are two basic approaches to examining aggregate demand. One is to view aggregate demand as the sum of total consumer spending by individuals and households (C), investment spending by businesses for new plants and equipment and for additions to inventory (I), and spending for goods and services by government (G). In this approach, aggregate demand is expressed as C + I + G*. A second approach is to view aggregate demand as reflecting the stock of money (M) multiplied by the velocity of circulation (V). The **velocity of circulation** is defined as the number of times the average dollar (consisting of checkable deposits as well as currency) is spent on final goods and services. Velocity can be calculated by dividing GDP by the average stock of money during the time period covered by GDP. In this approach, aggregate demand is expressed as M x V.

It is important to note that the C + I + G and the M x V approaches to aggregate demand simply express two different ways of looking at the same thing. Since, by definition, both C + I + G and M x V are equal to aggregate demand, this identity can be expressed symbolically as: C+ I + G = M x V. As we explain later, government fiscal

---

* As explained, net exports (exports minus imports) is also a component of this approach to total spending and aggregate demand.

policy (concept 18) influences aggregate demand by working on C, I, and G, the variables on the left-handed side of this identity, and government monetary policy (concept 17) influences aggregate demand by working on M and V, the variables on the right-hand side of this identity.

A list of nine content statements dealing with the concept of *Aggregate Supply and Aggregate Demand*, suggested for inclusion in the K-12 curriculum, is in Chapter IV. Chapters V, VI, and VII indicate placement in grades K-4, 5-8, and 9-12.

15. UNEMPLOYMENT

Unemployment is defined in U.S. statistics as the number of people without jobs who are actively seeking work. The **unemployment rate** is the number of people who are unemployed expressed as percentage of the number of people who are in the labor force. The **labor force** consists of people at least 16 years who are employed or actively looking for work. A high unemployment rate usually means that there are also idle machines and other unused means of production in the economy. The existence of unemployment does not imply that the basic problem of scarcity has disappeared. Rather, it implies that the nation is not using its scarce resources as effectively as possible. This is reflected in the opportunity cost of unemployed resources, which is the loss of all of the goods and services that these resources could be producing if they were employed. Moreover, unemployed workers lose the income, respect, and self-esteem they would enjoy if they were working. At the same time, the rest of society is confronted with the problem of what, if anything, to do about providing support to workers who are not earning any income of their own.

Not all people who are unemployed have lost their jobs. Some voluntarily left their previous positions and have not yet found new ones, others are looking for work for the first time, still others previously left the labor force and are now returning to it. Likewise, not all people who have lost a job are counted as unemployed. Job-seekers who become discouraged and quit looking for work, for example, are considered to have left the labor force and therefore are not counted as unemployed.

Wide differences exist in the unemployment rates of different groups in the U.S. labor force. The unemployment rate for teenagers 16-19, for example, is usually about three times as high as that for the labor force as a whole. An increase in the percent of the labor force that is under 20 years of age, therefore, might be expected to result in an increase in the overall unemployment rate, and vice versa.

Since the absolute size and composition of the labor force can change in response to different economic and social conditions, many economists have begun to emphasize the employment rate as well as the unemployment rate. The **employment rate** is defined as the percent of the *entire population* age 16 or over that is employed. The U.S. Bureau of Labor Statistics, which issues the nation's employment data, now publishes this measure as well as the more familiar unemployment rate described above.

Because people can become unemployed for different reasons, economists sometimes distinguish between frictional unemployment, structural unemployment, and cyclical unemployment.

Frictional unemployment is the more or less unavoidable unemployment that occurs in a market economy as people change jobs, new entrants into the labor force seek their first job, and people are temporarily laid off from seasonal jobs.

Structural unemployment refers to the situation of people who are unemployed because their present ability, skills, training, and location do not "match up" with available job openings that reflect the basic structure of the economy. Change in consumer preferences, changes in technology, the expansion of new industries and the decline of old ones, and shifts in the economic roles of different geographic regions, all influence the economy's structure and, hence, the types and locations of available jobs. If new jobs require different skills and training than did old ones, and if the new jobs are located in different parts of the country, structural unemployment may result.

Cyclical unemployment is unemployment associated with changes in the overall rate of economic activity. As the economy contracts, the total demand for goods and services falls, and the falling demand causes unemployment to rise. Contrariwise, during economic expansions, the total demand for goods and services rises, and the rising demand causes unemployment to fall.

Cyclical unemployment explains major fluctuations in the economy's overall unemployment rate, but the changing size and composition of the labor force and the existence of frictional unemployment and structural unemployment have made it difficult to get agreement on a specific numerical target for "full employment" in the U.S. economy.

During the late 1970s and early 1980s the U.S. economy was plagued with both high unemployment and rapid inflation at the same time. This caused many economists to re-evaluate traditional economic policies that have been used to deal with such problems.

Considered alone, a low rate of unemployment is desirable, but some economists now argue that there is a "natural rate of unemployment" that is consistent with a stable rate of inflation. In this view, attempts to reduce the unemployment rate below the so-called "natural rate" will cause inflation to accelerate. This theory, however, remains controversial, and attempts to reach agreement on a specific figure for the natural rate of unemployment have not been successful.

A list of 14 content statements dealing with the concept of *Unemployment*, suggested for inclusion in the K-12 curriculum, is in Chapter IV. Chapters V, VI, and VII indicate placement in grades K-4, 5-8, and 9-12.

16. INFLATION AND DEFLATION

Inflation is a sustained increase in the average price level of the entire economy; **deflation** is a sustained decrease in the average price level of the entire economy. Prices in some markets (e.g., pocket calculators) can fall even in times of inflation, and prices in some markets (e.g., medical care) can rise even in times of deflation. But it is not the change in individual prices that determines the extent to which an economy in experiencing inflation or deflation; it is the upward or downward movement in the average prices of all goods and services combined that determines the extent of inflation or deflation.

As the price level rises during an inflation, a dollar buys fewer goods and services than before. Hence, inflation reduces the dollar's real purchasing power. As the price level falls during deflation, a dollar buys more goods and services than before. Hence, deflation increases the dollar's real purchasing power. Because money is used as a unit of account and as a medium of exchange in most economies, changes in the purchasing power of money generally have several adverse consequences. Since inflation has been a more serious problem than deflation in recent years, some of the adverse consequences of inflation deserve mention.

Inflation can produce misleading information in business accounting. Since business is conducted in money terms, figures using changing prices can give deceptive signals. If goods and materials that firms bought at lower prices must be replaced at higher prices, profit figures are often overstated if the profits are calculated on the basis of the lower prices. Such a calculation implicitly assumes that goods and materials can continue to be purchased (replaced) at lower prices when, in fact, they cannot. Depreciation charges based on the original cost of equipment may not provide sufficient funds to replace this equipment after it wears out if inflation has caused equipment prices to rise. Firms that do not or cannot increase their depreciation charges will find it difficult to maintain, let alone expand, their investment in capital goods.

Inflation hurts people living on fixed money incomes and people who have saved fixed amounts of money for specific purposes such as financing their children's college education or their own retirement. Inflation hurts people who have lent out money at a rate of interest that did not include an allowance for an increase in the average price level. Lenders in that situation are without protection against a decline in the purchasing power of the loan when it is repaid. People who borrowed money under the conditions just mentioned will benefit, since the borrowers will repay their loans in dollars that have less purchasing power than the dollars originally borrowed. In general, if long-term contracts are negotiated in fixed dollar terms, buyers tend to gain and sellers tend to lose during periods of unanticipated inflation.

In large part, as suggested above, the adverse effects of inflation depend on the extent to which inflation is correctly anticipated and the extent to which it is unanticipated. If inflation is correctly anticipated, contracts can be negotiated to include "inflation premiums." Such premiums are designed to protect lenders and other recipients of future money payments from declines in the purchasing power of the money to be repaid to them. Lenders, for example, will insist on higher interest rates if they anticipate inflation, and the greater the inflation they anticipate the higher the rate of interest they will ask. Borrowers who agree to the lender's terms presumably share similar anticipations of inflation. However, it is often difficult to anticipate a future rate of inflation correctly, and if a mistake is made, there can be an unintended gain to either the lender or the borrower, depending on the direction of the mistake.

In addition to increasing the possibility of misleading accounting statements in business reports and of capricious windfall gains or losses of real income, inflation also encourages "shortsightedness." Under inflationary conditions, predicting future costs and profits of a major investment that will take a long time to pay off, such as an electronics plant or an oil refinery, becomes an even riskier process than it might otherwise be. In general, the increased risks and the higher interest rates that accompany inflation tend to discourage long-range planning as well as investment in long-term projects. These effects, in turn, hinder the expansion of the economy's total productive capacity.

Inflation can occur for several reasons, and economists sometimes distinguish between demand-pull inflation and cost-push inflation. People's expectations and the way their expectations are formed also may influence the occurrence and rate of inflation in the economy.

Demand-pull inflation occurs when aggregate demand in the economy increases faster than the economy's productive capacity at full employment. If aggregate demand exceeds aggregate supply, the average prices of goods and services are pulled up by the "excess" demand. Demand-pull inflation is generally associated with rapid increases in a nation's money supply and is often described as "too much money chasing too few goods."

Cost-push inflation occurs when higher prices for the factors of production increase costs. Most sellers try to push these higher costs on into higher prices even if there is no change in aggregate demand in the economy. Supply shocks, such as widespread and severe crop failure or the sharp increases in the price of oil instituted by a cartel that were experienced in the 1970s, can be sources of cost-push inflation if these shocks lead to reduced supply and higher prices throughout the economy.

Price expectations and changes in them can also influence the rate of inflation. If consumers, investors, and businesses begin to anticipate more inflation than currently exists, that expectation can make the anticipated increase in inflation a self-fulfilling prophecy. If consumers think that prices are going to increase, for example, they may rush out to buy before the prices go up. This surge in buying increases demand and speeds an inflationary spiral of prices. Or if businesses, workers, and lenders raise prices, wages, and interest rates to match the anticipated inflation, other sellers will in turn try to protect themselves by raising their prices. Inflationary expectations can play a key role in generating and maintaining inflation.

We still have much to learn about the process of inflation, as well as about its relation to other macroeconomic problems such as economic growth and unemployment. When conflicts occur, dilemmas in economic policy arise. Should policy, for example, be aimed primarily at achieving long-run price stability or high employment? Primary focus on avoiding inflation may mean higher employment. Primary focus on reducing unemployment may generate increasing inflation. Such dilemmas are especially hard to deal with because of their political implications: high and rising rates of unemployment or inflation, or both, are likely to adversely affect the party in power.

A list of 11 content statements dealing with the concept of *Inflation and Deflation,* suggested for inclusion in the K-12 curriculum, is in Chapter IV. Chapters V, VI, and VII indicate placement in grades K-4, 5-8 and 9-12.

17. MONETARY POLICY

Monetary policy seeks to affect the amount of money available in the economy and its cost (interest rates). Monetary policy in the United States is the responsibility of the Federal Reserve System, a quasi-independent agency of the federal government.

As we have indicated, exactly how "money" should be defined in the U.S. economy today is uncertain. The narrowest definition of money (known as M-1) is the sum of currency (cash), checkable deposits in banks and other financial institutions, and traveler's checks. Currency is printed or coined by the federal government, but the bulk of the nation's money supply, checkable deposits, is created by the lending activities of banks and certain other financial institutions (see next paragraph). In addition to checkable deposits, however, other financial assets, such as money market mutual funds and savings accounts are easily convertible into cash or checking accounts. Figures for broader definitions of money (known as M-2, M-3, etc.), therefore, are published in addition to those for M-1.

The financial system increases the money supply by making loans to individuals, businesses, and governments. These loans appear as new, additional checkable deposits in the borrowers' checking accounts and thus increase the spending power—or aggregate demand—of the nation's economic units. All institutions that take checkable deposits are required to keep reserves—in the form of vault cash or deposits at a Federal Reserve Bank—behind a stipulated portion of the checkable deposits they hold. Control over the size of these reserves is the principal but not the only means by which the Federal Reserve carries out the nation's monetary policy. If the Federal Reserve provides financial institutions with more reserves, their ability to lend to the public is increased, thus making possible growth in the money supply and in aggregate demand. Conversely, if the Federal Reserve holds down the amount of reserves or lowers its additions to them, the size of the money supply and of aggregate demand are restrained.

Monetary policy today is a subject of considerable controversy. Economists are divided on what Federal Reserve policy ought to be and how it should be executed. Conventional wisdom once said that the Fed should "lean against the wind"—that is, increase the money supply when aggregate demand falls and the economy needs stimulation, and hold the money supply down when aggregate demand rises and inflation threatens. Such a policy, it was felt, would enable the Federal Reserve to keep aggregate demand at a level that would promote price stability and encourage a more stable and desirable level of economic growth. More recently, however, economists who believe in the theory of "rational expectations," and another group of economists known as "monetarists," have argued that it is not possible for the Federal Reserve to be effective by following a "lean against the wind" policy. The rational expectationists argue that whenever consumers, investors, and businesses correctly anticipate shifts in economic policy, they will act in ways that will offset the effects of such shifts. Monetarists believe that the Federal Reserve should take a long-run view and steadily increase the money supply at approximately the same rate as the growth of the nation's productive capacity. They believe the Federal Reserve should not attempt to make frequent short-term changes in the money supply in response to changing economic conditions. The monetarists feel that changes in monetary policy create more economic instability than would a fixed policy of steady monetary expansion. These differences of opinion, plus current problems with defining and controlling the money supply, have been making the task of conducting effective monetary management a difficult one.

A list of 13 content statements dealing with the concept of *Monetary Policy*, suggested for inclusion in the K-l2 curriculum, is in Chapter IV. Chapters V, VI, and VII indicate placement in grades K-4, 5-8, and 9-12.

18. FISCAL POLICY

Fiscal policy consists of changes in taxes, in government expenditures on goods and services, and in transfer payments that are designed to affect the level of aggregate demand in the economy. Fiscal policy can also be used to provide incentives for increasing aggregate supply, such as providing special tax concessions to firms that invest in new plant and equipment, or offering low-cost student loan in order to encourage people to pursue a college education. Although the president makes proposals regarding fiscal policy in annual budget messages, the Congress of the United States is largely responsible for ultimate decisions on fiscal policy.

When the government increases spending on goods and services or on transfer payments but does not increase tax receipts correspondingly—and if no other significant changes occur—total aggregate demand will rise and the economy will experience more employment of its resources or more inflation or both. Conversely, when government reduces expenditures without reducing tax receipts, aggregate demand will decline and the economy will experience less employment of its resources or less inflation or both. Similar effects can be obtained by reducing or increasing tax receipts while holding government expenditures constant. A reduction in tax receipts will raise people's disposable income and thus increase aggregate demand in the economy. An increase in tax receipts will reduce people's disposable income and thus lower aggregate demand. But those who emphasize rational expectations (mentioned in the previous section) argue that to the extent that people recognize what these policies are intended to accomplish, fiscal policy can *not* work effectively in the manner just described. The monetarists (also mentioned in the previous section) argue that fiscal policy will not be effective unless it is accompanied by appropriate changes in the money supply.

Apart from the theoretical differences among some economists, the actual task of altering government expenditures and tax receipts to promote overall economic stability and growth has proven difficult to carry out in practice. It usually takes a long time to get legislation through Congress and signed by the president, and changes in taxes and spending often become entangled with questions of income distribution and political expediency as well as with questions of macroeconomic stability and growth. The large federal deficits of recent years also make it increasingly difficult to coordinate monetary and fiscal policy for the purpose of stabilizing the economy. Thus, as with monetary policy, we still have much to learn about fiscal policy and how it can be best used to achieve macroeconomic objectives.

A list of 10 content statements dealing with the concept of *Fiscal Policy*, suggested for inclusion in the K-12 curriculum, is in Chapter IV. Chapters V, VI, and VII indicate placement in grades K-4, 5-8, and 9-12.

International Economic Concepts

International economics is the study of economic relationships among nations, including international trade and investment and international monetary relations. In general, economists use the same tools of analysis to understand the world economy as they do to understand a national economy. These include opportunity cost, specialization and exchange, markets and prices, supply and demand, and competition and market structure. The principles underlying trade between countries are the same as those underlying trade between regions within a country. Capital and labor move between countries for the same reasons they move from one part of a country to another. Inflation and unemployment may spread around the world just as they do around one country—and for similar reasons. Special problems, however, which do not exist within a country, arise in international economic relationships because the world is divided into more than 180 political units. Most of these political units place restrictions on international trade that they do not place on domestic trade. Since almost every country has its own monetary system, there must be a "linkage mechanism" permitting people and businesses in one country to change their money into the currencies of other countries with which they wish to carry out economic transactions. This "linkage mechanism" is the network of foreign exchange markets in which different currencies are bought and sold at a "price" called the foreign exchange rate.

19. ABSOLUTE AND COMPARATIVE ADVANTAGE AND BARRIERS TO TRADE

Economists use the concepts of **absolute advantage** and **comparative advantage** to explain why trade takes place between countries (and between different regions in the same country). These concepts are based on the difference between the opportunity costs of producing goods and services in different areas.

Productive resources are distributed unevenly around the world just as they are within a country. These differences in resource distribution give rise to differences in opportunity costs which make it desirable to specialize and exchange. For example, Wyoming has open spaces suited to cattle-raising but has few people whereas Rhode Island has little space but many skilled workers, a situation that makes it worthwhile to develop industry. Thus, Wyoming has an absolute advantage over Rhode Island in cattle raising while Rhode Island has an absolute advantage over Wyoming in industry.

If necessary, Rhode Island probably could raise cattle and Wyoming could develop industry. But the opportunity cost of raising cattle in Rhode Island would be the loss of a large amount of industrial output, and the opportunity cost of Wyoming's using its existing resources to develop industry would be the loss of a large amount of cattle production. Each state would be worse off than if each specialized and traded with the other.

The concept of absolute advantage explains why trade takes place between countries with very different economies, such as raw material producers like Indonesia, which produces coffee, sugar, and minerals, and industrialized nations like Japan, which produces machinery. But the greatest volume of international trade today is actually between countries with rather similar economies—that is, between the industrialized nations of North America, Western Europe, and Japan. To explain the basis of this trade we must use the more sophisticated concept of comparative advantage. This can best be understood by considering it first in the context of individual specialization.

Sharon Smith is a top-flight advertising executive. It happens that she can also type faster than any of the secretaries in her offices. Yet, even though she is superior in both skills, it would still pay Ms. Smith to concentrate on her advertising work and let a secretary type her letters. An hour spent typing is an hour not spent on advertising work, and the opportunity cost of this for Ms. Smith would be very high. So she will concentrate on the skill in which her comparative advantage is the greatest and let the secretary specialize in the work in which her disadvantage is the least. In this way the total output of advertising work and typing will be greater than if each person tried to do both jobs.

Applying comparative advantage to countries, it will pay the United States, for example, to specialize in producing jet aircraft and leave the manufacture of lace to Belgium, even if the United States can make both products more cheaply than Belgium. The United States has a greater margin of efficiency over Belgium in jet aircraft than in lace, so the opportunity cost of diverting productive resources away from aircraft and into lace would be very high.

Among nations, as among individuals and regions, the concept of comparative advantage relates to the opportunity cost involved in producing more of one good or service and less of another. If each nation specializes in the production and export of those goods and services in which it has a comparative advantage and imports from other nations those goods and services in which it has a comparative disadvantage, several important consequences follow. World production, world economic growth, and efficiency in the use of limited resources will all be maximized. As a result, consumers everywhere will have access to a greater amount of goods and services at lower prices.

In principle, internationally traded goods and services should be sold in competitive markets at prices determined by supply and demand. Just as they do in a domestic economy, prices in international markets "tell" producers what it is profitable to produce and "tell" consumers on what it is advantageous to spend their money. The changing pattern of prices in international trade should thus determine what will be produced, how it will be produced, and to whom it will be distributed as these prices interact with the mechanisms that perform these same functions within different countries.

In fact, however, international markets are beset by more complexities than domestic markets. One reason is that most governments erect artificial barriers to the free flow of goods and services and productive resources. These **barriers to trade** include tariffs or special taxes on imported goods, quotas, import licenses, export subsidies, state trading, the formation of cartels, controls on the freedom to exchange currencies, and restrictions on immigration. Such obstacles distort the pattern of prices, production, consumption, and the distribution of income in international markets. If the United States restricts the importation of Japanese cars and Philippine sugar, for example, the production of American automobiles and sugar will be encouraged. American workers and sugar growers will have more jobs and higher incomes, but American consumers will pay higher prices for cars and sugar, and American exporters of aircraft and cotton, for example, may suffer reduced sales to Japan and the Philippines. Patterns of production in all three countries may change in an undesirable way, with productive resources moving from more efficient into less efficient uses.

Monopoly also may affect international markets. The government of the former Soviet Union, for example, had a monopoly on its foreign trade. As a result, foreign private businesses that engaged in trade with the Soviet Union found themselves dealing with one seller (a monopoly) or one buyer (a monopsony). After 15 independent countries emerged from the Soviet Union, each of them had to develop new ways of dealing with international buyers and sellers, and foreign governments and private businesses had to offer assistance to help them adapt to a non-monopoly, non-monopsony way of engaging in foreign trade.

Sometimes international prices are rigged by international agreement among governments, as is done with tin through the International Tin agreement and with oil through the organization of Petroleum Exporting Countries (OPEC).

A list of 10 content statements dealing with the concept of *Absolute and Comparative Advantage and Barriers to Trade*, suggested for inclusion in the K-12 curriculum, is in Chapter IV. Chapters V, VI, and VII indicate placement in grades K-4, 5-8, and 9-12.

20. EXCHANGE RATES AND THE BALANCE OF PAYMENTS

An **exchange rate** is the price of one nation's currency in terms of another nation's currency. (The British pound may be worth $1.80 in U.S. dollars, while the Canadian dollar may be worth $0.85, etc.). When exchange rates change, both the level of domestic economic activity and the international flow of goods, services, and productive resources are affected.

Some foreign exchange markets are completely free, which means that exchange rates are determined by the forces of supply and demand emanating from many buyers and sellers. In other foreign exchange markets, governments intervene to influence exchange rates. A government may actually fix the rates for its own currency by requiring all those who earn foreign currencies to surrender them to a government authority at a government-determined exchange rate. The government then rations or sells the currencies taken in at fixed prices to those who wish to make payments abroad. Other governments may "peg" their exchange rates by buying or selling their own currencies in foreign exchange markets in sufficient quantities to maintain a given set of rates

From 1946 to 1973, under the Bretton Woods agreement, which was signed by most of the world's countries , governments did intervene continuously in foreign exchange markets in order to maintain a world-wide system of fixed exchange rates. Since 1973, rates have been more or less flexible. Governments have been intervening in foreign exchange markets periodically or sporadically rather than continuously. Because rates neither float freely in response to supply and demand at all times nor are fixed, this practice has been called a "managed float."

An alteration in exchange rates can have a significant effect on the flow of world trade as well as on the domestic economy of a country. If, for example, the U.S. dollar strengthens in terms of the German mark (DM), with the exchange rate moving from say $1.00 equals DM 2.00 (DM equals $0.50) to $1.00 equals DM 2.50 (DM equals $0.40), German goods will become cheaper for Americans. They can now obtain DM 2.50 for $1.00 instead of DM 2.00. This will cause German imports into the United States to increase. Meanwhile, U.S. exports to Germany will fall because the change in exchange rates has made the U.S dollar more expensive in terms of German marks, causing imports from the United States to become more expensive to Germans. These changes in exports and imports will stimulate employment in Germany and may reduce employment in the United States. But the greater supply of German goods will help hold down inflationary pressures in the United States. (If the U.S. dollar weakens in terms of the German mark, the effects in each country will be reversed.)

The **balance of payments** (B/P) of a country is a statistical accounting which records, for a given period, all the payments that the residents, businesses, and government of one country make to the rest of the world as well as all the receipts which they receive from the rest of the world. Just as the GDP accounts provide information on the functioning of a national economy, so the B/P helps a nation to understand the state of its economic relationships with the rest of the world. It also helps nations to make appropriate decisions about their policies concerning world trade and finance.

The transactions recorded in the B/P are commonly separated into two portions: the current account and the capital account. The **current account** includes exports and imports of merchandise, receipts and payments relating to services such as tourism, shipping, banking, and insurance, income received from investments abroad, investment income transferred abroad to foreigners, payments and receipts in the form of royalties, government foreign aid given or received, military pension payments as well as charitable contributions. The **capital account** consists of movements of long-term capital between countries, such as business investments and purchases of stocks and bonds, as well as of short-term capital movements—which often consist mainly of banking transactions.

The terms "deficit" or "surplus" commonly used in reference to a country's B/P usually designate the relationship between current account receipts and payments. If receipts are less than expenditures, the country is running a deficit on current account. If receipts are greater than expenditures, the country is running a surplus. Deficits or surpluses in the current account may be offset in the capital account. A surplus or deficit on the entire B/P is recorded as, and results in, a gain or loss in official government reserves—chiefly gold and holdings of foreign exchange.

A study of the B/P reveals much information on the state of the demand for and supply of currencies in foreign exchange markets which, in turn, as we have seen, determine exchange rates. U. S. imports, investments abroad, foreign travel, and military spending for troops stationed in foreign countries, for example, all add to the supply of dollars in foreign exchange markets. These dollars constitute part of the demand for other currencies, say, Japanese yen. When foreigners buy our exports, visit our country, or invest in the United States, or when foreign businesses, banks or governments repay loans to Americans, then foreign currencies are being supplied and dollars are being demanded in foreign exchange markets. In a free market, the dollar's rate of exchange for foreign currencies depends on the relationship of both sets of demands and supplies just described. In this regard it is important to emphasize that it is the B/P as a whole, and not any one item taken separately that is important. The state of the balance of trade (exports-imports) alone, for example, does not determine a country's supply of and demand for foreign exchange. That is determined by all payments and all receipts taken together.

A list of 10 content statements dealing with the concept of *Exchange Rates and the*

Balance of Payment, suggested for inclusion in the K-12 curriculum, is in Chapter IV. Chapters V, VI, and VII indicate placement in grades K-4, 5-8, and 9-12.

21. INTERNATIONAL ASPECTS OF GROWTH AND STABILITY

The international economic concepts of comparative advantage, barriers to trade, exchange rates, and balance of payments are more important today than in the past because all nations are now so much more interdependent. The international transfer of investment capital and technology from rich and developed countries to poor and developing countries where capital and modern technology are scarce is vital to both the developing countries and the entire world economy. International investment takes place through both private and public channels. Private investments are made by businesses, particularly large multinational corporations, as well as by private purchases of foreign stocks and bonds. Public transfers of capital are made by governments through foreign-aid programs and by official lending by international organizations, of which the World Bank is the largest.

In some cases the flow of labor across international borders can also promote economic growth. This was true during the years of unlimited immigration into the United States in the nineteenth century. More recent examples are Australia after World War II and the flow of Italian and Turkish workers into West Germany in the 1960s. The large volume of Mexican immigration into the United States, both legal and illegal, in recent years reflects the working of the market mechanism. Labor is flowing from an area where wages are relatively low and job opportunities relatively limited to an area where wages are relatively high and job opportunities relatively plentiful.

A war can change economic opportunities in a very short time. After the brief Persian Gulf War, fought in early 1991, millions of workers from many countries lost their jobs in the countries around the Persian Gulf area and beyond. Some workers lost their jobs because their work could not be carried on during the war, but enormous numbers of people were expelled from the countries in which they worked because they were foreign nationals and therefore were considered to be untrustworthy. Repercussions of the displacement of people were felt in these workers' countries of origin, where their incomes made a great difference in their nations' economies.

Like economic growth, both inflation and unemployment—so important in Western industrial nations—are no longer purely domestic phenomena. They can be—and are—transmitted from one country to another through flows of trade and money. If the United States and other Western industrialized nations go into recession, as they did in 1974-75 and 1981-82, for example, the incomes of their citizens and the output of their industries drop. Their imports decline. This decline hits many less developed countries hard, for they depend heavily on sales of their primary products (copper, bauxite, sugar, wool, and the like) to the industrialized countries. Falling sales and prices bring the recession to the developing countries. Their foreign exchange earnings fall; they are unable to pay for needed imports; and they may become unable to repay their debts—or even the interest on them. Thus, worldwide recession tends to become a cumulative process. Conversely, if the economics of industrial countries are all booming, the demand for primary products increases in world markets, and the product prices rise. Such booms also tend to cumulate.

In theory, the major industrial powers acting in concert could use monetary and fiscal policies to maintain high-level output and employment without inflation. That would help achieve world economic stability at high levels of output. In practice, countries usually follow somewhat different—and sometimes incompatible—monetary and fiscal policies that frequently result in different rates of growth and inflation (or deflation) and thereby produce fluctuations in foreign exchange rates.

In sum, the complex world economy can be understood by using much the same concepts of economic analysis as for a domestic economy. The special problems of the world economy arise because the world is divided into numerous countries. Each has sovereign powers over the flow of goods, services, capital, and people across its borders, and each has its own monetary and fiscal policies which influence exchange rates and the balances of payments among nations.

A list of six content statements dealing with the concept of *International Aspects of Growth and Stability*, suggested for inclusion in the K-12 curriculum, is in Chapter IV. Chapters V, VI, and VII indicate the placement in grades K-4, 5-8, and 9-12.

Measurement Concepts and Methods

Economists and other analysts use a number of measurement concepts and methods to explain economic developments and to assess economic performance. Many of these are included in the mathematics curriculum, though in some cases they are described there using somewhat different terminology. The same concepts and methods can be taught with an emphasis on their applicability and usefulness in understanding economics rather than by following the more traditional approach of drawing examples almost exclusively from the physical sciences and engineering.

Several examples of the application of measurement concepts in economics are provided in Chapters V, VI, and VII in the activities shown under the heading "Evidence of Student Learning."

TABLES

Tables are used to present numbers in a concise fashion and to reveal particular relationships among sets of numerical data. Exhibit 8 illustrates two common forms of presentation. The title of each table provides a general indication of its subject and/or purpose. The source note below the table states where the data come from; lettered footnotes present qualifications or more detailed explanations as needed.

EXHIBIT 8

TABLE 1
Employment and Unemployment of the Civilian Labor Force in the United States, 1990–1993
(thousands of persons)

Year	Employed	Unemployed	Total
1990	117,914	6,874	124,788
1991	116,877	8,426	125,303
1992	117,598	9,384	126,982
1993	119,306	8,734	128,040

SOURCE: Bureau of Labor Statistics, U.S. Dept. of Labor

TABLE 2
Employment and Unemployment of the Civilian Labor Force in the United States, 1993

	Thousands of Persons	Percentage of Total Persons
Total	128,040	100.0%
Employed	119,306	93.2
Unemployed	8,734	6.8

SOURCE: Bureau of Labor Statistics, U.S. Dept. of Labor

Table 1 is a **times series.** Tables of this kind show data by time period—day, month, quarter, year—for a number of periods. The information in the first column gives the time period; in this case, the period is yearly, beginning with 1990. The labels at the tops of the next three columns describe what sort of data are given for each time period; in this example, employment, unemployment, and total civilian labor force in the United States. The numerical data themselves are then presented in the rows and columns of the table.

Table 2 shows a **cross section** of some of the data in Table 1, i.e., a snapshot of the information in one particular time period. As before, the labels in the first column and at the tops of the second and third columns describe the data provided. Exhibit 6 on page 24 provides other examples of cross-section tables. The two tables in that exhibit present data on income distribution in the United States in 1992 and 1993.

Tables can also be used to show relationships between economic variables. Exhibit 5 on page 21, for example, presents supply and demand data in the form of a table or "schedule."

CHARTS AND GRAPHS

Charts are used to present relationships among quantitative data in pictorial form. Exhibit 9 illustrates some common types. Chart 1 on page 42 pictures the data that appear in Table 1. This is a **line chart**, in this case showing time along the horizontal axis and employment along the vertical axis. The title and footnotes serve the same purposes as their counterparts in Table 1. Line charts are often called **graphs**. Chart 2 depicts the same data as Chart 1, but in the form of a **bar chart**: differently marked or differently colored bars replace the simple lines used in Chart 1. Chart 3 pictures the data in Table 2 in the form of a **pie chart**. It answers the question: What percentage of the total civilian labor force was employed in 1993?

There are other ways of picturing economic relationships apart from those illustrated here. Exhibits 4 and 7 on pages 20 and 28, for example, show flow charts to illustrate the interrelationships of market exchanges in the U. S. economy.

RATIOS AND PERCENTAGES

Ratios express the relationship of one numerical value to another. The data in Table 2, for example, indicate that the ratio of civilian employment to the total civilian labor force in 1993 was 119,306/128,040. A ratio can also be expressed as a decimal fraction, i.e., 119,306/128,040=.932. Multiplying a decimal fraction by 100 restates it as a percentage, i.e., .932 x 100 = 93.2%. The latter tells us that 93.2% of the total civilian labor force was employed in 1993.

Percentages (often represented by the symbol %), therefore, are a simple way of expressing ratios or proportions between numbers in terms of hundredth parts. What proportion of $100 is $50? It is 50/100 =0.5 x 100 = 50%.

PERCENTAGE CHANGES

Percentage changes are used to measure the relative change in economic variables from one time period to another. Thus, the percentage change in teachers' average salary during the period 1970 to 1992, displayed in Table 3, on the following page, is 450 percent. This number is calculated by dividing the *change* in average salary during the period ($34,100 - $6,200, or $27,900) by the average salary in 1970: 27,900/6,200 = 4.50; multiplying by 100 yields 450 percent.

Percentages can be useful aids in making comparisons. At the same time, however, one must pay careful attention to the base numbers—the denominators—used in calculating percentage changes. Equal percentage changes do not imply equal changes in the underlying absolute numbers, unless all the comparisons use the same base number. For example, a 10 percent increase from 100 is a change of 10 (from 100 to 110), but a 10 percent increase from 1,000 is a change of 100 (from 1,000 to 1,100). Likewise, equal changes in absolute numbers do not signify equal percentage changes unless, as noted before, all the comparisons use the same base number. For example, an increase of 10 from 10 to 20 is a 100 percent increase, but an increase of 10 from 20 to 30 is a 50 percent increase. These cautions about making comparisons when the percentage changes consist of increases also apply when the percentage changes consist of decreases. There is no limit to how large a percentage increase can be, but a percentage decrease can never be larger than 100 percent.

EXHIBIT 9

CHART 1

Line Chart

Employment and Unemployment in the U.S. Civilian Labor Force, 1990-93

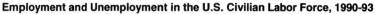

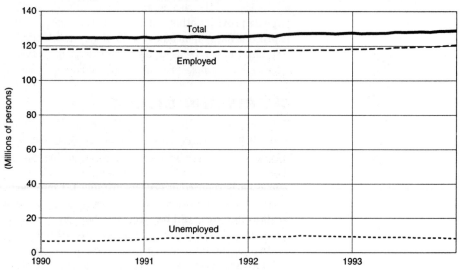

Source: Bureau of Labor Statistics, U.S. Dept. of Labor

CHART 2

Bar Chart

Employment and Unemployment in the U.S. Civilian Labor Force, 1990-93

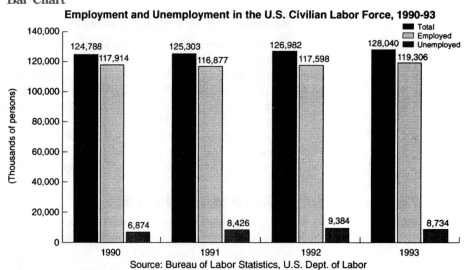

Source: Bureau of Labor Statistics, U.S. Dept. of Labor

CHART 3

Pie Chart

Employment and Unemployment in the U.S. Civilian Labor Force, 1993

Unemployed, 6.8%

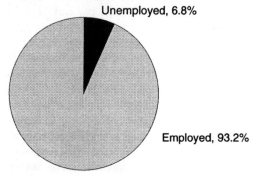

Employed, 93.2%

Source: Bureau of Labor Statistics, U.S. Dept. of Labor

INDEX NUMBERS

Index numbers measure changes in economic variables using a fixed base value for comparisons. The base value can be for a single year, or it can be an average of several years. With rare exceptions, the base index number is set at a value of 100, and all other numbers are expressed as a percentage of the base period value. We can construct an index of the teachers' salaries shown in Table 3 (Exhibit 10), for example, by setting the 1970 value equal to 100 and expressing the 1980, 1990, and 1992 values as percentages of the 1970 value. As shown in Table 3, the index of teachers' salaries in 1980 is 258, in 1990 it is 503, and in 1992 it is 550 when 1970 is given the base year value of 100.

Calculating percentage changes from the base year is easier using index numbers than using the standard percentage change formula explained earlier. The percentage change in average teachers' salaries from 1970 to 1992, which we calculated earlier as 450 percent, for example, can be read directly from Table 3 by subtracting the 1970 index number of 100 from the 1992 index number of 550. To calculate percentage changes from years other than the base year, however, use the procedure explained in the first paragraph under "percentage changes" above.

REAL VS. NOMINAL VALUES

Monetary variables in economics can be expressed in "nominal" values or in "real" values. **Nominal** monetary values are measured in **current prices**, that is, in the prices prevailing in the period represented by the variable. **Real** monetary values are measured in **constant prices**, that is, in prices of a given—or base—period. When the level of any set of prices changes, the difference between nominal values and real values (or the difference between current prices and constant prices) can be substantial.

Real (or constant) monetary values are obtained by adjusting or "deflating" nominal monetary values with an appropriate index of prices. (See Table 4, which shows the average teachers' salaries presented earlier along with figures for the Consumer Price Index.) The **Consumer Price Index** (CPI) measures the change from some base period in the average level of prices for a fixed collection of goods and services bought by urban families and individuals. For ease of comparison, we use 1970 as the base year for the CPI data shown in Table 4.

The real value of teachers' salaries (in constant 1970 prices) is obtained by dividing the nominal salary values by the Consumer Price Index and multiplying the result by 100 to get the decimal in the right place, that is, to convert the figure back to a dollar amount. For 1970 the calculation is $6,200/100 = 62.00; 62.00 x 100 = $6,200. For 1980 the calculation is $16,00/213 = 75.12; 75.12 x 100 = $7,512. For 1990 the calculation is $31,00/337 x 100 = $9,258. For 1992 the calculation is $34,100/362 x 100 = $9,420.

The resulting figures for the real value of teachers' salaries indicate that the increase between 1970 and 1992 was much less that the increase shown by the nominal values. The average salary increase in nominal terms was 450 percent. The average salary increase in real terms was 52 percent ($3,220/6,200 = .52; .52 x 100 = 52 percent).

AVERAGES AND DISTRIBUTIONS AROUND THE AVERAGE

"Average" is a general term for a single number that is used to summarize the meaning of a large amount of numerical data. The two most common measures of averages used in economics are the median and the arithmetic mean.

The **median** is the middle-most value when the individual values in a set of data are arranged by magnitude from the lowest value to the highest value. Such an arrangement is called an "array." Half the values in the array are above the median; half are below. The **arithmetic mean** (sometimes called the "mean" or simply the "average") is the sum of all values in a set of data divided by the number of values included. Table 5 shows an array of the 1993 sales receipts of the top 25 corporations in Fortune magazine's list of the 500 largest U. S. industrial corporations. The median sales figure for this array of 25 values is the thirteenth, the $25,336 million shown for Amoco. The arithmetic mean for these 25 sales figures is $40,285 million.

Extreme values in a set of data have a stronger influence on the arithmetic mean than on the median. That is why there is a big difference between the mean and the median values in the data just cited. Therefore, careful interpretation of any average value usually requires some knowledge of the distribution of values around the average.

EXHIBIT 10

The 25 Largest U.S. Industrial Corporations, Ranked by Sales, 1993

	Sales (millions of dollars)
General Motors	$133,622
Ford Motor	108,521
Exxon	97,825
International Business Machines	62,716
General Electric	60,823
Mobil	56,576
Philip Morris	50,621
Chrysler	43,600
Texaco	34,359
E.I. du Pont de Nemours	32,621
Chevron	32,123
Procter & Gamble	30,433
Amoco	25,336
Boeing	25,285
Pepsico	25,021
Conagra	21,519
Shell Oil	20,853
United Technologies	20,736
Hewlett-Packard	20,317
Eastman Kodak	20,059
Dow Chemical	18,060
Atlantic Richfield	17,189
Motorola	16,963
USX	16,844
RJR Nabisco Holdings	15,104

SOURCE: Fortune, April 18, 1994, p. 220

Broad Social Goals

The broad social goals that relate to economics and that are given considerable importance in American society today are economic freedom, economic efficiency, economic equity, economic security, economic stability (full employment and the absence of inflation), and economic growth. These goals, and the importance attached to each of them, guide individuals and society in the making of decisions. The goals provide targets and a sense of direction in formulating the means for reaching these targets.

These goals can also be thought of as criteria for evaluating the performance of the economic system (or parts of the system) and for examining the usefulness of new as well as existing programs. Some of the goals, such as freedom or equity, are difficult to state in quantitative form. Others, such as full employment or price stability, can be articulated as numerical targets. Indeed, in 1978 Congress for the first time established specific numerical goals for unemployment and inflation. The 1978 legislation, popularly known as the Humphrey-Hawkins Act, had set the target for the unemployment rate at 4 percent, to be achieved by 1983. The rate of inflation, as measured by the consumer price index, was to be reduced to 3 percent by 1983 and to zero by 1988.

A comparison of the goals of the Humphrey-Hawkins Act with what has happened since 1978 makes it clear that economic goals are rarely if ever fully attained; if they are, it is usually for short periods of time only. Nevertheless, the results point up the conclusion that only by attempting to set clear, specific goals is it possible to measure the progress made in attaining them.

Examples of the use of broad social goals to evaluate the performance of an economy are in Chapter III and in several activities in Chapter VII under "Evidence of Student Learning."

ECONOMIC FREEDOM

Freedom as an economic goal concerns the freedoms of the marketplace—the freedom of consumers to decide how they wish to allocate their spending among various goods and services, the freedom of workers to choose to change jobs, join unions, and go on strike, the freedom of individuals to establish new businesses and to decide what to produce and when to change the pattern of production, the freedom of savers to decide how much to save and where to invest their savings. Of particular interest is the effect of actions by individuals, groups, or governments to enhance or restrict freedom in the marketplace and thereby affect the possible attainment of the other goals of efficiency, equity, security, stability, and growth. A number of people argue that government regulation limits the freedom of some people to make their own choices. Others argue that government policies may free some people to take greater advantage of the opportunities provided in a market economy. Given the differences in viewpoint, it is essential to define the kinds of freedom under discussion and whose behavior is most likely to be affected.

ECONOMIC EFFICIENCY

Efficiency can have two meanings. The term can refer to **technical efficiency**, which focuses on using the smallest input of resources to obtain some stated level of output, or obtaining the highest level of output using fixed inputs of specified resources. Since technical efficiency does not take into account the different costs of various inputs or the different benefits of various outputs, considerations of technical efficiency alone cannot indicate the most appropriate decision to make. An economy might be technically efficient in producing good A, for example, but if consumers do not want good A and prefer good B instead, then it would not be economically efficient to produce good A.

Economic efficiency is a broader concept than technical efficiency. Economic efficiency goes beyond technical efficiency and takes into account the costs and benefits associated with various market preferences and decisions. In order to obtain maximum benefits from using our limited resources, we should undertake only these economic actions which result in additional benefits that exceed the additional costs. By this standard, economic actions should not be undertaken if the additional costs exceed the additional benefits. The concept of economic efficiency is central in economics, and it should receive heavy emphasis in both individual and social decision making.

ECONOMIC EQUITY

Equity, which deals with what is "fair" and what is "unfair," or what is "right" and what is "wrong," is difficult to define precisely. **Economic equity** can be described as the application of our concepts of what is fair and what is unfair—or of what "ought to be" and "ought not to be"—to economic policy. To be sure, people differ in their conception of what represents equity or fairness. However, in evaluating economic performance, the concept serves as a reminder to investigate which or what kinds of people are made better or worse off as a result of, for example, a change in prices or the introduction of a new government program. Though two actions may appear to be equally efficient from an economic standpoint, one could benefit the old and another the young, one might benefit consumers and another producers, and so on. Many people would not be indifferent to who benefits from a policy, because they harbor some general idea of what is equitable. From the viewpoint of economics, equity ultimately deals with the distribution of income and wealth. One way of dealing with this question is simply to examine the effects of economic actions on the distribution of income and wealth: Who gains and who loses? The distinction between equality of opportunity and the equality of results is also important when economic equity is addressed.

ECONOMIC SECURITY

The goal of **economic security** concerns the desire of people to be protected against economic risks over which they may have little or no control. Such risks include accidents on their jobs, unemployment, destitution in old age, business failures, bank failures, precipitous price declines for one's product, as well as disasters caused by natural or human agency. Economic security is enhanced by individual efforts, such as savings and the purchase of insurance, as well as by the growth of the economy, through which the mass of people receive more material well-being. Various government programs such as worker's compensation, unemployment compensation, social security, aid to families with dependent children, federal insurance of bank deposits, and farm price supports are also aimed at increasing economic security in the United States. Nations also engage in the quest for economic security by seeking international agreements which assure them of access to key resources or of adequate prices for their exports. In the last analysis, it is the possession of real goods and access to services or assured claims to goods and services that provides economic security.

FULL EMPLOYMENT

Full employment prevails when all of an economy's resources are utilized to capacity, but most discussion turns on the employment or unemployment of people. In practice, an unemployment rate for people that reflects normal frictional unemployment— unemployment that occurs as workers change jobs or enter the labor force— has come to be viewed as full employment. Debate continues as to what unemployment rate—at present suggestions range from 5 to 7 percent of the labor force—constitutes full employment. But keeping the goal of full employment in mind helps to remind us of the costs in lost output to the economy and in economic hardship to individuals that result from rates of unemployment that are too high.

PRICE STABILITY

As we have indicated, overall **price stability** means the absence of inflation or deflation, not the absence of changes in relative prices in particular markets. In reality, overall price-level changes are not often likely to be zero. Not only do our price indexes fail to reflect some improvements in product quality that in effect lower certain prices, but more important, price changes reflect the push and pull of market forces as changes occur in supply and demand. What constitutes "reasonable" price stability is the subject of much discussion. Nonetheless, this goal recognizes that sharp price changes necessitate costly adjustments in the behavior of individuals and businesses in order to cope with the effects that such changes produce.

ECONOMIC GROWTH

Economic growth means producing increasing amounts of goods and services over the long term. If the people of a society want to raise their level of living, they must produce more goods and services. If the population is growing, the amount produced must be still greater to provide for the additional people. This is why changes in total GDP per capita (that is, per person) are usually more meaningful than changes in total GDP as a measure of growth.

Economic growth is an important goal in virtually all countries, and it is closely related to several of the other goals discussed above. Both individuals and nations try to increase their economic security and well-being by expanding output. Individuals seek ways to enhance their earning ability while nations seek to stimulate the growth of per capita output and income. Economic growth helps provide jobs for a growing labor force, and economic growth also makes it easier for a society to devote some of its output to promoting greater economic equity and greater economic security by assisting the disadvantaged, the disabled, or other groups that need help. If output does not grow, one person or one group can obtain more goods and services only if another person or group receives less. But, to revert to an often-used metaphor, when a larger economic pie is baked, everyone can have a larger slice.

On the supply side, the upper limit to economic growth is determined by the availability of productive resources, the efficiency with which these resources are used, and the economic, social, and political factors that either encourage or discourage an increase in productive capacity. These latter factors include the size of the market, the value system of the people, and the degree of political stability or instability. Once the productive capacity of an economy is established, the actual rate of growth in a market economy will be determined by the level of aggregate demand. If an economy is in a recession and aggregate demand is too low to employ existing resources fully, there will be little market incentive to increase productive capacity. Thus, there is a close relationship between the short-run goal of full employment and the long-run goal of economic growth. As we have indicated, the existence of rapid inflation also hinders the long-run expansion of a nation's total productive capacity.

OTHER GOALS

The foregoing broad social goals are not immutable. As economic conditions change and as social patterns shift, goals are constantly being rethought and sometimes redefined. From time to time other goals appear and take priority. In the early 1940's, for example, the United States' main objective was to mobilize the economy to win World War II. Strengthening our nation's defenses also became an increasing concern in the early 1980's, as did improving the quality of education. In the 1960s, President Kennedy committed the nation to putting a human on the moon, and President Johnson emphasized the need to build a "great society," including improving the treatment of women and minorities in the marketplace. In the 1970s, environmental concerns received increasing attention, and the world's attention was focused on energy supplies.

Not only do broad social goals change, but the relative importance attached to these goals also shifts from time to time. When inflation is rampant, for example, concern about unemployment tends to decline; when equity considerations become uppermost in people's minds, concern about economic efficiency lessens; when environmental concerns increase, the emphasis on economic growth tends to diminish. Moreover, we constantly face the problem of trade-offs among our broad social goals.

Trade-offs among Goals

The pursuit of any goal requires calculating the costs of achieving it versus the value of the expected benefits. In this way economic analysis enables us to make clear-minded decisions about goals that reflect our individual as well as our national values and objectives. Since many of our broad social goals conflict, difficult trade-offs frequently have to be made in making specific policy decisions. Some examples: farm price supports, which promote security for some farmers but may reduce efficiency in agriculture and raise prices for consumers; minimum wage laws, which are an attempt to increase equity (by trying to raise the wages of lower-paid workers) but may do so at the cost of increased unemployment; and wage-price controls in order to restrain inflation, which do so only temporarily and reduce economic efficiency and freedom.

Economic growth also involves costs and trade-offs as well as benefits. Protection of the environment seems almost always to involve a trade-off. If we wish to preserve or clean up the environment, we may have to pay the price of having less—for example, going without the coal we would have if strip-mining were permitted. If the government requires automobile manufacturers to install anti-pollution devices, the car costs the consumer more. If a city builds a water purification plant, citizens may have to pay higher taxes to finance it. In general, cleaning up and preserving the environment is likely to divert resources into environmental protection and away from growth, and this will affect our measurements of the GDP. Spending on growth, e. g., for an additional factory, will have the consequence of increasing future GDP through the inclusion of the future output of the new factory. Spending on a cleaner environment, e. g., for the reduction of air pollution, will improve the quality of life, but since the cleaner air is not sold in the market, it will not be included as an addition to GDP. Thus, society's choice of trade-offs has different effects on the statistics we conventionally use to measure economic growth.

We may conclude that any particular economic goal must be viewed as one of several goals that individuals and societies try to reach and recognize that trade-offs are inherent in pursuing multiple goals. Economic analysis seeks to inform people about what they must give up with respect to one goal as they consider the gains from attaining another. Such analysis helps people make more intelligent decisions by clarifying the nature of the trade-offs among various goals.

Self-Interest and Personal Values

The idea of self-interest differs from the goals discussed above. Self-interest reflects the concern of individuals for their own well-being and personal values, whereas the other goals we have noted reflect broader social concerns. The achievement of social goals often comes at the expense of particular individuals or groups. The individuals or groups adversely affected may well oppose steps to achieve the goals. This means that the positions people ultimately take on economic issues will be affected by their own self-interest as well as by the weight they put on broad social goals. It is important to try to separate these two types of goals in order to understand why people ultimately reach the decisions they do on economic issues.

Chapter III

Applying Economic Understanding to Specific Issues

The purpose of teaching economics at the elementary and secondary school levels is not only to impart a general understanding of how our economy works, but also to improve economic decision making by students through the use of an orderly reasoned approach. The kind of systematic diagnosis Malcolm used in the case described in Chapter I applies to most economic problems, whether personal or public. The following cases extend the use of such a decision-making model to two economic issues involving public policy.

The first deals with a microeconomic issue: the extent, if any, to which a state should exert control over the price of eggs that are produced within its borders. The second deals with a macroeconomic issue: how the economy might adjust to a large, permanent decline in defense spending by the federal government. These cases illustrate the opportunities citizens in a democratic society have to influence decisions about important public policies by making their views known to legislators and other public officials, by voting, or by both means.

The Case of Egg Diversion

Some years ago, a newspaper in State A reported that the price of eggs had declined from 72 to 65 cents per dozen. The reason was reduced consumer demand because of an economic recession. As a result of the price decline, several local egg producers were forced out of business and others complained about the difficulty of earning a reasonable profit. One rural legislator called for an investigation of the slide in egg prices and its impact, but nothing had come of his suggestion.

Another report appeared in State B, stating that a state board had decided to continue diverting 5 percent of the state's weekly egg production from the consumer market in order to keep egg prices up. The report continued:

> The 16-member State Egg Advisory Board, on a 9-5 vote with two abstentions, turned down a motion from consumer representatives to quit buying up and thereby diverting 10,000 cases of eggs a week—30 dozen eggs to the case—from the consumer marketplace for later sale abroad at lower prices. The policy, in effect since November, helps hold prices in the state up to about 72 cents a dozen.

Inflation-squeezed egg farmers, hurt by soaring grain and feed prices, said that ending the diversion policy would depress prices, probably as much as 5 to 8 cents a dozen, and would force smaller egg producers out of business.

The issues described represent the problems raised by federal farm policy in respect to several major agricultural products. People must make up their own minds about such policies after considering the probable gains and costs to producers, to consumers, and to any others concerned. The key question in the case is: would it be better to let competition govern the market for farm products or to employ government intervention? The answer depends on which course is deemed to provide the most benefit to the individuals directly concerned and to society as a whole. Or, to put it another way, which course will prove to be the least detrimental in achieving the foregoing objectives.

Individuals can use the five-step reasoned approach outlined in Chapter I to reach their own conclusions.

1. STATE THE PROBLEM OR ISSUE

The basic question raised in this case is whether a state should buy eggs and thereby divert supply from the consumer market in order to maintain prices above where they would otherwise be. Closely related questions are how a system of egg diversion helps or hurts various groups: domestic egg producers, domestic egg consumers, state taxpayers, foreign egg producers, and foreign egg consumers.

2. DETERMINE THE PERSONAL OR BROAD SOCIAL GOALS TO BE ATTAINED

The most relevant broad social goals seem to be efficiency, equity, and security; the most relevant personal goals are the self-interest of domestic egg producers and consumers, foreign egg producers and consumers, and state taxpayers.

3. CONSIDER THE PRINCIPAL ALTERNATIVE MEANS OF ACHIEVING THE GOALS

This case presents only two alternatives. One is to allow the price of eggs to fluctuate in response to changing market conditions, as they do in State A. The other is to have a State Egg Advisory Board use taxpayers' money to buy up to 10,000 cases of eggs a week in order to hold the price near 72 cents per dozen, as is done in State B. In the second alternative, the Egg Advisory Board sells the "surplus" eggs abroad at a price below 72 cents per dozen.

4. SELECT THE ECONOMIC CONCEPTS NEEDED TO UNDERSTAND THE PROBLEM AND USE THEM TO APPRAISE THE MERITS OF EACH ALTERNATIVE.

The concept of opportunity cost (number 2 in the list that appears in Chapter II) lies at the heart of nearly all issues of economic choice. In addition, this case requires use of the concepts of markets and prices (7), supply and demand (8), competition and market structure (9), income distribution (10), and the role of government (12).

A decision-making grid similar to the one discussed earlier can be used to structure the analysis. In the grid shown in Exhibit 11, the broad goals of efficiency, equity, and security are entered across the row at top. The alternatives of relying on competitive market forces or of supporting prices by state egg board purchases are entered in the left-hand column. Since the goals of equity and security may have different implications for state taxpayers, domestic producers, domestic consumers, foreign producers, and foreign consumers, a grid containing a total of at least 20 cells is necessary to analyze this case.

By definition, economic efficiency involves satisfying consumer preferences with minimum resources. Since a competitive market usually ensures that consumers as a whole will be able to satisfy their preferences at the lowest possible prices, we have entered a plus sign (+) in the cell that relates competitive market forces to the goal of efficiency. We have entered a minus (-) in the cell that relates regulated prices to efficiency because holding the price up to 72 cents per dozen keeps more producers in the egg business; and in the absence of government intervention about 10,000 cases of eggs each week go unsold at that price. The opportunity cost of the unsold eggs in State B is the loss of the other things the surplus resources in the egg business could

EXHIBIT 11
Sample Decision-making Grid for the Egg Diversion Case

ALTERNATIVES	Efficiency	Equity					Security			
		Help Domestic Producers	Help Domestic Consumers	Help Domestic Taxpayers	Help Foreign Producers	Help Foreign Consumers	Help Domestic Producers	Help Domestic Consumers	Help Foreign Producers	Help Foreign Consumers
Rely on competitive market forces (State A)	+	−	+	0	0	0	−	+	0	0
Support prices by state egg board purchases (State A)	−	+	−	−	−	+	+	−	−	+
Other										

53

have produced instead of the eggs. In State A, however, the egg producers who are driven out of business are forced to find other uses for their resources. In State B, resources are used to continue producing eggs that must be bought with taxpayers' money for resale abroad at a lower price. The need to devote resources to the buying and selling of the surplus eggs is another source of inefficiency in State B. This inefficiency does not occur in State A, since the forces of supply and demand result in a market-clearing price that does not leave a surplus of unsold eggs on grocer's shelves. Other aspects of market structure and the role of government can also be used to assess economic efficiency in this case. In the absence of externalities or other types of market failures, none of which appear to be present in this case, our society usually relies on competitive markets to promote efficiency. In State B, however, government intervention reduces competition, and has the effect of holding the price up in what would otherwise be a competitive market.

With regard to equity (or fairness), views will differ. Some people may think that all existing egg farmers should be able to cover their costs and make a reasonable profit after selling their output. Some may believe that the competitive process should operate, thereby rewarding the most efficient producers and causing those who cannot make a reasonable profit in an unregulated market to fail and try to employ their resources elsewhere. A competitive market would also provide domestic consumers with eggs at a lower price. While one group of people may feel it is unfair to consumers or taxpayers to use tax dollars to keep egg prices higher than they would otherwise be, another group may believe that the side effect of helping foreign countries keep their food costs down is a worthy one. This list does not exhaust all possible views, but illustrates some main issues.

Posing the question of "who gains and who loses?" clarifies the broader issue of economic equity, but it does not assure a resolution of the question. In terms of helping domestic egg producers, the competitive market alternative is clearly a minus (-), which we have entered in the appropriate cell of Exhibit 11: producers do not want lower prices. But this alternative is a plus (+) for domestic consumers, who would buy eggs for 65 cents instead of 72 cents per dozen. The competitive market alternative would not directly involve state taxpayers or foreign producers or consumers, so we have entered a zero (0) in each of these cells under the heading of "equity."

Still under equity, adoption of the state board purchase plan is a plus (+) in helping domestic egg producers, but the plan receives a minus (-) for its effects on domestic consumers and state taxpayers. Consumers clearly lose because they pay 72 cents rather than 65 cents for eggs. At 72 cents they can buy fewer eggs. They may have less money to buy other things as well. State taxpayers will have to pay the difference between the 72 cents the egg board pays for eggs and the lower price received when the eggs are sold abroad. Taxpayers also pay for the administration, storage, and shipping costs associated with the purchase of eggs for resale abroad. Another consequence of the egg board's foreign sales is the impact on foreign egg producers and consumers. The effect on foreign egg producers would be a minus (-) because supply would increase and price would decline in their markets. At the same time, the lower price would be a plus (+) for foreign egg consumers.

The effects of the two policies on the economic "security" of various groups are much the same as the effects on equity, as the completed grid indicates. In brief, compared to the competitive market alternative, the economic security of domestic egg producers (and of foreign consumers) is helped by egg purchases for resale abroad, but this comes at the expense of the economic security of foreign egg producers and domestic consumers.

The completed grid in Exhibit 11 shows three pluses, two minuses, and five zeros for the competitive market alternative; it shows four pluses and six minuses for the price support alternative. Different sets of pluses and minuses would no doubt be obtained if different goals or criteria had been employed. We use this grid only to illustrate the use of an orderly method of problem solving. Such a grid cannot be relied on to resolve an issue completely, but it does help clarify the choices and trade-offs, often revealing the need for additional alternatives and criteria to analyze specific cases.

5. DECIDE WHICH ALTERNATIVE BEST LEADS TO THE ATTAINMENT OF THE MOST GOALS OR THE MOST IMPORTANT GOALS

Individuals may assign different weights to the various pluses and minuses shown in Exhibit 8 and thus reach different conclusions about the case. People for whom economic efficiency is the most important goal would choose the competitive market alternative. People who think that the government should promote rather than reduce competition would make the same choice. Egg producers and others who believe the government should help support their income would choose the egg purchase alternative. If not, they might suggest an equity or a security alternative for egg producers that is less adverse to efficiency and to the interest of taxpayers and consumers. Orderly problem solving not only clarifies choices and trade-offs but also reveals the sources of disagreements about various policies.

The Cold War Ends—Economic Consequences

In December 1991, the Soviet Union ceased to exist as a country. Even before that time, the United States and the Soviet Union had begun to discuss the reduction of arms on both sides. Early in 1992, Russia, Ukraine, Belarus, and Kazakhstan, formerly republics of the Soviet Union, now the independent countries in the region with the greatest stocks of nuclear weapons, agreed to destroy many of these weapons and disarm others. After its chief adversary was no longer a military threat, the United States had to consider whether to reduce defense spending, how rapidly any such reduction should take place, and what to do about the money saved by not spending on national defense. Although many of the economic concepts employed in making such a decision are different from those employed in the egg case, the orderly, reasoned approach to reaching a decision is the same.

In many respects, the situation was similar to the one facing the U.S. economy at the end of World War II, when military spending fell from 42 percent of GDP in 1944 to 4 percent of GDP in 1948, but there were important differences. On the one hand, an annual reduction in defense spending in 1992 would cause a far smaller reduction in the percentage of military spending to GDP. On the other hand, the economy in 1992 did not have a huge pent-up consumer demand similar to that caused by the Great Depression of the 1930s and the widespread unavailability of consumer goods in the early 1940s during World War II. We will use the five-step reasoned approach to examine the alternatives for dealing with the issue in this case.

1. STATE THE PROBLEM OR ISSUE

In the absence of any other action, a decrease in defense spending of a hypothetical amount of $30 billion a year for each of three years would cause a decrease in aggregate demand in the economy. (Using the C + I + G approach to aggregate demand, this would be a decrease in G, which might later spread to decreases in C and I. Using the M x V approach to aggregate demand, the cut in defense spending would show up as a decline in V since there is nothing in this situation that would reduce the stock of money per se.*) If the decrease in aggregate demand did not lead to widespread price reductions throughout the economy, the macroeconomic aspect of this problem would involve the need to offset the decrease in aggregate demand. There is also a microeconomic aspect to the problem, since it is desirable to move resources from defense industries to non-defense industries as efficiently and as equitably as possible.

2. DETERMINE THE PERSONAL OR BROAD SOCIAL GOALS TO BE ATTAINED

The macroeconomic goals of full employment, price stability, and economic growth, realized before the cuts in defense spending, should continue to be realized, along with

* The symbols used here are defined and discussed in Chapter II as part of concept 14, aggregate supply and aggregate demand.

the microeconomic goals of efficiency and equity. In addition to these broad goals, people's relative preferences for private goods and services compared to public goods and services have to be considered as well as their preferences for direct or indirect government policies. The speed with which new government policies could be put into effect and the diffusion of the impact of government policies throughout the economy also have to be taken into account.

3. CONSIDER THE PRINCIPAL ALTERNATIVE MEANS OF ACHIEVING THE GOALS

Monetary policy is one of the two broad means for maintaining aggregate demand. The other is fiscal policy. Fiscal policy presents the options of (a) shifting government spending from defense to nondefense government programs, or (b) cutting taxes and letting individual taxpayers and businesses spend the revenue that was previously used for defense purposes, or (c) redirecting some of the money saved by not spending on military needs toward reducing the deficit in the federal government budget and retiring some of the national debt, or (d) some combination of these options. Consequently, in addition to the task of maintaining the overall level of aggregate demand, there is the question of the new composition of aggregate demand. Monetary policy and tax cuts work through the private sector. Reliance on these two options would put the policy emphasis on increased consumer spending and increased investment spending by private businesses. Reliance on a shift in government spending or continued borrowing, of course, would operate through the public sector and put the policy emphasis on the provision of public goods, services, transfers, and interest payments.

At some point, however, it may be suggested that if the excess resources in defense industries are to be transferred efficiently to match shifts in demand, the government would have to provide temporary help through special unemployment benefits, retraining programs, moving allowances, tax write-offs for capital equipment in defense industries that has become useless, and the like.

4. SELECT THE ECONOMIC CONCEPTS NEEDED TO UNDERSTAND THE PROBLEM AND USE THEM TO APPRAISE THE MERITS OF EACH ALTERNATIVE

As we have indicated, the concept aggregate supply and aggregate demand (14 in the Chapter II list), unemployment (15), inflation and deflation (16), monetary policy (17), fiscal policy (18), markets and prices (7), and the role of government (12) are clearly relevant to analyzing this case. To pursue a more detailed analysis than is provided here, add the concepts of opportunity cost and trade-offs (2), competition and market structure(9), income distribution (10), and market failures (11) in order to explore the differences between the defense and nondefense sectors of our economy.

Since the alternatives of using monetary policy and fiscal policy to maintain aggregate demand are not mutually exclusive, and since various combinations of tax cuts and shifts in government spending are also possible, we do not present a detailed decision-making grid for this case. Instead, we analyze briefly how each of the main possible policies squares with the goals we would like to achieve in adjusting to a world of reduced defense spending.

Monetary Policy

Some increase in the money supply would probably be necessary to offset the likely decrease in the velocity of circulation immediately following the cut in defense spending, and the Federal Reserve would also want to try to lower interest rates temporarily to encourage more business investment. A drawback in employing monetary policy to ease the economic adjustment being considered is that it often takes some time for changes in monetary policy to work their way through the system; further, changes in monetary policy affect certain sectors of the economy more than others. The housing and durable goods industries are particularly affected by the alterations in interest rates brought about by changes in monetary policy.

Shifts in Government Spending

Shifting government spending from defense industries to nondefense industries or to transfer programs might seem to be relatively easy to carry out, but experience suggests that Congress can be slow in making budgetary decisions, especially when powerful special-interest groups vie for the benefits of new government programs. People or groups who favor private spending over public spending would oppose this policy route. Moreover, it frequently takes considerable time to launch new government programs even after the appropriations have been approved. Specific government projects tend to have a more concentrated initial impact than do transfer programs or tax reduction policies whose effects are widely spread through the entire economy. Some types of spending help increase our productive capacity and thus aggregate supply as well as aggregate demand, and some do not.

Tax Reductions to Stimulate Private Spending

Experience suggests that people would probably save part of any tax reductions; so the government would need to cut taxes by more than $30 billion a year to get an immediate increase of $30 billion in private consumer spending. Proposals to change taxes are also prone to run into delays in congressional decision-making. Once enacted, however, tax reductions can have immediate and widespread economic effects throughout the economy. As with shifts in government spending, some tax cuts can favor investment in new plants and equipment rather than consumer spending and thus increase our productive capacity and aggregate supply as well as aggregate demand.

5. DECIDE WHICH ALTERNATIVE BEST LEADS TO THE ATTAINMENT OF THE MOST GOALS OR THE MOST IMPORTANT GOALS

As the preceding analysis makes clear, an appropriate combination of monetary and fiscal policy can maintain aggregate demand so as to help promote full employment, price stability, and economic growth. Selecting the optimum combination of policies, however, is not without difficulties, and the actual combination selected will depend on the weight given to the various broad social goals we have discussed earlier.

Chapter IV

Overview: Scope and Sequence Guidelines

The curriculum guidelines in this and subsequent chapters provide assistance to school districts committed to the **Economics**America program. The guidelines are also for any district planning a systematic study of economics, kindergarten through twelfth grade.

For decades economists and educators have emphasized the need for economic literacy in a society whose members have great freedom to make choices that affect their lives and the lives of others. The guidelines assist schools in developing programs to help students achieve economic literacy.

Content Selection and Sequencing

The scope and sequence guidelines address two basic questions:

1. What are the fundamental concepts and generalizations that an economically literate person should know?
2. At what grade levels should these concepts and generalizations be introduced within the curriculum?

The answer to the first question is in the conceptual framework in Chapter II. The 21 concept clusters identified there provide a basis for understanding the operations of economic forces in the world in which we live. Recommendations for sequencing content are based on the commitment of the National Council on Economic Education and its network of affiliated state councils and centers to developmental economic education. Repeated exposure to and elaboration of important organizing ideas help students to develop an integrated intellectual structure to use in analyzing the meaning and implications of specific facts, enabling them to deal effectively with the economic issues they will confront throughout their lives.

A single concept can vary in difficulty, depending upon the level of sophistication at which it is presented. "Price," for example, means at the simplest level a number attached to a product that is for sale; however, at the highest level it is a number that reflects the relative scarcity of the product compared to all other goods and services.

Concepts that are concrete and within the immediate experience of the learner are more easily understood than abstract concepts. As an example, the concept "bulldozer," which can be physically observed, is easier to learn than the more abstract "capital."

Categorical concepts, which define something in terms of its attributes (the characteristics necessary for something to be considered an example of that concept), are easier to understand than concepts that define a relationship. Thus, educational theory predicts that students will have less difficulty in learning the concept of "good," which is defined by the attributes "has a physical presence" and "can be used to satisfy a want," than the concept "scarcity," which is a relationship between the amount of something that is available and the amount that people want. The most difficult concepts are probably those that involve several relationships, such as "comparative advantage," which requires that students relate the relative costs of production of two products in one country to the relative costs of producing the same two products in another country.

Two or more concepts can be linked together to make a "generalization," a statement about how those concepts are related to each other. (Most of the content statements in these guidelines are generalizations.) The discipline of economics is made up of a vast number of generalizations that are accepted in varying degrees by economists and that describe or provide insights into economic events. "When price goes down, the quantity demanded of a particular good or service usually goes up," is an example of such a generalization. Statements such as these make possible a clearer understanding of how an economic society operates, and they can be changed or modified to include other variables or to deal with new situations. Since each generalization consists of a number of related concepts, a basic principle is that the concepts involved must be understood thoroughly before a generalization can be understood and applied.

While every effort was made to use research to guide content placement, existing research on children's understanding of economic ideas is incomplete, and in many areas fragmentary. The guidelines are intended to serve as a basis for further and more systematic research in this area.

Current school practices were assessed by examining numerous state and local curriculum guides to determine the range and extent of economic content now included in the curricula of the nation's schools. Where possible, grade level placements for content statements were influenced by the kinds of social studies most commonly taught at those grade levels.

The Use of Models in Economics

To analyze economic relationships, economists often use "models"—simplified versions of reality that allow them to isolate the most important variables in an economic situation for the purpose of making judgments about causes or predicting outcomes. Like a road map or a blueprint, an economic model eliminates much distracting information to concentrate on essentials. For example, many factors affect a consumer's decision to buy a certain product. However, consumer demand is modeled on the assumption that price is the single most important factor in that decision. Other things affecting buyer behavior, such as preferences or income, are deliberately assumed to remain constant while the effects of price changes are studied, in order to separate out these effects from changes of other kinds. Typically, then, content statements in economics, such as those provided in this volume, are made on the assumption that only the variables specified in the statements are allowed to change. This is known as the *ceteris paribus* assumption, which translates roughly as "other things being equal." Of course, assumptions can be changed to study the effects of other variables.

Treatment of Values

As mentioned in Chapter I, the scope and sequence guidelines are limited to a discussion of positive economics, statements that reflect "what is," rather than "what ought to be." Of course, normative ideas are introduced in the context of goals and discussion of public policy measures, but no judgments are made about the superiority of one economic decision over another.

While the guidelines avoid prescriptive instruction on the relative importance of broad social goals such as freedom, security, growth, equity, or efficiency, they do discuss how specific policy measures may affect these goals. Students should learn that certain economic goals are endorsed in varying degrees by all modern societies and that there are often trade-offs in terms of these goals. For example, an action that promotes security may have negative effects on freedom or equity. Finally, students should be able to appreciate the difficulties of what has been called the "art of economics"—developing private or public policies to achieve a given set of goals at the lowest possible cost and with the fewest possible undesirable side effects.

Students' ability to distinguish between positive and normative statements increases with age and practice. Thus, decision-making activities that involve value dimensions have been included for many content areas, based upon levels of reasoning appropriate for given age groups.

Summary and Use of the Guidelines

This chapter provides a complete list of content statements for economic education programs. Content statements are organized according to the 21 concept clusters identified and discussed in Chapter II. Exhibit 12 on the following page shows the grade level at which each of the content areas is introduced. Used together, the list of content statements and Exhibit 12 provide a quick, yet comprehensive overview of the content recommended for the K-12 curriculum. They also enable those who use the guidelines in developing curriculum for the upper grades to determine prerequisites for planned courses of study.

Subsequent chapters present separate lists of content statements for three grade levels: K-4, 5-8, and 9-12. Accompanying each content statement in these chapters are a sample activity for assessing student understanding and a list of materials from **Economics**America/National Council on Economic Education for teaching the content.

As every teacher knows, students within a given grade vary widely in intellectual maturity. The suggested placements should be modified to fit the actual ability levels of the students. A gifted child will be able to understand difficult concepts at a younger age than the suggested levels in the guidelines, and a slower learner will profit more from studying the same concepts later in his or her school career. Teachers should try, insofar as their classroom situations permit, to match concepts with the levels of understanding of individual students.

The scope and sequence guidelines should be used flexibly to meet the needs of individual school districts. Some districts might elect to integrate a few economic ideas into every grade, while others might target three or four specific grades at which fairly intensive economic education programs would be developed. Economic concepts and generalizations can be meaningfully taught in a variety of subjects, from social studies to mathematics, language arts, home economics, and many others. Because economic factors are such a pervasive part of our lives, economic ideas can broaden and enrich the curriculum in many areas.

EXHIBIT 12

DEVELOPMENT OF BASIC ECONOMIC CONCEPTS IN THE K-12 CURRICULUM

	GRADE LEVEL		
CONCEPTS	K–4	5–8	9–12
1. Scarcity and Choice	N	R/N	R/N
2. Opportunity Cost and Trade-offs	N	R/N	R/N
3. Productivity	N	R/N	R/N
4. Economic Systems	N	R/N	R/N
5. Economic Institutions and Incentives	N	R/N	R/N
6. Exchange, Money, and Interdependence	N	R/N	R/N
7. Markets and Prices	N	R/N	R/N
8. Supply and Demand		N	R/N
9. Competition and Market Structure	N	R/N	R/N
10. Income Distribution		N	R/N
11. Market Failures		N	R/N
12. The Role of Government	N	R/N	R/N
13. Gross Domestic Product		N	R/N
14. Aggregate Supply and Aggregate Demand			N
15. Unemployment		N	R/N
16. Inflation and Deflation		N	R/N
17. Monetary Policy			N
18. Fiscal Policy		N	R/N
19. Absolute and Comparative Advantage and Barriers to Trade		N	R/N
20. Exchange Rates and the Balance of Payments		N	R/N
21. International Aspects of Growth and Stability		N	R/N

N = New Content Introduced   R = Content Reinforced/Reviewed/Extended

Content Statements, K-12

1. SCARCITY AND CHOICE

1.1 Scarcity is the condition of not being able to have all of the goods and services that you want.

1.2 Economic wants are desires that can be satisfied by consuming a good or service.

1.3 Goods are objects that can satisfy people's wants.

1.4 Services are activities that can satisfy people's wants.

1.5 Scarcity requires people to make choices about using goods and services to satisfy wants.

1.6 People whose wants are satisfied by using goods and services are called consumers.

1.7 People who make goods and provide services are called producers.

1.8 Productive resources are all natural resources, human resources, and human-made resources (capital) used in the production of goods and services.

1.9 Natural resources (also collectively referred to as "land") are "gifts of nature"; they are present without human intervention.

1.10 Human resources (also called labor) represent the quantity and quality of human effort directed toward producing goods and services.

1.11 Capital resources are goods made by people and used to produce other goods and services.

1.12 Scarcity results from the imbalance between relatively unlimited wants and relatively limited resources. There are not enough productive resources to satisfy all of our wants.

1.13 Like individuals, governments and societies experience scarcity because their productive resources are limited and their wants are virtually unlimited.

1.14 Entrepreneurship refers to the human resources that assume the risk of organizing other resources to produce goods and services.

1.15 Because federal, state and local governments have limited budgets, they must compare their revenues to the costs of public projects their citizens desire.

1.16 Scarcity of resources necessitates choice at both the personal and the societal levels.

1.17 The quality of labor resources (known as human capital)can be improved through investments in education, training, and health care.

2. OPPORTUNITY COST AND TRADE-OFFS

2.1 Opportunity cost is the highest valued alternative that must be forgone because another option is chosen.

2.2 Whenever someone makes a personal decision to use limited resources (i.e., an economic choice), an opportunity cost is incurred.

2.3 Whenever resources are used to produce a particular good or a service, the opportunity cost is not being able to produce the next most valued alternative that could have been made with the same resources.

2.4 Few choices are all-or-nothing propositions; they usually involve trade-offs—i.e., getting a little more of one option in exchange for a little less of something else.

2.5 All decisions involve opportunity costs; weighing the costs and the benefits associated with alternative choices constitutes effective economic decision making.

3. PRODUCTIVITY

3.1 Economic specialization occurs when people produce a narrower range of goods and services than they consume.

3.2 The level of output in an economy can be increased through specialization.

3.3 Productivity refers to a ratio of output (goods and services)produced per unit of input(productive resources) over some time period.

3.4 Specialization and division of labor usually increase labor productivity.

3.5 Productivity can also be increased by providing labor with additional capital goods such as tools and machines to work with.

3.6 Creating new capital goods involves a trade-off of fewer consumer goods or services in the present in return for higher expected productivity in the future.

3.7 Investment in human capital occurs when resources are devoted to increasing the quality of labor resources, thus enhancing their productivity.

3.8 Although investments in capital goods and in human capital can increase productivity, such investments have significant opportunity costs and economic risks.

3.9 Technological change is a leading cause of long-run increases in productivity.

3.10 Technological change depends heavily on incentives to reward innovation and on investments in research and development and in capital goods.

3.11 Government expenditures, regulations, and tax policy influence productivity.

3.12 Technological change and investments in capital goods and human capital increase productivity.

3.13 Living standards are directly related to productivity.

4. ECONOMIC SYSTEMS

4.1 The United States economy is organized around a system of private markets in which prices for goods and services are determined.

4.2 An economic system is the institutional framework that a society uses to allocate its resources to produce and distribute goods and services.

4.3 In a tradition-based economic system, production and distribution decisions are largely determined by custom, i.e., the way things have been done in the past.

4.4 In a command economic system, a central authority makes the major production and distribution decisions.

4.5 In a market economic system, the major decisions about production and distribution are made in a decentralized manner by individual households and business firms following their own self-interest.

4.6 Every modern economy is a "mixed system," having some features characteristic of traditional, command, and market economies. The "mix" varies from one economy to another.

4.7 Although wages and prices are found in all economic systems, they are determined in fundamentally different ways in traditional, command, and market economies.

4.8 Economic systems based on tradition do not adapt quickly to change or promote rapid economic growth.

4.9 Economic systems can be evaluated by their ability to achieve broad social goals such as freedom, efficiency, equity, security, and growth.

5. ECONOMIC INSTITUTIONS AND INCENTIVES

5.1 Households are individuals or family units which, as consumers, buy goods and services from firms and, as resource owners, sell productive resources to firms.

5.2 Profit-seeking firms are the basic production units in a market economy.

5.3 Profit is the difference between revenues and the costs entailed in producing or selling a good or service; it is a return for risk-taking.

5.4 The hope of earning profit motivates business firms to incur the risks involved in producing goods and services for the market.

5.5 To earn income, households own and sell productive resources in a market economy and also lend money to people or firms.

5.6 Several kinds of specialized economic institutions such as corporations, banks, and other financial organization are found in market economies.

5.7 In a market economy, the pursuit of economic self-interest is a basic motivation that leads people and businesses to provide goods and services that other people want.

5.8 Economic incentives, including the desire to achieve financial or material gain and to avoid loss, are powerful motivating forces.

5.9 Cultural traditions and customs influence the patterns of economic behavior in a society.

5.10 An economic institution is an enduring organization, practice, or relationship established by people to cope with basic economic problems.

5.11 Economic institutions include such organizations as corporations, labor unions, banks, the stock market, cooperatives, and partnerships.

5.12 Private ownership of property is a basic institution in a market economy; property rights are defined, enforced, and limited through the process of government.

5.13 Specific financial and nonfinancial incentives often influence individuals differently.

5.14 In every economic system, consumers, producers, workers, savers, and investors seek to allocate their scarce resources to obtain the highest possible return, subject to the institutional constraints of their society.

6. EXCHANGE, MONEY, AND INTERDEPENDENCE

6.1 Trading goods and services with people for other goods and services or for money is called exchange.

6.2 Money is a good that can be used to buy all other goods and services.

6.3 People voluntarily exchange goods and services because they expect to be better off after the exchange.

6.4 The simplest and most primitive form of exchange is barter—the direct trading of goods and services between people.

6.5 Money is any generally accepted medium of exchange.

6.6 Money eliminates the need for the "double coincidence of wants" that must occur for barter to take place.

6.7 Exchanges made through barter face problems of divisibility, portability, and storage that are greatly reduced by the use of money.

6.8 Money has generally replaced barter as a more efficient system for exchange.

6.9 As a unit of account, money can be used to express the market value of different goods and services.

6.10 As a store of value, money retains its buying power and its "liquidity"—i.e., it can easily be traded for goods and services at any time.

6.11 The basic money supply is usually measured as the total value of coins, currency, and checkable deposits held by the public.

6.12 Banks play a key role in providing currency and other forms of money to consumers, and serve as intermediaries between savers and borrowers.

6.13 Greater specialization leads to increasing interdependence between producers and consumers

6.14 Money encourages specialization by decreasing the opportunity costs of exchange.

6.15 Specialization is limited by the extent of the market for different goods and services.

6.16 When interdependence is present, a single economic unit is ultimately affected by many of the decisions or events that initially affect its trading partners.

*6.17 Transaction costs are those costs other than price associated with the purchase of a good or service (e.g., legal restrictions on trading, costs of gathering or disseminating information on products, transportation costs paid by the consumer). When transaction costs decrease, more exchanges will be made, thus enlarging the scope of markets.

7. MARKETS AND PRICES

7.1 A price is the amount of money that people pay when they buy a good or service.

7.2 A market exists whenever buyers and sellers exchange goods and services.

7.3 The market clearing or equilibrium price is the one price at which quantity supplied equals quantity demanded.

7.4 Relative prices refer to the price of one good or service compared to the prices of other goods and services, and are the basic measure of the relative scarcity of a product when prices are set by market forces (supply and demand).

7.5 Relative prices provide the key signals used by consumers and producers to answer the three basic economic questions: What to produce? How to produce it? Who will consume it?

7.6 The circular flow model shows the interactions between households and producers in product and resource markets.

7.7 In a market system, prices provide information to consumers and producers, which encourages the efficient production and allocation of the goods and services consumers demand.

8. SUPPLY AND DEMAND

8.1 If the price of a product increases, quantity demanded will decrease and quantity

* Indicates statements that would normally be covered in a one-semester Capstone course in economics.

supplied will increase. If the price of a product decreases, quantity demanded will increase and quantity supplied will decrease.

8.2 Forces of supply and demand determine prices, which are measures of the relative scarcity of different products.

8.3 Demand is the schedule of how much consumers are willing and able to buy at all possible prices in a given period of time.

8.4 Supply is the schedule of how much producers are willing and able to sell at all possible prices in a given period of time.

8.5 Market demand and supply schedules are based on the sum of decisions made by all of the individual consumers and producers in a market.

8.6 Prices for different products are interrelated.

8.7 The level of competition among producers or buyers affects supply and demand and prices for different products.

8.8 The demand curve shows an inverse, or negative, relationship between price and quantity demanded.

8.9 Demand for a product will normally change (the demand curve will shift) if there is a change in consumers' incomes, tastes and preferences, or the prices of related (complementary or substitute) products.

8.10 The short-run supply curve shows a direct, or positive, relationship between price and quantity supplied because of the law of diminishing returns.

8.11 The supply of a product will normally change (the supply curve will shift) if there is a change in technology or prices of inputs, or in the prices of other products that could be made and sold by producers.

8.12 In the long run, all factors of production are variable.

8.13 Prices set by supply and demand are measures of the relative scarcity of products.

8.14 Shortages or surpluses usually result in price changes for products in a market economy.

8.15 When price controls are enforced, shortages and surpluses occur and create long-run allocation problems in the economy.

*8.16 Economists describe the demand and supply schedules for various goods and services as elastic if the quantity responses to a change in price are relatively large compared to the change in price. If the quantity responses are relatively small, demand or supply is described as inelastic.

*8.17 Demand for products that have few close substitutes and that make up a small part of the consumer's budget tends to be inelastic, as does the demand for items that are regarded as necessities. Demand for large expenditure items, products with many close substitutes, and items regarded as luxuries tends to be elastic.

*8.18 Demand and supply are usually more elastic in the long run than in the short run.

9. COMPETITION AND MARKET STRUCTURE

9.1 A market is a setting where buyers and sellers establish prices for identical or very similar products.

9.2 The level of competition in a market is largely determined by the number of buyers and sellers in the market.

* Indicates statements that would normally be covered in a one-semester Capstone course in economics.

9.3 An industry is made up of all the producers of identical or very similar products in a market area.

9.4 Active competition among sellers results in lower prices and profit levels.

9.5 A monopoly exists when only one producer sells a product that has no close substitutes.

9.6 Competition among buyers of a product results in higher prices for the product.

9.7 Sellers engage in both price and nonprice competition.

9.8 Collusion among buyers or sellers reduces the level of competition in a market. Collusion is more difficult in markets with large numbers of buyers and sellers.

9.9 Oligopoly exists when only a few relatively large producers sell a product that has no close substitutes.

9.10 Cartels are explicit forms of collusion concerning product price, output, service or sales.

9.11 In the United States laws and government regulations have been adopted to maintain competition. However, many laws and regulations also have had the effect, often unanticipated, of reducing competition.

9.12 The level of competition in an industry is, in the long run, determined largely by how difficult and expensive it is for new firms to enter the market.

*9.13 Monopolistic competition exists when many sellers provide similar products that are differentiated to some extent by nonprice competition.

*9.14 A monopsony exists when there is only one buyer of a product or resource in a market area; an oligopsony exists when there are only a few large buyers.

10. INCOME DISTRIBUTION

10.1 There are four basic categories of earned income: wages and salaries, rent, interest, and profit. Wages and salaries are payments for labor service; rent is the payment for the use of land (natural resources); interest is the payment for the use of capital, including financial capital (money); and profit is the return to business enterprise (entrepreneurship) when the value of sales exceeds the cost of the goods and service sold.

10.2 Transfer payments are monetary payments or the direct provision of goods and services made by one party to another without receiving money, goods or services in return.

10.3 The functional distribution of income classifies the income received by individuals and business firms according to the type of productive resources sold in resource markets.

10.4 The personal distribution of income classifies the population according to the amount of income they receive, including transfer payments.

10.5 The functional distribution of income has, over time, reflected changes in the occupational structure of the economy and changing economic conditions related to the business cycle.

10.6 The personal distribution of income has remained relatively stable in the United States over long periods of time.

10.7 Decisions about the distribution of income are made by individuals and firms making exchanges in resource markets, and also by governments through the political process.

10.8 Public policies that can be used to redistribute income include taxation (e.g., progressive or negative income taxes), spending and assistance programs targeted at particular income groups, and programs designed to provide training to workers or to encourage private investments in education or other kinds of human capital.

* Indicates statements that would normally be covered in a one-semester Capstone course in economics.

11. MARKET FAILURES

11.1 Governments provide public goods, due to the shared consumption and nonexclusion properties of these products.

11.2 Shared consumption (or non-rival) products are those that can be used simultaneously by more than one person without reducing the amount of the product available for others to consume.

11.3 A nonexclusive product is one that, once produced, cannot be withheld even from those who do not pay for it.

11.4 Externalities exist when some of the costs or benefits associated with the production or consumption of a product "spill over" to third parties other than the direct producers and consumers of the product. Positive externalities (external benefits) result in the underproduction or under consumption of a product, since not all benefits are reflected in consumers' demand for the product. Negative externalities (external costs) result in the overproduction or over consumption of a product, since not all costs are reflected in producers' supply of the product.

11.5 A natural monopoly exists when one producer can supply total output in a market at a cost that is lower than if two or more producers divided the production of this output.

11.6 Because competition cannot serve to regulate the price, output, and quality of goods and services produced by natural monopolies, government regulatory agencies are generally established to perform these roles.

*11.7 Government can correct for the over or underproduction/consumption of products affected by externalities through the use of tax policies, subsidies or regulations.

*11.8 Perfect competition does not eliminate the problem of market failures.

*11.9 Establishing and implementing government policies and programs to correct for market failures is itself a costly activity, and only when the expected benefits of such programs are greater than the costs involved are these actions economically justified. Economic analysis can help determine where market failures are important enough to justify corrective actions by government.

12. THE ROLE OF GOVERNMENT

12.1 Some goods and services are provided by the government.

12.2 The government pays for the goods and services it provides through taxing and borrowing.

12.3 In a market economy, the government defines and enforces property rights and provides standard units of weights, measures, and money.

12.4 Operating government requires shifting scarce resources from the private sector of the economy to the public sector.

12.5 Other economic roles of government include providing public goods and services; correcting for externalities; maintaining competition; redistributing income; and promoting full employment, stable prices, and reasonable rates of economic growth.

12.6 Different taxes affect different income groups differently. Progressive taxes levy higher tax rates on high-income groups; regressive taxes levy higher tax rates on low-income groups; and proportional taxes levy identical tax rates on all income groups.

12.7 The economic efficiency of a government policy is determined by comparing its costs and benefits.

* Indicates statements that would normally be covered in a one-semester Capstone course in economics.

12.8 Public policies involve economic and political choices and are influenced by both positive and normative concepts as well as by the actions of special interest groups.

12.9 Government policies often affect the well-being of people, businesses, and regions differently as a result of the impact of different kinds of taxes, transfer payments, laws, regulations, and the provision of goods and services that are not used equally by all groups.

12.10 The legal and economic incidence of a tax are often different.

12.11 Benefits of government spending programs are often shifted away from those who were initially intended to receive them.

13. GROSS DOMESTIC PRODUCT

13.1 When purchases are made, goods and services are transferred from businesses to households in exchange for money payments. The money is used by businesses to pay for factors of production: land, labor, capital, and entrepreneurship. This is often depicted in a circular flow diagram.

13.2 Gross Domestic Product (GDP) is a basic measure of economic output. It is used as an indicator of the state of the economy.

13.3 GDP is the total market value, expressed in dollars, of all final goods and services produced in an economy in a given year.

13.4 Nominal GDP is stated in current dollars; thus, an increase in GDP may reflect not only increases in the production of goods and services, but also increases in prices. GDP can be adjusted for price level changes; the resulting statistic is called "real GDP."

13.5 A country's potential GDP depends on the quantity and quality of natural resources available, the size and skills of the labor force, and the size and quality of its capital stock.

13.6 Measures of per capita real GDP (real GDP divided by population) are often compared across countries to evaluate the performance of economies and the well-being of their citizens. However, there are limitations to this approach. The measurement of GDP does not account for differences in the types of goods produced, nor for differences in the distribution of income.

13.7 In the United States and other industrialized economies, the rate of economic growth overlong periods of time has been relatively steady. However, short-run fluctuations in business activity, called business cycles, are not smooth nor completely predictable.

13.8 A recession is said to occur when real GDP declines for a period of at least six months.

13.9 Government may attempt to reduce the fluctuations of the business cycle (stabilize economic activity) by implementing policies that can affect the level of real GDP.

*13.10 GDP is not a perfect measure of how well-off people are.

*13.11 GDP can be calculated by adding up all sales of final products. With minor adjustments, the same total is achieved by adding up all income paid to factors of production.

*13.12 Disposable income is the income available for use after taxes have been paid. It is either spent on consumption or saved.

* Indicates statements that would normally be covered in a one-semester Capstone course in economics.

14. AGGREGATE SUPPLY AND AGGREGATE DEMAND

14.1 The relationship between potential aggregate supply and aggregate demand is an important determinant of the levels of unemployment and inflation in an economy.

14.2 Aggregate supply is the total quantity of goods and services produced in an economy in a given time period. Constraints on potential aggregate supply are the quantity and quality of productive resources and the level of available technology.

14.3 Aggregate demand equals consumption, investment, and government spending, plus net exports.

14.4 When aggregate demand is equal to aggregate supply at a level that just employs all available productive resources with no changes in the overall price level, the economy is at a full-employment, noninflationary equilibrium.

14.5 When aggregate demand falls below the full-employment level of aggregate supply, production declines and some resources become unemployed in the short run. A reduction in aggregate demand below the full-employment level is the cause of cyclical unemployment.

14.6 When aggregate demand rises above the full-employment level of aggregate supply, competition for productive resources increases and costs and prices rise in the short run. An increase in aggregate demand above the full-employment level is the cause of demand-pull inflation.

*14.7 One person's spending becomes another person's income. This process eventually results in a multiple change in aggregate income whenever spending in any one sector of the economy changes.

*14.8 Aggregate demand changes when there are changes in consumer, investment or government spending, in net exports, or in price expectations.

*14.9 Aggregate supply changes when there are changes in the quantity or quality of resources, productivity, tax policies or profit expectations.

15. UNEMPLOYMENT

15.1 Unemployed people are those who are willing and able to work at current wage rates, but do not have jobs.

15.2 People who are unemployed usually have less income to buy goods and services than those who have jobs.

15.3 Governments provide income to some unemployed workers until they can find jobs.

15.4 The labor force is composed of people age 16 and over who are either employed or actively seeking work.

15.5 The unemployment rate is the percentage of the labor force considered to be unemployed.

15.6 The unemployment rate rises during a recession.

15.7 The standard measure of the unemployment rate is imperfect: it does not include discouraged workers, it does not weight part-time and full-time employment differently, nor does it account for differences in the intensity with which people look for jobs.

15.8 Because of regional economic differences and labor force immobility, unemployment rates differ across the country.

15.9 Unemployment rates differ for people of different ages, races, and sexes. This reflects differences in work experience, training, and skills, as well as discrimination.

* Indicates statements that would normally be covered in a one-semester Capstone course in economics.

15.10 There are four types of unemployment: frictional, seasonal, structural, and cyclical. Different policies may be required to reduce each.

15.11 The rate of unemployment is affected by the costs and benefits of searching for a job.

15.12 Currently full employment is considered to be the employment of about 93–95 percent of the labor force, allowing for frictional unemployment of about 5-7 percent.

15.13 Policies designed to deal with structural unemployment include education and training programs. Not increasing the minimum wage and reducing discrimination might also help.

15.14 Cyclical unemployment may be reduced through policies that stimulate demand (e.g., tax cuts, government spending for public works programs).

16. INFLATION AND DEFLATION

16.1 Inflation is a sustained increase in the average price level of the entire economy; deflation is a sustained decrease in the average price level of the entire economy.

16.2 The Consumer Price Index (CPI) is the most commonly used measure of price level changes. It compares prices in one year with some earlier period (a base period).

16.3 The CPI is not a perfect measure of how inflation affects individual households.

16.4 Inflation creates uncertainty because it affects different groups differently.

16.5 There are two general types of inflation: demand-pull and cost-push. Demand-pull inflation occurs when total spending rises faster than total production. Cost-push inflation occurs when increases in the overall costs of making and selling goods and services raise the price level.

16.6 Demand-pull inflation may result from expansive monetary or fiscal policies, or from expectations of businesses and consumers that prices will rise in the future.

16.7 Cost-push inflation may result from the effects of monopolization in product or factor markets, or from supply shocks.

16.8 A variety of policy options is available to combat inflation; these include monetary and fiscal policies, wage and price controls, antitrust actions, and tax incentives. Alternatively, policy-makers may decide to rely upon automatic adjustment mechanisms.

16.9 Many economists believe that there is a trade-off between unemployment and inflation, at least in the short run. If the government stimulates demand to fight unemployment, inflation is likely to increase; if the government restrains demand to fight inflation, unemployment is likely to increase.

16.10 Stagflation is the combination of high unemployment (a stagnant economy) and high inflation in the same time period. It may result from reductions in aggregate supply.

16.11 People form expectations using both past experience and predictions about present and future government policies. This may have an impact upon the effectiveness of government policy actions.

17. MONETARY POLICY

17.1 Policies that change the size of the money supply can be used to promote price stability, maximum employment, and reasonable economic growth.

17.2 When the banking system makes loans, the money supply increases; when loans are paid off, the money supply decreases. Banks may lend the money deposited with them that is in excess of the reserves they are required to keep by the Federal Reserve System, the central banking system of the United States.

17.3 Monetary policy refers to actions by the Federal Reserve System that lead to changes in the supply of money and availability of credit.

*17.4 One of the tools of monetary policy is raising or lowering the reserve requirement.

*17.5 A second tool of monetary policy is increasing or decreasing the discount rate.

*17.6 A third tool of monetary policy is open market purchase or sale of government securities.

*17.7 An initial increase or decrease in the money supply has a multiplier effect on the total money supply.

*17.8 The Federal Reserve's ability to control the total amount of money in the economy is not complete; the actions of individuals, firms, and foreign investors all influence the money supply.

17.9 Changes in the money supply may influence the levels of spending, employment, prices, and economic growth in the economy by leading to changes in interest rates and in individual and corporate spending.

*17.10 One of the limitations of monetary policy is that policies cannot be immediately determined, implemented, or evaluated. Instead there exist long and variable lags associated with each stage of the process.

17.11 Federal reserve policies can cause serious economic problems if they are inconsistent or inappropriate.

17.12 The conduct of monetary policy is influenced by political as well as economic conditions.

*17.13 Disagreements among economists about the effectiveness of monetary policy can be evaluated using the equation of exchange, which relates the money supply and its velocity (rate of turnover) to the nominal GDP.

18. FISCAL POLICY

18.1 Fiscal policy involves the use of national government spending and taxation programs to affect the level of economic activity in such a way as to promote price stability, maximum employment, and reasonable economic growth.

18.2 Tax reductions and increases in government spending increase aggregate demand and nominal income; tax increases and decreases in government spending reduce aggregate demand and nominal income.

18.3 The government budget is balanced when revenues equal expenditures. The government runs a budget deficit when its expenditures exceed its tax revenues. It must then borrow from individuals, corporations, or financial institutions to finance the excess of expenditures over tax revenues. When revenues exceed expenditures, the government has a budget surplus.

18.4 The national debt is the total amount of money the government owes; it is the accumulated annual deficits.

18.5 Foreigners and foreign governments may lend money to the United States government to finance its deficits. Repayment of loans from abroad results in a transfer of income from United States citizens to foreign economies.

18.6 Fiscal policies are often a result of political factors as well as economic factors.

18.7 Fiscal policy requires time to affect the economy.

---

* Indicates statements that would normally be covered in a one-semester Capstone course in economics.

18.8 Fiscal policies may be reinforced or offset by monetary policies.

*18.9 An expansionary fiscal policy may "crowd out" private spending if interest rates are raised by the increased government demand for credit.

*18.10 Fiscal policy can have a powerful impact on aggregate demand and national income if the government implements the proper policy, at the appropriate time, and at a level commensurate with needs and goals, and if crowding out effects are small.

19. ABSOLUTE AND COMPARATIVE ADVANTAGE AND BARRIERS TO TRADE

19.1 The quantity and quality of productive resources available in different nations vary widely.

19.2 International trade is the exchange of goods and services between people and institutions in different nations.

19.3 Exports are goods and services produced in one nation but sold to buyers in another nation.

19.4 Imports are goods or services bought from sellers in another nation.

19.5 International trade promotes greater specialization, and specialization increases total world output.

19.6 International differences in factor endowments and relative prices are the basis for international trade.

19.7 A nation has an absolute advantage if it can produce more of a product with the same amount of resources than another nation can.

19.8 A nation has a comparative advantage when it can produce a product at a lower opportunity cost than another nation.

19.9 Despite the benefits of international trade, many nations restrict the free flow of goods and services through a variety of devices known as trade barriers which include tariffs and quotas.

19.10 While free trade among nations will raise worldwide production levels and material standards of living, in the short run some groups are likely to be hurt by the effects of increased international competition.

20. EXCHANGE RATES AND THE BALANCE OF PAYMENTS

20.1 Different currencies are used in different countries.

20.2 Extensive international trade requires an organized system for exchanging money between nations.

20.3 An exchange rate is the price of one nation's currency in terms of another nation's currency.

20.4 A change in exchange rates can have a significant effect on the flow of trade between nations and on a nation's domestic economy. When the exchange rate between currencies changes, it changes the relative prices of goods and services traded by the two countries.

20.5 A nation's balance of payments is an accounting of all international transactions that involve the payment or receipt of foreign exchange.

*20.6 Exchange rates can be set in a free market, or established through controls imposed by

---

* Indicates statements that would normally be covered in a one-semester Capstone course in economics.

national governments, or allowed to fluctuate within certain price ranges before triggering government action designed to stabilize the exchange rates between currencies.

*20.7 The balance of payments accounts are reported in three sections. These sections distinguish trade involving basic goods and services from trade involving capital resources and financial assets issued by businesses and government, and official transactions of reserve currencies and other assets.

*20.8 Countries often run surpluses or deficits in either their current or capital accounts, but the overall balance of payments account for a country must balance.

*20.9 The balance of trade figures regularly reported in the media include only the deficit or surplus position of merchandise exports. Therefore, this figure reflects only a small part of a nation's overall balance of payments account.

*20.10 Increasingly, we live in a global economy where what is done in this nation affects the rest of the world, and what is done there affects this nation. Economic issues associated with this trend must be analyzed by examining trends in trading levels, investments, foreign exchange values, and changes in public policies affecting these sectors.

21. INTERNATIONAL ASPECTS OF GROWTH AND STABILITY

21.1 Economic growth is a sustained rise in the production of goods and services.

21.2 Technological change and improvements in a society's stock of productive resources promote economic growth.

21.3 The level of real GDP per capita is frequently used to compare the level of economic development in different nations.

21.4 The international transfer of technology and the exchange of productive resources and finished goods and services have led to increased interdependence among nations.

21.5 Increasing international economic interdependence causes economic conditions and policies in one nation to affect economic conditions in many other nations.

21.6 Public policies affecting foreign trade impose costs and benefits on different groups of people; decisions on these policies reflect economic and political interests and forces.

* Indicates statements that would normally be covered in a one-semester Capstone course in economics.

Chapter V

Scope and Sequence Guidelines, K-4

Although the content statements for the primary grades are stated as verbal definitions and propositions, the main focus of primary school instruction should be on providing experiences that can serve as a basis for the development of ideas. Simple definitions of concepts such as "scarcity," "opportunity cost" or "exchange" provide young children with labels that can be enriched in later grades. Probably the most important economic education task in the early grades is to give students experiences in producing, buying, and selling, which can be a foundation for more abstract ideas in the upper elementary grades and beyond.

Economic education in the earliest grades can be integrated into many areas. The social studies curriculum, of course, is a natural place to teach about how families and communities acquire the economic goods and services that they want. There are numerous stories with economic ideas that can be used in reading instruction, and many arithmetic problems can be enriched if they are linked to economic concepts such as prices.

As students mature, they are increasingly capable of understanding economic relationships such as the idea that scarcity results because people's wants are greater than are the productive resources available to satisfy those wants. Since economic life is an important part of the experiences of all people, economic ideas may be integrated into social studies; however, mathematics lessons may also be built around economic concepts, and economic ideas may be incorporated into language arts or science instruction.

The content statements are presented in two different ways:

1. To provide the user a quick and comprehensive overview of the economic content recommended for grades K-4, the content statements are organized according to the concept clusters discussed in Chapter II and are listed in the order in which they should be introduced in the curriculum.

2. In the second presentation, each concept statement is accompanied by a sample activity which suggests the kind of behavior that would indicate that students have mastered the content. The verb in each activity is highlighted to assist teachers in determining cognitive levels.

Also included is a list of materials from the National Council on Economic Education to use in teaching the content statements.

Evaluating Student Learning. The *Basic Economics Test* (Grades 4–6), published by the National Council on Economic Education, is a nationally normed test based on the content categories of the conceptual framework in Chapter II. It is available in two equivalent forms for pretesting and posttesting upper elementary students. An examiner's manual is also available.

Content Statements, K-4

1. SCARCITY AND CHOICE

1.1 Scarcity is the condition of not being able to have all of the goods and services that you want.

1.2 Economic wants are desires that can be satisfied by consuming a good or service.

1.3 Goods are objects that can satisfy people's wants.

1.4 Services are activities that can satisfy people's wants.

1.5 Scarcity requires people to make choices about using goods and services to satisfy wants.

1.6 People whose wants are satisfied by using goods and services are called consumers.

1.7 People who make goods and provide services are called producers.

1.8 Productive resources are all natural resources, human resources, and human-made resources (capital) used in the production of goods and services.

1.9 Natural resources (also collectively referred to as "land")are "gifts of nature"; they are present without human intervention.

1.10 Human resources (also called labor) represent the quantity and quality of human effort directed toward producing goods and services.

1.11 Capital resources are goods made by people and used to produce other goods and services.

2. OPPORTUNITY COST AND TRADE-OFFS

2.1 Opportunity cost is the highest valued alternative that must be forgone because another option is chosen.

2.2 Whenever someone makes a personal decision to use limited resources (i.e., an economic choice), an opportunity cost is incurred.

2.3 Whenever resources are used to produce a particular good or a service, the opportunity cost is not being able to produce the next most valued alternative that could have been made with the same resources.

3. PRODUCTIVITY

3.1 Economic specialization occurs when people produce a narrower range of goods and services than they consume.

3.2 The level of output in an economy can be increased through specialization.

4. ECONOMIC SYSTEMS

4.1 The United States economy is organized around a system of private markets in which prices for goods and services are determined.

5. ECONOMIC INSTITUTIONS AND INCENTIVES

5.1 Households are individuals or family units which, as consumers, buy goods and services from firms and, as resource owners, sell productive resources to firms.

5.2 Profit-seeking firms are the basic production units in a market economy.

5.3 Profit is the difference between revenues and the costs entailed in producing or selling a good or service; it is a return for risk-taking.

6. EXCHANGE, MONEY, AND INTERDEPENDENCE

6.1 Trading goods and services with people for other goods and services or for money is called exchange.

6.2 Money is a good that can be used to buy all other goods and services.

6.3 People voluntarily exchange goods and services because they expect to be better off after the exchange.

6.4 The simplest and most primitive form of exchange is barter—the direct trading of goods and services between people.

6.5 Money is any generally accepted medium of exchange.

6.6 Money eliminates the need for the "double coincidence of wants" that must occur for barter to take place.

6.7 Exchanges made through barter face problems of divisibility, portability, and storage that are greatly reduced by the use of money.

6.8 Money has generally replaced barter as a more efficient system for exchange.

6.12 Banks play a key role in providing currency and other forms of money to consumers, and serve as intermediaries between savers and borrowers.

6.13 Greater specialization leads to increasing interdependence between producers and consumers

7. MARKETS AND PRICES

7.1 A price is the amount of money that people pay when they buy a good or service.

7.2 A market exists whenever buyers and sellers exchange goods and services.

9. COMPETITION AND MARKET STRUCTURE

9.1 A market is a setting where buyers and sellers establish prices for identical or very similar products.

12. THE ROLE OF GOVERNMENT

12.1 Some goods and services are provided by the government.

Teaching Resources, K-4

1. SCARCITY AND CHOICE

Content Statement

1.1 Scarcity is the condition of not being able to have all of the goods and services that you want.

Evidence of Student Learning

Students will *state* orally all of the toys they want, which of those toys they have, and *explain* why they can't have all the toys they want.

EconomicsAmerica *Materials*

Choices and Changes: Work, Human Resources, and Choices, Part 1, "I Am a Worker," pp. 1-32.
Econ and Me, Lesson 1, "Scarcity."
KinderEconomy+, Chapter 1, "Scarcity," pp. 2-9
MCG, K-2, Lesson 1, "Wants from A to Z," p. 3; Lesson 4, "Learning Center: Winning Wants," p. 15; Lesson 11, "Alligator Annie and the Scarcity Alternatives," p. 49; Lesson 12, "Opportunities for Appreciation," p. 53; Lesson 14, "Learning Center: Choice Train," p. 61.

Content Statement

1.2 Economic wants are desires that can be satisfied by consuming a good or service.

Evidence of Student Learning

From pictures or a collection of different types of items, such as baseball cards, comic books, miniature boxes of raisins, and apples, students will *select* one and *describe* how they feel when they receive that item.

EconomicsAmerica *Materials*

Econ & Me, Lesson 3, "Consumption."
KinderEconomy+, Chapter 3, "Production: Goods and Services, Substitutes and Complements," pp. 20-25.
MCG, K-2, Lesson 1, "Wants from A to Z," p. 3; Lesson 3, "Foods Around the World," p. 11; Lesson 4, "Learning Center: Winning Wants," p. 15.
MCG, 3-4, Lesson 1, "Everybody Wants Everything," pp. 1-2.

Content Statement

1.3 Goods are objects that can satisfy people's wants.

Evidence of Student Learning

Students will *describe* five objects that they would like to buy at a local store and *explain* why they want these objects.

EconomicsAmerica *Materials*

Choices & Changes: Work, Human Resources, and Choices, Part 1, "I Am a Worker," pp. 1-32.
Econ and Me, Lesson 3, "Consumption."
KinderEconomy+, Chapter 3, "Production: Goods and Services, Substitutes and Complements," pp. 20-25.
MCG, K-2, Lesson 2, "Consumer Reflections," p. 7; Lesson 3, "Foods Around the World," p. 11; Lesson 4, "Learning Center: Winning Wants," p. 15.
MCG, 3-4, Lesson 2, "Service With a Smile," pp. 3-6.

Content Statement

1.4 Services are activities that can satisfy people's wants.

Evidence of Student Learning

Students will *state* five services that their teacher provides for them, and *name* other ways that these services might be provided if the teacher did not perform them.

EconomicsAmerica *Materials*

Econ and Me, Lesson 3, "Consumption."
KinderEconomy+, Chapter 3, "Production: Goods and Services, Substitutes and Complements," pp. 20-25.
MCG, K-2, Lesson 2, "Consumer Reflections," p. 7; Lesson 3, "Foods Around the World," p.11; Lesson 4, "Learning Center: Winning Wants," p. 15; Lesson 5, "People Movers Bulletin Board," p. 17.
MCG, 3-4, Lesson 2, "Service With a Smile," pp. 3-6.

Content Statement

1.5 Scarcity requires people to make choices about using goods and services to satisfy wants.

Evidence of Student Learning

Given a list of 20 goods and services, and only ten slips of paper representing paper dollars, students will *select* the goods and services they want most, *explain* their choices to a partner, and *cite* scarcity as the reason why they had to make choices.

EconomicsAmerica *Materials*

Choices & Changes: Work, Human Resources, and Choices, part 2, "I Can Improve My Human Resources," pp. 33-70.
The Community Publishing Company, Lesson 2, "Community Resources," pp. 11-14.
Econ and Me, Lesson 1, "Scarcity."
KinderEconomy+, Chapter 1, "Scarcity," pp. 2-9.
MCG, K-2, Lesson 11, "Alligator Annie and the Scarcity Adventure," p. 49; Lesson 12, "Opportunities for Appreciation," p. 53; Lesson 14, "Learning Center: Choice Train," p. 61; Lesson 15, "Scarcity Bulletin Board: Balloon Trip," p. 65.
MCG, 3-4, Lesson 4, "Olympic-Minded Decisions," pp. 11-14.

Content Statement

1.6 People whose wants are satisfied by using goods and services are called consumers.

Evidence of Student Learning

Given pictorial examples of people using goods and services, students, working in pairs, will *explain* why the people depicted are called consumers and *identify* the goods and services being consumed.

EconomicsAmerica *Materials*

The Community Publishing Company, Lesson 5, "My Community," pp. 37-43; Lesson 6, "Our Community," pp. 45-47.
Econ and Me, Lesson 3, "Consumption."
MCG, K-2, Lesson 2, "Consumer Reflections," p. 7; Lesson 3, "Foods Around the World," p. 11.

Content Statement

1.7 People who make goods and provide services are called producers.

Evidence of Student Learning

Students will *identify* five different types of producers of goods and five different types of producers of services.

EconomicsAmerica *Materials*

Choices & Changes: You Can Be an Inventor: Human Capital and Entrepreneurship, Part 2, pp. 29-49.
The Community Publishing Company, Lesson 5, "My Community," pp. 37-43; Lesson 6, "Our Community," pp. 45-47.
MCG, K-2, Lesson 6, "Mystery Workers," p. 25; Lesson 8, "Producer Charades," p. 33; Lesson 9, "Learning Center: Producer Pigs," p. 37; Lesson 10, "Bulletin Board: Art Gallery," p. 41.
Econ and Me, Lesson 4, "Production."

Content Statement

1.8 Productive resources are all natural resources, human resources, and human-made resources (capital) used in the production of goods and services.

Evidence of Student Learning

Students will *list* all the resources that would be needed to build their school and *categorize* them as natural, human, and human-made (capital) resources.

EconomicsAmerica *Materials*

Choices & Changes: You Can Be an Inventor: Human Capital and Entrepreneurship, Part 1, "Creativity and Invention," pp. 1-28.
The Community Publishing Company, Lesson 2, "Community Resources," pp. 19-24; Lesson 3, "Communities Change, pp. 25-30; Lesson 4, "Communities Today," pp. 31-35; Lesson 21, "Resources for the Publishing Company," pp. 143-150.
Econ and Me, Lesson 4, "Production."
MCG, 3-4, Lesson 2, "Service With a Smile," pp. 3-6.

Content Statement

1.9 Natural resources (also collectively referred to as "land") are "gifts of nature"; they are present without human intervention

Evidence of Student Learning

Students will *list* five different natural resources and *identify* at least five different uses for trees and for water in producing goods and services for people.

EconomicsAmerica *Materials*

The Community Publishing Company, Lesson 2, "Community Resources," pp. 19-24; Lesson 3, "Communities Change," pp. 25-30; Lesson 4, "Communities Today," pp. 31-35.
Econ and Me, Lesson 4, "Production."
MCG, K-2, Lesson 7, "Gifts of Nature," p. 29; Lesson 9, "Learning Center: Producer Pigs," p. 37.
MCG, 3-4, Lesson 2, "Service With a Smile," pp. 3-6.

Content Statement

1.10 Human resources (also called labor) represent the quantity and quality of human effort directed toward producing goods and services.

Evidence of Student Learning

Given pictures of people in several different occupations, students will *name* the types of skills these people need in order to do their jobs.

EconomicsAmerica *Materials*

Choices and Changes: Work, Human Resources, and Choices, Part 1, "I Am a Worker," pp. 1-32; Part 2, "I Can Improve My Human Resources," pp. 33-70; Part 3, I Can Set and Reach My Goals," pp. 71-100.
Choices and Changes: You Can Be an Inventor: Human Capital and Entrepreneurship, Part I, "Creativity and Invention, pp. 1-28; Part 2, "Producing a

Product," pp. 29-49; Part 3, "Human Capital," pp. 50-73.

The Community Publishing Company, Lesson 2, "Community Resources," pp. 19-24; Lesson 3, "Communities Change," pp. 25-30; Lesson 4, "Communities Today," pp. 31-35; Lesson 27, "Job Application," pp. 183-185; Lesson 28, "Preparation for Production," pp. 187-193; Lesson 29, "The Production Process," pp. 195-197.

MCG, K-2, Lesson 6, "Mystery Workers," p. 25; Lesson 8, "Producer Charades," p. 33; Lesson 9, "Learning Center: Producer Pigs," p. 37.

MCG, 3-4, Lesson 2, "Service With a Smile," pp. 3-6; Lesson 13, "The Working World, pp. 55-58.

Content Statement

1.11 Capital resources are goods made by people and used to produce other goods and services.

Evidence of Student Learning

From a group of classroom items such as desk, chair, flag, clothes hanger, etc., students will *name* all the products that had to be made (such as hammers, axes, nails, glue) in order to make these classroom items.

Economics America *Materials*

Choices & Changes: Work, Human Resources, and Choices, Part 1, I Am a Worker," pp. 1-32; Part 2, "I Can Improve My Human Resources," pp. 33-70.
Choices & Changes: You Can Be an Inventor: Human Capital and Entrepreneurship, Part 3, "Human Capital," 50-73.
The Community Publishing Company, Lesson 2, "Community Resources," pp. 19-24; Lesson 4, "Communities Today," pp. 31-35.
MCG, K-2, Lesson 6, "Mystery Workers," p. 25; Lesson 9, "Learning Center: Producer Pigs," p. 37.
MCG, 3-4, Lesson 2, "Service With a Smile," pp. 3-6.

2. OPPORTUNITY COST AND TRADE-OFFS

Content Statement

2.1 Opportunity cost is the highest valued alternative that must be forgone because another option is chosen.

Evidence of Student Learning

Given a choice between going to the movies, going to a pizza parlor, or going to an amusement park, students will *choose* the most favored alternative and will *explain* which activity is the opportunity cost of the choice.

Economics America *Materials*

Choices & Changes: Work, Human Resources, and Choices, Part 2, "I Can Improve My Human Resources," pp. 33-70.
The Community Publishing Company, Lesson 8, "Mini-Mall," pp. 59-65; Lesson 21, "Resources for the Publishing Company," pp. 143-150; Lesson 32, "Choice Making," pp. 215-219.
Econ and Me, Lesson 2, "Opportunity Cost."
KinderEconomy+, Chapter 2, "Opportunity Cost and Cost-Benefit Analysis," pp. 10-19.
The Community Publishing Company, Lesson 2, "Community Resources," pp. 19-24; Lesson 3, "Communities Change," pp. 25-30; Lesson 4, "Communities Today," pp. 31-35.
MCG, K-2, Lesson 12, "Opportunities for Appreciation," p. 53; Lesson 13, "We Decide...," p. 57; Lesson 14, "Learning Center: Choice Train," p. 61.
MCG, 3-4, Lesson 3, "Wooden Opportunities," pp. 7-9.

2.2 Whenever someone makes a personal decision to use limited resources (i.e., an economic choice), an opportunity cost is incurred.

Evidence of Student Learning

Given an imaginary amount of money (e.g., $10.00), students will *decide* what to buy with the money and *identify* the next highest valued alternative as the opportunity cost of the decision.

EconomicsAmerica *Materials*

The Community Publishing Company, Lesson 8, "Mini-Mall," pp. 59-65; Lesson 10, "The Pencil Choice," pp. 75-81.
Econ and Me, Lesson 2, "Opportunity Cost."
KinderEconomy+, Chapter 2, "Opportunity Cost and Cost-Benefit Analysis," pp. 10-19.
MCG, K-2, Lesson 12, "Opportunities for Appreciation," p. 53; Lesson 13, "We Decide...," p. 57; Lesson 14, "Learning Center: Choice Train," p. 61.
MCG, 3-4, Lesson 3, "Wooden Opportunities," pp. 7-9.

2.3 Whenever resources are used to produce a particular good or a service, the opportunity cost is not being able to produce the next most valued alternative that could have been made with the same resources.

Evidence of Student Learning

Given a list of goods and services, students will *name* alternative uses for the productive resources used to make them and *identify* the forgone goods and services as the opportunity cost of the goods and services actually produced. For example, wood used to make a table might have been used instead in building a house, and the worker(s)who built the table might instead have been employed in building the house.

EconomicsAmerica *Materials*

The Community Publishing Company, Lesson 32, "Choice Making," pp. 215-219.
Econ and Me, Lesson 2, "Opportunity Cost."

3. PRODUCTIVITY

3.1 Economic specialization occurs when people produce a narrower range of goods and services than they consume.

Evidence of Student Learning

Given two or more examples of adults in the school or community who specialize in the production of a good or service (e.g., baker, law enforcement officer, teacher, etc.), students will *name* other goods and services that these individuals consume but do not produce for themselves.

EconomicsAmerica *Materials*

The Community Publishing Company, Lesson 11, "The Badge Factory," pp. 83-88; Lesson 7, "Job Application," pp. 183-185; Lesson 28, "Preparation for Production," pp. 187-193; Lesson 29, "The Production Process, pp. 195-197.
Econ and Me, Lesson 5, "Interdependence."
KinderEconomy+, Chapter 3, "Production: Goods and Services, Substitutes and Complements," pp. 20-25; Chapter 4, "Production and Banking: From Civil Service to Entrepreneurship," pp. 26-31,
MCG, K-2, Lesson 16, "An Interdependent Branch," p. 73; Lesson 17, "Spotlight on Specialists," p.77; Lesson 18, "The Baker Wants a Pair of Shoes," p. 81; Lesson 19,

"Learning Center: School Connections," p. 83; Lesson 20, "Bulletin Board: Showcasing Specialists," 85.

Content Statement

3.2 The level of output in an economy can be increased through specialization.

Evidence of Student Learning

After performing the following activity, students will *explain* how it illustrates the concept of specialization: The class is divided into groups of four and each group is given blank paper and told to make as many paper airplanes as possible in ten minutes. In order to make an airplane, each sheet of paper must be folded in half, then stapled, and then folded into the shape of an airplane and stapled again. In some groups, students should be required to work individually, while in others, students should be allowed to specialize.

EconomicsAmerica *Materials*

The Community Publishing Company, Lesson 11, "The Badge Factory," pp. 83-88. *MCG, 3-4*, Lesson 5, "Getting More Out of Less," pp. 15-16.

4. ECONOMIC SYSTEMS

Content Statement

4.1 The United States economy is organized around a system of private markets in which prices for goods and services are determined.

Evidence of Student Learning

Given a situation in which a seller of bicycles wants to sell them to a buyer, students will *explain* that the price reached will be satisfactory to both the seller and the buyer and that the transaction represents a market. Students will also give other examples of markets.

EconomicsAmerica *Materials*

MCG, 3-4, Lesson 6, "Circles Within Circles," pp. 21-25.
Choices & Changes: Choices, the Economy, and You, Part 1, "The Economy and My Place in It," pp. 1-27.

5. ECONOMIC INSTITUTIONS AND INCENTIVES

Content Statement

5.1 Households are individuals or family units which, as consumers, buy goods and services from firms and, as resource owners, sell productive resources to firms.

Evidence of Student Learning

Students will *name* at least five goods or services that parents, other family members, or neighbors help to produce or provide, and also will *list* several local businesses where the adults they have discussed frequently buy goods or services.

EconomicsAmerica *Materials*

MCG, 3-4, Lesson 6, "Circles Within Circles," pp. 21-25.

Content Statement

5.2 Profit-seeking firms are the basic production units in a market economy.

Evidence of Student Learning

Students will *explain* the difference between the neighborhood police department and the neighborhood grocery store or supermarket in terms of goods and services provided, ownership and the role of profits.

EconomicsAmerica *Materials*

KinderEconomy+, Chapter 9, "Business Ventures," pp. 55-58.
MCG, 3-4, Lesson 6, "Circles Within Circles," pp. 21-25.

Content Statement

5.3 Profit is the difference between revenues and the costs entailed in producing or selling a good or service; it is a return for risk-taking.

Evidence of Student Learning

After a classroom visit by a local entrepreneur, students will *write* a paragraph describing how profit is calculated and a paragraph describing risks common to most small business enterprises.

EconomicsAmerica *Materials*

The Community Publishing Company, Lesson 22, "Production Questions," pp. 151-155; Lesson 23, "Production and Pricing Decisions," pp. 157-162; Lesson 32, "Choice Making," pp. 215-219.
KinderEconomy+, Chapter 9, "Business Venture," pp. 55-57.

6. EXCHANGE, MONEY, AND INTERDEPENDENCE

Content Statement

6.1 Trading goods and services with people for other goods and services or for money is called exchange.

Evidence of Student Learning

Students will *name* five different items produced by a farmer, baker, and one other person chosen by the class; *name* five different items each one of those persons might want, such as a house, car, bread, milk, etc., and *explain* how each person can get what he or she wants through exchange.

EconomicsAmerica *Materials*

Econ and Me, Lesson 5, "Interdependence."
MCG, K-2, Lesson 21, "His Barter Is Worse Than His Bite!" p. 91; Lesson 22, "Birthday Barter," p. 93

Content Statement

6.2 Money is a good that can be used to buy all other goods and services.

Evidence of Student Learning

Given a list of five goods and services they desire and asked to describe ways for obtaining these goods and services, students will *cite* the use of money as one means for obtaining each of the items listed.

EconomicsAmerica *Materials*

Econ and Me, Lesson 3, "Consumption."
KinderEconomy+, Chapter 4, "Production and Banking: From Civil Service to Entrepreneurship," pp. 26-31; Chapter 5, "Consumption and Earning Money," pp. 32-35; Chapter 6, "Exchange and Money versus Barter," pp. 36-39.
MCG, K-2, Lesson 22, "Birthday Barter," p. 93.

Content Statement

6.3 People voluntarily exchange goods and services because they expect to be better off after the exchange.

Evidence of Student Learning

Students will *select* examples of voluntary exchange from the following list: (1) Richard mows Mr. Smith's grass for $5.00 a week; (2) John offers to fix Bill's stereo if

Bill will fix John's car; (3) John cleans up Joe's sporting goods store in return for lessons from the tennis professional; (4) Sally broke Jerry's toy truck and helped him with his chores for three days so he wouldn't tell her mother that she broke his truck.

EconomicsAmerica *Materials*

KinderEconomy+, Chapter 6, "Exchange: Money Versus Barter," pp. 36-39.
MCG, *K-2*, Lesson 21, "His Barter Is Worse Than His Bite!" p. 91; Lesson 23, "To Market, To Market," p. 97.
MCG, *3-4*, Lesson 7, "Let's Trade," pp. 27-30.

Content Statement

6.4 The simplest and most primitive form of exchange is barter—the direct trading of goods and services between people.

Evidence of Student Learning

Students will *state* the difficulties involved in bartering after engaging in the following activity: Explain to students that each will be given something he or she can trade. Distribute a number of different items in varying quantities to members of the class (e.g., two pencils, four small boxes of raisins, one apple, etc.). Ask students to identify which of the items distributed they would like to have most and then attempt to trade with the person who has the item.

EconomicsAmerica *Materials*

KinderEconomy+, Chapter 6, "Exchange: Money Versus Barter," pp. 36-39.
MCG, *K-2*, Lesson 21, "His Barter Is Worse Than His Bite!" p. 91.
MCG, *3-4*, Lesson 7, "Let's Trade," pp. 27-30.

Content Statement

6.5 Money is any generally accepted medium of exchange.

Evidence of Student Learning

Students will *define* the basis for money as anything that is acceptable by everyone and *cite* several examples from history such as cloth, corn, seashells, porpoise teeth, etc.

EconomicsAmerica *Materials*

MCG, *3-4*, Lesson 7, "Let's Trade," pp. 27-30.

Content Statement

6.6 Money eliminates the need for the "double coincidence of wants" that must occur for barter to take place.

Evidence of Student Learning

Students will *explain* why using money would work better than barter in the following scenario: Mrs. Mulligan has more tomatoes in her garden than she can use, but the rabbits ate all her green beans this year and her family likes green beans. Mr. Swanson has extra green beans, but also all the tomatoes he wants. He does, however, want a bird feeder for his front lawn. Mrs. Greenberg has a nice bird feeder that she doesn't want any longer because she is moving to an apartment. She would really like an antique vase to decorate her new apartment. Mrs. Signorelli has just inherited an antique vase, but her furniture is all modern. She has a family reunion planned this weekend and would like to serve fresh, home-grown tomatoes, but she doesn't have a garden herself. Which would be a more efficient system of meeting the wants of all these people, bartering or using money? Why?

EconomicsAmerica *Materials*

MCG, *3-4*, Lesson 7, "Let's Trade," pp. 27-30.

6.7 Exchanges made through barter face problems of divisibility, portability and storage that are greatly reduced by the use of money.

Evidence of Student Learning

After discussion of the use of money instead of barter, students will state at least three reasons why use of money is preferable.

EconomicsAmerica *Materials*

MCG, 3-4, Lesson 7, "Let's Trade," pp. 27-30; Lesson 8, "Money Is What Money Does," pp. 31-34.

6.8 Money has generally replaced barter as a more efficient system for exchange.

Evidence of Student Learning

Students will explain why the use of money is more efficient than barter.

EconomicsAmerica *Materials*

MCG, 3-4, Lesson 7, "Let's Trade," pp. 27-30; Lesson 8, "Money Is What Money Does," pp. 31-34.

6.12 Banks play a key role in providing currency and other forms of money to consumers, and serve as intermediaries between savers and borrowers.

Evidence of Student Learning

Students will *name* and *describe* the types of financial functions the local bank performs. Students will also *explain* how the services provided help people.

EconomicsAmerica *Materials*

The Community Publishing Company, Lesson 25, "Obtaining a Bank Loan," pp. 169-176; Lesson 26, "Study Trip," pp. 177-180.

6.13 Greater specialization leads to increasing interdependence between producers and consumers.

Evidence of Student Learning

From the following example, students will *analyze* the effects of specialization on interdependence: The Lopez family owns a cattle ranch and members of the family spend all their time raising cattle. What other people and businesses do the Lopezes have to rely on in order to specialize in raising cattle?

EconomicsAmerica *Materials*

The Community Publishing Company, Lesson 7, "Community Interdependence," pp. 49-57; Lesson 9, "Visiting a Business," pp. 67-74; Lesson 12, "Interviewing People in the Community," pp. 89-97; Lesson 13, "Results of the Community Interviews," pp. 99-101; Lesson 27, "Job Application," pp. 183-185; Lesson 28, "Preparation for Production," pp. 187-193; Lesson 29, "The Production Process," pp. 195-197.
Econ and Me, Lesson 5, "Interdependence."
MCG, K-2, Lesson 16, "An Interdependent Bunch," pp. 73-75; Lesson 17, "Spotlight on Specialists," pp. 77-79; Lesson 18, "The Baker Wants a Pair of Shoes," pp. 81-82; Lesson 19, "Learning Center: School Connections," pp. 83-84.

7. MARKETS AND PRICES

Content Statement

7.1 A price is the amount of money that people pay when they buy a good or service.

Evidence of Student Learning

Students will *define* "price" and will *name* five items they would buy, giving the price of each item.

EconomicsAmerica *Materials*

KinderEconomy+, Chapter 7, "Distribution," pp. 40-45.

Content Statement

7.2 A market exists whenever buyers and sellers exchange goods and services.

Evidence of Student Learning

Students will correctly *label* the following: (1) If you went to the grocery store and bought two oranges for fifteen cents each, is that a market? (2) If Mrs. Jones bought her son John a frozen yogurt at the drug store, is that a market? (3) If two farmers sold tomatoes at a roadside stand to Mr. Jones, is that a market? (4) If Mrs. Jones had a tooth pulled at the dentist's office, is that a market?

EconomicsAmerica *Materials*

Children in the Marketplace, Grades 3 and 4, Lesson 5.
Community Publishing Company, Lesson 8, "Mini-Mall," pp. 59-65; Lesson 13, "Results of the Community Interviews," pp. 99-101.
KinderEconomy+, Chapter 4, "Production and Banking: From Civil Service to Entrepreneurship," pp. 26-31; Chapter 7, "Distribution," pp. 40-45.
MCG, K-2, Lesson 23, "To Market, to Market," p. 97.
MCG, 3-4, Lesson 6, "Circles Within Circles," pp. 21-25.

9. COMPETITION AND MARKET STRUCTURE

Content Statement

9.1 A market is a setting where buyers and sellers establish prices for identical or very similar products.

Evidence of Student Learning

Students will *identify* places near their own homes where specific goods such as food, toys or clothes are sold.

EconomicsAmerica *Materials*

KinderEconomy+, Chapter 4, "Production and Banking: From Civil Service to Entrepreneurship," pp. 26-31; Chapter 7, "Distribution," pp. 40-45.
12. "The Role of Government."

12. THE ROLE OF GOVERNMENT

Content Statement

12.1 Some goods and services are provided by the government.

Evidence of Student Learning

Students will *identify* from the following list which goods and services are provided by the government: a bag of groceries; the fire department; the police department; a television set.

EconomicsAmerica *Materials*

Econ and Me, Lesson 3, "Consumption."
MCG, 3-4, Lesson 10, "A Taxing Situation," pp. 39-43.

Chapter VI

Scope and Sequence Guidelines, 5-8

Students in fifth through eighth grades are beginning to develop an understanding of how systems work and an ability to generalize from specific facts to abstract principles. Economics instruction can facilitate this change from the concrete reasoning of the child to the abstract reasoning of the adult.

Instruction in middle schools or junior high schools should reinforce the fundamental economic concepts of scarcity and opportunity cost, concepts which ideally have been taught in lower grades but can only now be understood fully in terms of their implications for the structure of societies. How different societies respond to the universal problem of scarcity should be an organizing idea in geography and world history or world cultures in the middle school/junior high school curriculum. The ideas upon which a market economy is based and the importance of supply and demand in a market economy should be learned by every student.

Mathematics teachers can use economics problems that show the relevance of mathematical concepts in the real world. Calculations of profit and loss, the Consumer Price Index or the Gross Domestic Product, or the graphing of supply and demand curves can show students that mathematical skills are necessary to describe and analyze real world problems.

The content statements are presented in two different ways

1. To provide the user a quick and comprehensive overview of the economic content recommended for grades 5–8, the content statements are organized according to the concept clusters discussed in Chapter II and are listed in the order in which they should be introduced in the curriculum.

2. In the second presentation, each concept statement is accompanied by a sample activity which suggests the kind of behavior that would indicate that students have mastered the content. The verb in each activity is highlighted to assist teachers in determining cognitive levels.

Also included is a list of materials from the National Council on Economic Education to use in teaching the content statements.

Evaluating Student Learning. The *Basic Economics Test* (Grades 4–6) and the *Test of Economic Knowledge* (Grades 7-9), published by the National Council on Economic Education are nationally normed tests based on the content categories discussed in Chapter II. Both tests are available in two equivalent forms for pretesting and posttesting middle school and junior high school students. An examiner's manual is also available.

Content Statements, 5-8

1. SCARCITY AND CHOICE

Same as for preceding grade level, and also:

1.12 Scarcity results from the imbalance between relatively unlimited wants and relatively limited resources. There are not enough productive resources to satisfy all of our wants.

1.13 Like individuals, governments and societies experience scarcity because their productive resources are limited and their wants are virtually unlimited.

1.14 Entrepreneurship refers to the human resources that assume the risk of organizing other resources to produce goods and services.

1.15 Because federal, state, and local governments have limited budgets, they must compare their revenues to the costs of public projects their citizens desire.

1.16 Scarcity of resources necessitates choice at both the personal and the societal levels.

1.17 The quality of labor resources (known as human capital)can be improved through investments in education, training, and health care.

2. OPPORTUNITY COST AND TRADE-OFFS

Same as for preceding grade level, and also:

2.4 Few choices are all-or-nothing propositions; they usually involve trade-offs—i.e., getting a little more of one option in exchange for a little less of something else.

2.5 All decisions involve opportunity costs; weighing the costs and the benefits associated with alternative choices constitutes effective economic decision making.

3. PRODUCTIVITY

Same as for preceding grade level, and also:

3.3 Productivity refers to a ratio of output (goods and services)produced per unit of input(productive resources) over some time period.

3.4 Specialization and division of labor usually increase labor productivity.

3.5 Productivity can also be increased by providing labor with additional capital goods such as tools and machines to work with.

3.6 Creating new capital goods involves a trade-off of fewer consumer goods or services in the present in return for higher expected productivity in the future.

3.7 Investment in human capital occurs when resources are devoted to increasing the quality of labor resources, thus enhancing their productivity.

4. ECONOMIC SYSTEMS

Same as for preceding grade level, and also:

4.2 An economic system is the institutional framework that a society uses to allocate its resources to produce and distribute goods and services.

4.3 In a tradition-based economic system, production and distribution decisions are largely determined by custom, i.e., the way things have been done in the past.

4.4 In a command economic system, a central authority makes the major production and distribution decisions.

4.5 In a market economic system, the major decisions about production and distribution are made in a decentralized manner by individual households and business firms following their own self-interest.

4.6 Every modern economy is a "mixed system," having some features characteristic of traditional, command, and market economies. The "mix" varies from one economy to another.

5. ECONOMIC INSTITUTIONS AND INCENTIVES

Same as for preceding grade level, and also:

5.4 The hope of earning profit motivates business firms to incur the risks involved in producing goods and services for the market.

5.5 To earn income, households own and sell productive resources in a market economy and also lend money to people or firms.

5.6 Several kinds of specialized economic institutions such as corporations, banks, and other financial organizations are found in market economies.

5.7 In a market economy, the pursuit of economic self-interest is a basic motivation that leads people and businesses to provide goods and services that other people want.

5.8 Economic incentives, including the desire to achieve financial or material gain and to avoid loss, are powerful motivating forces.

5.9 Cultural traditions and customs influence the patterns of economic behavior in a society.

6. EXCHANGE, MONEY, AND INTERDEPENDENCE

Same as for preceding grade level, and also:

6.9 As a unit of account, money can be used to express the market value of different goods and services.

6.10 As a store of value, money retains its buying power and its "liquidity"—i.e., it can easily be traded for goods and services at any time.

6.11 The basic money supply is usually measured as the total value of coins, currency, and checkable deposits held by the public.

6.14 Money encourages specialization by decreasing the opportunity costs of exchange.

6.15 Specialization is limited by the extent of the market for different goods and services.

6.16 When interdependence is present, a single economic unit is ultimately affected by many of the decisions or events that initially affect its trading partners.

7. MARKETS AND PRICES

Same as for preceding grade level, and also:

7.3 The market clearing or equilibrium price is the one price at which quantity supplied equals quantity demanded.

7.4 Relative prices refer to the price of one good or service compared to the prices of other goods and services, and are the basic measure of the relative scarcity of a product when prices are set by market forces (supply and demand).

7.5 Relative prices provide the key signals used by consumers and producers to answer the three basic economic questions: What to produce? How to produce it? Who will consume it?

7.6 The circular flow model shows the interactions between households and producers in product and resource markets.

8. SUPPLY AND DEMAND

8.1 If the price of a product increases, quantity demanded will decrease and quantity supplied will increase. If the price of a product decreases, quantity demanded will increase and quantity supplied will decrease.

8.2 Forces of supply and demand determine prices, which are measures of the relative scarcity of different products.

8.3 Demand is the schedule of how much consumers are willing and able to buy at all possible prices in a given period of time.

8.4 Supply is the schedule of how much producers are willing and able to sell at all possible prices in a given period of time.

8.5 Market demand and supply schedules are based on the sum of decisions made by all of the individual consumers and producers in a market.

8.6 Prices for different products are interrelated.

8.7 The level of competition among producers or buyers affects supply and demand and prices for different products.

9. COMPETITION AND MARKET STRUCTURE

Same as for preceding grade level, and also:

9.3 An industry is made up of all the producers of identical or very similar products in a market area.

9.4 Active competition among sellers results in lower prices and profit levels.

9.5 A monopoly exists when only one producer sells a product that has no close substitutes.

9.6 Competition among buyers of a product results in higher prices for the product.

9.7 Sellers engage in both price and nonprice competition.

10. INCOME DISTRIBUTION

10.1 There are four basic categories of earned income: wages and salaries, rent, interest, and profit. Wages and salaries are payments for labor service; rent is the payment for the use of land (natural resources); interest is the payment for the use of capital, including financial capital (money); and profit is the return to business enterprise (entrepreneurship) when the value of sales exceeds the cost of the goods and service sold.

11. MARKET FAILURES

11.1 Governments provide public goods, due to the shared consumption and non-exclusion properties of these products.

11.2 Shared consumption (or non-rival) products are those that can be used simultaneously by more than one person without reducing the amount of the product available for others to consume.

11.3 A nonexclusive product is one that, once produced, cannot be withheld even from those who do not pay for it.

11.4 Externalities exist when some of the costs or benefits associated with the production or consumption of a product "spill over" to third parties other than the direct producers and consumers of the product. Positive externalities (external benefits) result in the underproduction or under consumption of a product, since not all benefits are reflected in consumers' demand for the product. Negative externalities (external costs) result in the overproduction or over consumption of a product, since not all costs are reflected in producers' supply of the product.

11.5 A natural monopoly exists when one producer can supply total output in a market at a cost that is lower than if two or more producers divided the production of this output.

11.6 Because competition cannot serve to regulate the price, output, and the quality of goods and services produced by natural monopolies, government regulatory agencies are generally established to perform these roles.

12. THE ROLE OF GOVERNMENT

Same as for preceding grade level, and also:

12.2 The government pays for the goods and services it provides through taxing and borrowing.

12.3 In a market economy, the government defines and enforces property rights and provides standard units of weights, measures, and money.

12.4 Operating government requires shifting scarce resources from the private sector of the economy to the public sector.

12.5 Other economic roles of government include providing public goods and services; correcting for externalities; maintaining competition; redistributing income; and promoting full employment, stable prices, and reasonable rates of economic growth.

13. GROSS DOMESTIC PRODUCT

13.1 When purchases are made, goods and services are transferred from businesses to households in exchange for money payments. The money is used by businesses to pay for factors of production: land, labor, capital, and entrepreneurship. This is often depicted in a circular flow diagram.

15. UNEMPLOYMENT

15.1 Unemployed people are those who are willing and able to work at current wage rates, but do not have jobs.

15.2 People who are unemployed usually have less income to buy goods and services than those who have jobs.

15.3 Governments provide income to some unemployed workers until they can find jobs.

15.4 The labor force is composed of people age 16 and over who are either employed or actively seeking work.

15.5 The unemployment rate is the percentage of the labor force considered to be unemployed.

15.6 The unemployment rate rises during a recession.

16. INFLATION AND DEFLATION

16.1 Inflation is a sustained increase in the average price level of the entire economy; deflation is a sustained decrease in the average price level of the entire economy.

16.2 The Consumer Price Index (CPI) is the most commonly used measure of price level changes. It compares prices in one year with some earlier period (a base period).

18. FISCAL POLICY

18.1 Fiscal policy involves the use of national government spending and taxation programs to affect the level of economic activity in such a way as to promote price stability, maximum employment, and reasonable economic growth.

19. ABSOLUTE AND COMPARATIVE ADVANTAGE AND BARRIERS TO TRADE

19.1 The quantity and quality of productive resources available in different nations vary widely.

19.2 International trade is the exchange of goods and services between people and institutions in different nations.

19.3 Exports are goods and services produced in one nation but sold to buyers in another nation.

19.4 Imports are goods or services bought from sellers in another nation.

19.5 International trade promotes greater specialization, and specialization increases total world output.

20. EXCHANGE RATES AND THE BALANCE OF PAYMENTS

20.1 Different currencies are used in different countries.

21. INTERNATIONAL ASPECTS OF GROWTH AND STABILITY

21.1 Economic growth is a sustained rise in the production of goods and services.

21.2 Technological change and improvements in a society's stock of productive resources promote economic growth.

Teaching Resources, 5-8

1. SCARCITY AND CHOICE

Same as for preceding grade level, and also:

Content Statement

1.12 Scarcity results from the imbalance between relatively unlimited wants and relatively limited resources. There are not enough productive resources to satisfy all of our wants.

Evidence of Student Learning

Students will *explain* why they cannot have all the games, clothes, and sporting equipment that they want, stated in terms of scarcity of the specific productive resources necessary to produce those items.

EconomicsAmerica *Materials*

Choices and Changes: You Can Be an Inventor: Human Capital and Entrepreneurship, Part I, "Creativity and Invention, pp. 1-28; Part 2, "Producing a Product," pp. 29-49; Part 3, "Human Capital," pp. 50-73.
Entrepreneurship in the U. S. Economy, Lesson 1, "What Is an Entrepreneur?" pp. 2-5; Lesson 2, "Scarcity: Everyone's Problem Is the Entrepreneur's Opportunity," pp. 6-9. Lesson 5, "Making Things Entrepreneurs Sell," pp. 17-20.
26, "Human Resource Management: The Entrepreneur's Perspective," pp. 113-116.

Content Statement

1.13 Like individuals, governments and societies experience scarcity because their productive resources are limited and their wants are virtually unlimited.

Evidence of Student Learning

Students will *list* all the services they think the government should provide ideally for the people in their community and *explain* why all of these services cannot be provided.

EconomicsAmerica *Materials*

The Elementary Economist, "Taxes and Taxation," Vol. 9, No. 2.

Content Statement

1.14 Entrepreneurship refers to the human resources that assume the risk of organizing other resources to produce goods and services.

Evidence of Student Learning

After a classroom visit by a local entrepreneur, students will *write* a short essay on the risk entrepreneurs take and the motivation they have in undertaking these risks.

EconomicsAmerica *Materials*

Choices & Changes: You Can Be An Inventor: Human Capital and Entrepreneurship, Part 3, "Human Capital," pp. 50-73.
Entrepreneurship in the U. S. Economy, Lesson 1, "What Is an Entrepreneur?" pp. 2-5; Lesson 5, "Making Things Entrepreneurs Sell," pp. 17-20.
The International News Journal, Lesson 7, "Trade Among Businesses," pp. 31-37.
United States History, Eyes on the Economy, Vol. 1, Unit 5, Lesson 3, "Entrepreneurship Case Study: George Mason," pp. 79-80; Vol. 1, Unit 6, Lesson 7, "Entrepreneurship Case Study: Samuel Slater," pp. 124-125.

1.15 Because federal, state, and local governments have limited budgets, they must compare their revenues to the costs of public projects their citizens desire.

Evidence of Student Learning

Given the following problem, students will *decide* which project the city should undertake and *state* the reasons for that choice.

A city needs new street lights in one neighborhood, but it also needs two daycare centers in opposite sections of town. Each project will cost $50,000.00, but the city has only enough money to pay for one of the projects. Fifty houses will benefit from the street lights. One-hundred families will use the daycare centers. Which project should the city choose?

EconomicsAmerica *Materials*

The Elementary Economist, "Taxes and Taxations," Vol. 9, No. 2.

1.16 Scarcity of resources necessitates choice at both the personal and the societal levels.

Evidence of Student Learning

Students will *list* things their families want and also the services that they think should be provided by their local, state or federal government. They will then *select* those family wants that they would be willing to give up in order to obtain the government services listed and *state* the reasons for their choices.

EconomicsAmerica *Materials*

Entrepreneurship in the U. S. Economy, Lesson 1, "What Is an Entrepreneur," pp. 2-5.
The International News Journal, Inc., Lesson 12, "Resources for the News Journal," pp. 53-56.
United States History, Eyes on the Economy, Vol. 1, Unit 2, Lesson 1, "The New World Was an Old World," pp. 26-32; Unit 4, Lesson 1, "Understanding the Colonial Economy," pp. 52-59.

1.17 The quality of labor resources (known as human capital) can be improved through investments in education, training, and health care.

Evidence of Student Learning

For a selected group of occupations, such as police officer, auto worker, secretary or doctor, students will *describe* how different levels of education and training contribute to the value of the goods or services these workers provide and to the income differentials for these occupations. Students will also *analyze* the effects of health care, or the lack of it, on human capital.

EconomicsAmerica *Materials*

The International News Journal, Inc., Lesson 19, "Getting Organized," pp. 83-90; Lesson 20, "Formulating Questions and Note Taking," pp. 91-93; Lesson 21, "Outlining," pp. 94-95; Lesson 22, "Rough Draft," pp. 96-97; Lesson 23, "Editing," pp. 98-99; Lesson 24, "Final Draft," pp. 103-104; Lesson 25, "Production Choices," pp. 105-106; Lesson 26, "Art/Graphics Project," pp. 107-111.

2. OPPORTUNITY COST AND TRADE-OFFS

Same as for preceding grade level, and also:

Content Statement

2.4 Few choices are all-or-nothing propositions; they usually involve trade-offs—i.e., getting a little more of one option in exchange for a little less of something else.

Evidence of Student Learning

Students will *apply* the concepts of "opportunity costs" and "trade-offs" in answering the following: Your grandmother gave you $30.00 for your birthday and you are trying to decide how to spend it. You are considering buying cassette tapes (price = $12.00 each), or going to the movies (matinee ticket price = $3.50 each time you go), or taking some friends out for pizza ($7.50 for each person you take, including yourself). You do not have to spend all your money on one thing; you can choose some of one thing and some of another. How would you spend your money so as to get the greatest satisfaction from your grandmother's present? Why would your choices satisfy you more than the things you gave up?

Content Statement

2.5 All decisions involve opportunity costs; weighing these costs and the benefits associated with alternative choices constitutes effective economic decision making.

Evidence of Student Learning

Students will *apply* the concept "opportunity cost" in responding to the following: You are a member of your state's legislature, and there is a $500,000 surplus in the state budget. How much of that $500,000 would you spend on each of the following programs: aid to the homeless, money to retrain unemployed workers, aid to schools in poor neighborhoods, improvement of state roads, or money for the state society for prevention of cruelty to animals? Explain why you chose to support certain programs and to spend no money on others. What is the opportunity cost of the choices that you made?

EconomicsAmerica *Materials*

Choices & Changes: Choices, the Economy, and You, Part 1, "The Economy and My Place in It," pp. 1-27; Part 2, "Making Choices," pp. 28-51; Part 3, "Choices: Influences and Consequences," pp. 52-76.
Choices & Changes: Choice Making, Productivity, and Planning, Part 1, "Making Choices," pp. 1-20; Part 3, "Choosing a Future You Prefer," pp. 45-67.
Entrepreneurship in the U. S. Economy, Lesson 4, "Successful Entrepreneurs Make Rational Choices," pp. 13-16; Lesson 22, "Cash Flow and the Successful Entrepreneur," pp. 94-98; Lesson 30, "The Costs and Benefits of Innovation," pp. 130-134; Lesson 35, You and Entrepreneurial Skills," pp. 155-160.
United States History, Eyes on the Economy, Vol. 1, Unit 1, Lesson 1, "Solving Mysteries in United States History: A User's Guide," pp. 2-9; Unit 4, Lesson 2, "The Costs and Benefits of Independence," pp. 60-66; Unit 6, Lesson 1, "The Tale of the Corset and the Necktie," pp. 88-93; Unit 8, Lesson 1, "Why Did the South Secede?" pp. 148-154; Unit 8, Lesson 2, "The Economic Effects of the Civil War," pp. 154-157.

3. PRODUCTIVITY

Same as for preceding grade level, and also:

Content Statement

3.3 Productivity refers to a ratio of output (goods and services) produced per unit of input (productive resources) over some time period.

Evidence of Student Learning

Students will *solve* the following problem: The Tanner factory and the Thacker factory both make baseball gloves. Both factories have the same kind of equipment and both employ 200 workers. Last month the Tanner factory produced 5,000 baseball gloves in 20 working days, while the Thacker factory produced 4,000 gloves in the same time period. What was the output per worker per day in each factory? Which factory was more productive, assuming equal quality?

EconomicsAmerica *Materials*

Choices & Changes: You Can Be an Inventor: Human Capital and Entrepreneurship, Part 3, "Human Capital," pp. 50-73.
Choices & Changes: Choice Making, Productivity, and Planning, Part 2, "Human Capital and Productivity," pp. 21-40.
Entrepreneurship in the U. S. Economy, Lesson 25, "How Entrepreneurs Measure Productivity," pp. 109-112.
United States History, Eyes on the Economy, Vol. 1, Unit 6, Lesson 2, "Productivity Raises Output," pp. 94-101.
MCG 5-6, Lesson 7, "Widget Production," pp. 29-32.

Content Statement

3.4 Specialization and division of labor usually increase labor productivity.

Evidence of Student Learning

After making a specific product as a member of a small group, students will *explain* why more goods are produced when each member of the group performs a particular task in making the good.

EconomicsAmerica *Materials*

Choices & Changes: Choice Making, Productivity, and Planning, Part 2, "Human Capital and Productivity," pp. 21-40.
Entrepreneurship in the U. S. Economy, Lesson 7, Entrepreneurship in Our Market Economy, pp. 27-30.
The International News Journal, Inc., Lesson 27, "Assembling the News Journal," pp. 116-117.
United States History, Eyes on the Economy, Vol. 1, Unit 4, Lesson 1, "Understanding the Colonial Economy," pp. 94-901; Unit 6, Lesson 2, "Productivity Raises Output," pp. 94-101; Unit 6, Lesson 3, "Lowell Workers and Producers Respond to Incentives," pp. 102-108.

Content Statement

3.5 Productivity can also be increased by providing labor with additional capital goods such as tools and machines to work with.

Evidence of Student Learning

Students will *explain* how a secretary's productivity can be increased by replacing a typewriter with a word processor.

EconomicsAmerica *Materials*

Entrepreneurship in the U. S. Economy, Lesson 25, "How Entrepreneurs Measure Productivity," pp. 109-112.
United States History, Eyes on the Economy, Vol. 1, Unit 6, Lesson 2, "Productivity Raises Output," pp. 94-101; Unit 6, Lesson 4, "Cost Cutting Is Fashionable," pp. 109-112.
MCG 5-6, Lesson 7, "Widget Production," pp. 29-32.

Content Statement

3.6 Creating new capital resources involves a trade-off of fewer consumer goods or services in the present in return for higher expected productivity in the future.

Evidence of Student Learning

Students will *explain the* following: Last year Mr. Smith took $2,400 out of the bank to buy two new ovens to increase productivity in his bakery. What trade-off did Mr. Smith make?

EconomicsAmerica *Materials*

United States History, Eyes on the Economy, Vol. 1, Unit 6, Lesson 6, "What Is Investment?" pp. 120-123.
MCG 5-6, Lesson 7, "Widget Production," pp. 29-32.

Content Statement

3.7 Investment in human capital occurs when resources are devoted to increasing the quality of labor resources, thus enhancing their productivity.

Evidence of Student Learning

Students will *explain in terms* of human capital why engineers make more money than taxi drivers and why teachers with master's degrees earn more money than teachers without master's degrees.

EconomicsAmerica *Materials*

Choices & Changes: Choices, the Economy, and You, Part 1, "The Economy and My Place in It," pp. 1-27.
Choices & Changes: Choice Making, Productivity, and Planning, Part 2, "Human Capital and Productivity," pp. 21-44.
Entrepreneurship in the U. S. Economy, Lesson 3, "Consumers, Businesses, Entrepreneurs, and Governments Face Opportunity Costs," pp. 10-12; Lesson 34, "Successful Entrepreneurs Develop Their Own Human Capital," pp. 150-154.
MCG 5-6, Lesson 7, "Widget Production," pp. 29-32.

4. ECONOMIC SYSTEMS

Same as for preceding grade level, and also:

Content Statement

4.2 An economic system is the institutional framework that a society uses to allocate its resources to produce and distribute goods and services.

Evidence of Student Learning

Students, working in small groups, will *decide* from a list of several products which one they will produce, how they will produce it, and for whom they will produce it. They will also *describe* how they arrived at their decisions and *state*, in terms of scarcity, why these decisions must be made by any group of people living and working together.

EconomicsAmerica *Materials*

Entrepreneurship in the U. S. Economy, Lesson 6, "Entrepreneurship in Different Economic Systems," pp. 22-26.
United States History, Eyes on the Economy, Vol. , Unit 1, Lesson 1, "Solving Mysteries in United States History: A User's Guide," pp. 2-9; Unit 1, Lesson 2, "The United States and the Global Economy," pp. 10-16; Unit 2, Lesson 1, "The New World Was an Old World," pp. 26-32.
MCG 5-6, Lesson 2, "What? How? For Whom?", pp. 7-9.

Content Statement

4.3 In a tradition-based economic system, production and distribution decisions are largely determined by custom, i.e., the way things have been done in the past.

Evidence of Student Learning

Students will *describe* how the three economic questions are answered in traditional societies of the past or present, such as Europe in the Middle Ages, the American Indian tribes before the arrival of European settlers, or the rural villages of the less-developed countries today.

EconomicsAmerica *Materials*

Entrepreneurship in the U. S. Economy, Lesson 6, "Entrepreneurship in Different Economic Systems," pp. 22-26.

Content Statement

4.4 In a command economic system, a central authority makes the major production and distribution decisions.

Evidence of Student Learning

Students will *describe* how the three economic questions are answered in command economies of the past and present, such as the mercantilist nations of early modern Europe or twentieth century communist nations.

EconomicsAmerica *Materials*

Entrepreneurship in the U. S. Economy, Lesson 6, "Entrepreneurship in Different Economic Systems," pp. 22-26.

Content Statement

4.5 In a market economic system, the major decisions about production and distribution are made in a decentralized manner by individual households and business firms following their own self-interest.

Evidence of Student Learning

Students will *describe* how the three economic questions are answered in a market economy such as the United States, Canada, or other western societies.

EconomicsAmerica *Materials*

Entrepreneurship in the U. S. Economy, Lesson 6, "Entrepreneurship in Different Economic Systems," pp. 22-26.

Content Statement

4.6 Every modern economy is a "mixed" system having some features characteristic of traditional, command, and market economies. The "mix" varies from one economy to another.

Evidence of Student Learning

Students will *list* some traditional or command features of the United States economy, such as the small number of women in jobs such as plumber or miner, or the goods and services provided by the government rather than by private firms.

EconomicsAmerica *Materials*

Entrepreneurship in the U. S. Economy, Lesson 6, "Entrepreneurship in Different Economic Systems," pp. 22-26.

5. ECONOMIC INSTITUTIONS AND INCENTIVES

Same as for preceding grade level, and also:

Content Statement

5.4 The hope of earning profit motivates business firms to incur the risks involved in producing goods and services for the market.

Evidence of Student Learning

Students will correctly *calculate* profit or loss for each of the following: (1) As the owner of a bicycle repair shop that made $80,000 in revenue last year, you had to pay $62,000 for spare parts, rent for your store, electricity, wages, and business taxes. How much was your profit or loss? (2) You own a doughnut shop. Last year the expenses of running your shop, including the wages you paid, the rent for your shop, your business taxes, the cost of the flour, eggs and sugar to make your doughnuts, and the cost of keeping your equipment in good order totaled $170,000.00. Your revenue from selling doughnuts was $152,000.00. How much was your profit or loss?

EconomicsAmerica *Materials*

Entrepreneurship in the U. S. Economy, Lesson 6, "Entrepreneurship in Different Economic Systems," pp. 22-25.
The International News Journal, Inc., Lesson 13, "Business Ownership," pp. 57-60; Lesson 32, "Profits and the Annual Report," pp. 135-138.
United States History, Eyes On the Economy, Vol. 1, Unit 6, Lesson 2, "Productivity Raises Output," pp. 94-101.
MCG 5-6, Lesson 8, "Creative Toy Production," pp. 35-38.

Content Statement

5.5 To earn income, households own and sell productive resources in a market economy and also lend money to people or firms.

Evidence of Student Learning

Students will *cite* specific examples of how a household could earn income by selling labor, by selling or renting a natural resource (such as farmland), by selling or renting capital equipment (such as a snow-plow), by running a business (single proprietor shop), or by putting money in a bank, stocks, or bonds and receiving a return.

EconomicsAmerica *Materials*

Entrepreneurship in the U. S. Economy, Lesson 9, "The Circular Flow Between Consumers and Entrepreneurs," pp. 36-39.
MCG 5-6, Lesson 3, "Dandy Dollars Takes a Trip," pp. 11-15.

Content Statement

5.6 Several kinds of specialized economic institutions are found in market economies.

Evidence of Student Learning

Students will *describe* in their own words at least one economic purpose that is served by each of the following institutions: corporations, partnerships, proprietorships, cooperatives, labor unions, banks, government organizations, nonprofit organizations.

EconomicsAmerica *Materials*

Entrepreneurship in the U. S. Economy, Lesson 18, "Entrepreneurs Choose Different Types of Business Organization," pp. 76-79.
The International News Journal, Inc., Lesson 13, "Business Ownership," pp. 57-60; Lesson 14, "Organizing the Corporation," pp. 61-63; Lesson 15, "Board of Directors and Corporate Officers," pp. 64-69; Lesson 16, "Selling Stock," pp. 70-73; Lesson 17, "Review of Corporations," pp. 74-75.

Content Statement

5.7 In a market economy, the pursuit of economic self-interest is a basic motivation that leads people and businesses to provide goods and services that other people want.

Evidence of Student Learning

In a one- or two-paragraph essay, students will *explain* the economic reasoning and *give examples* of the following generalization: The fact that people are motivated by their own economic self-interest is a major reason why market-oriented economies can continue to function.

EconomicsAmerica *Materials*

United States History, Eyes on the Economy, Vol. 1, Unit 1, Lesson 1, "Solving Economic Mysteries in United States History: User's Guide," pp. 2-9; Unit 6, Lesson 3, "Lowell Workers and Producers Respond to Incentives," pp. 102-108; Unit 7, Lesson 1, "Saving and Investing in Razorback," pp. 130-133.

Content Statement

5.8 Economic incentives, including the desire to achieve financial or material gain and to avoid loss, are powerful motivating forces.

Evidence of Student Learning

Students will *list* economic incentives that have recently affected their behavior, such as taking a part-time job (mowing lawns, delivering newspapers, etc.) to get money to buy something they want.

EconomicsAmerica *Materials*

Choices & Changes: Choices, the Economy, and You, Part 3, "Choices: Influences and Consequences," pp. 52-76.
Choices & Changes: Choice Making, Productivity, and Planning, "Making Choices," pp. 1-20.
United States History, Eyes on the Economy, Vol. 1, Unit 2, Lesson 2, "Did Native Americans Act Economically?" pp. 33-36; Unit 3, Lesson 2, "Be a Planet Planner," pp. 45-49; Unit 6, Lesson 3, "Lowell Workers and Producers Respond to Incentives," pp. 102-108.
MCG 5-6, Lesson 8, "Creative Toy Production," pp. 35-38.

Content Statement

5.9 Cultural traditions and customs influence the patterns of economic behavior in a society.

Evidence of Student Learning

Students will *explain* the following generalization in terms of cultural tradition: Although a majority of American elementary and middle school teachers are women, most principals of elementary schools and middle schools are men.

EconomicsAmerica *Materials*

United States History, Eyes on the Economy, Vol. 1, Unit 2, Lesson 2, "Did Native Americans Act Economically?' pp. 33-36; Unit 3, Lesson 1, "Why Do Economies Grow?" pp. 40-44.

6. EXCHANGE, MONEY, AND INTERDEPENDENCE

Same as for preceding grade level, and also:

Content Statement

6.9 As a unit of account, money can be used to express the market value of different goods and services.

Evidence of Student Learning

Students will *explain* that money has value because everyone accepts it as the unit of account and will *give examples* of how three specific products are valued by buyers and sellers based upon their relative prices.

EconomicsAmerica *Materials*

United States History, Eyes on the Economy, Vol. 1, Unit 5, Lesson 2, "The Constitution: Ground Rules for the Economy," pp. 74-78.

6.10 As a store of value, money retains its buying power and its "liquidity"—i.e., it can be used as final payment for goods and services.

Evidence of Student Learning

Students will *demonstrate* their understanding of money as a "store of value" in responding to the following: A tomato farmer wants to save money for his five-year-old daughter's college education. Why is he better off selling his tomatoes for money and saving the money than he would be if he saved tomatoes to exchange for his daughter's tuition when she was eighteen?

EconomicsAmerica *Materials*

United States History, Eyes on the Economy, Vol. 1, Unit 7, Lesson 2, "What Role Does Money Play," pp. 134-138.

6.11 The basic money supply is usually measured as the total value of coins, currency, and checkable deposits held by the public.

Evidence of Student Learning

After reviewing a circle graph depicting percentages of the money supply, students will *identify* the components of the basic money supply and *describe each* component.

EconomicsAmerica *Materials*

United States History, Eyes on the Economy, Vol. 1, Unit 7, Lesson 2, "What Role Does Money Play?" pp. 134-138; Unit 7, Lesson 3, "Boom and Bust in the 1830s," pp. 139-143.

6.14 Money encourages specialization by decreasing the opportunity costs of exchange.

Evidence of Student Learning

Students will *explain* how money makes it possible for an economics teacher to get her car repaired, even though she may not be able to find an auto mechanic who wants to learn economics.

EconomicsAmerica *Materials*

United States History, Eyes on the Economy, Vol. 1, Unit 2, Lesson 2, "Did Native Americans Act Economically?" pp. 33-36; Unit 7, Lesson 2, "What Role Does Money Play?" pp. 134-138.

6.15 Specialization is limited by the extent of the market for different goods and services.

Evidence of Student Learning

Students will *explain* the following situations in terms of the limits of specialization: (1) John Smith wants to be a history teacher. He likes Chinese history best, but in college he also takes courses in American history and the history of other parts of the world. (2) Marilyn Robinson opens an auto dealership that carries large luxury automobiles, station wagons and small economy cars.

EconomicsAmerica *Materials*

The International News Journal, Inc., Lesson 12, "Resources for the News Journal," pp. 53-56.

6.16 When interdependence is present, a single economic unit is ultimately affected by many of the decisions or events that initially affect its trading partners.

Evidence of Student Learning

Students will *list* ten ways in which the United States economy would be affected if the OPEC countries cut off all trade with the United States.

EconomicsAmerica *Materials*

The International News Journal, Inc., Lesson 27, "Preparation for the Assembly Process," pp. 112-115.

7. MARKETS AND PRICES

Same as for preceding grade level, and also:

Content Statement

7.3 The market clearing or equilibrium price is the one price at which quantity supplied equals quantity demanded.

Evidence of Student Learning

Students will *interpret* the following demand and supply schedules to determine the market price for peaches.

Quantity of peaches demanded:
2 bushels for $4.00 a bushel
4 bushels for $3.50 a bushel
6 bushels for $3.00 a bushel
8 bushels for $2.50 a bushel
10 bushels for $2.00 a bushel
Quantity of peaches supplied:
2 bushels for $2.00 a bushel
4 bushels for $2.50 a bushel
6 bushels for $3.00 a bushel
8 bushels for $3.50 a bushel
10 bushels for $4.00 a bushel

EconomicsAmerica *Materials*

Entrepreneurship in the U. S. Economy, Lesson 14, "Entrepreneurs and Equilibrium," pp. 58-61; Lesson 15, "Entrepreneurs and Changing Prices," pp. 62-65. MCG 5-6, Lesson 11, "Market Balance," pp. 51-54; Lesson 12, "Market Madness." pp. 57-61.

Content Statement

7.4 Relative prices refer to the price of one good or service compared to the prices of other goods and services, and are the basic measure of the relative scarcity of a product when prices are set by market forces (supply and demand).

Evidence of Student Learning

From the following list of paired items, students will *identify* which items will have higher prices than others and will *explain* why in terms of relative scarcity: diamonds and salt; steak and hamburger;gold and silver.

Content Statement

7.5 Relative prices provide the key signals used by consumers and producers to answer the three basic economic questions: What to produce? How to produce it? Who will consume it?

Evidence of Student Learning

Students will *state* the economic reasons for what happened in each of the following situations: (1) The price of peanuts rose. Consumers bought fewer peanuts, and farmers decided to plant more peanuts. Why did consumers and farmers behave the way they did? (2) The price of oil fell. Consumers drove more, and oil-drilling companies reduced their exploration for new oil. Why did consumers and oil producers behave the way they did?

EconomicsAmerica *Materials*

United States History, Eyes on the Economy, Vol. 1, Unit 2, "The Hula Hoop Market of 1958," pp. 17-22.

Content Statement

7.6 The circular flow model shows the interactions between households and producers in product and resource markets.

Evidence of Student Learning

Students will *draw* the circular flow diagram and *explain* the interrelated roles of households and businesses in the economy.

EconomicsAmerica *Materials*

Entrepreneurship in the U. S. Economy, Lesson 8, "Entrepreneurial Behavior in Other Settings," pp. 31-34.
MCG 5-6, Lesson 3, "Dandy Dollars Takes a Trip," pp. 11-15.

8. SUPPLY AND DEMAND

Same as for preceding grade level, and also:

Content Statement

8.1 If the price of a product increases, quantity demanded will decrease and quantity supplied will increase. If the price of a product decreases, quantity demanded will increase and quantity supplied will decrease.

Evidence of Student Learning

Based on the data collected in the following exercises, students will *describe* the relationship between price and the quantity demanded and the relationship between price and the quantity supplied. (1) There is a new fruit drink called "Delicious." It gives you lots of energy and really tastes good. How many 8 oz. cups would you buy at the following prices: $1.00;$0.75; $0.50; $0.25; $0.15; $0.10; $0.05? (2) Now you are the producer/seller of this fruit drink. How many cups would you be willing to supply at the following prices: $1.00; $0.75; $0.50; $0.25; $0.15; $0.10; $0.05? (3) Based on your answers, what do you think normally happens to the amount of a product that is bought if the price goes up? What normally happens to the amount that is sold if the price goes down?

EconomicsAmerica *Materials*

Choices & Changes: You Can Be an Inventor: Human Capital and Entrepreneurship, Part 2, "Producing a Product," pp. 29-48.
Entrepreneurship in the U. S. Economy, Lesson 10, "The Nature of Consumer Demand," pp. 40-43; Lesson 12, "Entrepreneurs Supply Goods and Services," pp. 49-52.
MCG 5-6, Lesson 4, "A Profusion of Confusion," pp. 17-19; Lesson 5, "Graphing Demand," pp. 21-23; Lesson 9, "Producers and Supply," pp. 41-44.
United States History, Eyes on the Economy, Vol. 1, Unit 6, Lesson 3, "Lowell Workers and Producers Respond to Incentives," pp. 102-108.

Content Statement

8.2 Forces of supply and demand determine prices, which are measures of the relative scarcity of different products.

Evidence of Student Learning

Given that one item is worth $5.00, another $1.00, and a third $.50, students will *describe* how supply and demand together set the market price of each and how the prices reflect relative scarcity of the three items.

EconomicsAmerica *Materials*

The International News Journal, Inc., Lesson 15, "Board of Directors and Corporate Officers," pp. 64-69.
MCG 5-6, Lesson 11, "Market Balance," pp. 51-54.

Content Statement

8.3 Demand is the schedule of how much consumers are willing and able to buy at all possible prices in a given period of time.

Evidence of Student Learning

Students will *construct a* demand schedule and a demand curve for peaches from the following information:

Price per pound: $1.00, .90, .80, .70, .60, .50, .40, .30, .20. Quantity demanded in pounds: 1,000; 1,500; 2,000; 2,750; 3,750; 5,000; 6,500; 8,250; 10,250.

EconomicsAmerica *Materials*

Entrepreneurship in the U. S. Economy, Lesson 10, "The Nature of Consumer Demand," pp. 40-43.
The International News Journal, Inc., "Board of Directors and Corporate Officers," pp. 64-69.
MCG 5-6, Lesson 4, "A Profusion of Confusion," pp. 17-19; Lesson 5, "Graphing Demand," pp. 21-23; Lesson 6, "Demand Changes," pp. 25-28.

Content Statement

8.4 Supply is the schedule of how much producers are willing and able to sell at all possible prices in a given period of time.

Evidence of Student Learning

Students will *construct a* supply schedule and a supply curve for peaches from the following information:

Price per pound: $1.00, .90, .80, .70, .60, .50, .40, .30. Quantity supplied in pounds: 10,250; 8,250; 6,500; 5,000; 3,750; 2,750; 1,500; 1,000.

EconomicsAmerica *Materials*

Entrepreneurship in the U. S. Economy, Lesson 12, "Entrepreneurs Supply Goods and Services.
MCG 5-6, Lesson 9, "Producers and Supply," pp. 41-44.

Content Statement

8.5 Market demand and supply schedules are based on the sum of decisions made by all of the individual consumers and producers in a market.

Evidence of Student Learning

After taking part in a simulation where half of the class members are buyers and half are sellers of a product such as apples, potatoes, or hamburgers, students will *describe* how market demand and supply schedules are obtained from adding up the demand of individual buyers and the supply of individual sellers.

EconomicsAmerica *Materials*

MCG 5-6, Lesson 4, "A Profusion of Confusion," pp. 17-19; Lesson 5, "Graphing Demand," pp. 21-23; Lesson 6, "Demand Changes," pp. 25-28; Lesson 9, "Producers and Supply," pp. 41-44.

Content Statement

8.6 Prices for different products are interrelated.

Evidence of Student Learning

Students will correctly *answer* the following questions: (1) If steak becomes more expensive, what is likely to happen to purchases of hamburger and the price of hamburgers? (2) If the price of hamburgers decreases, then what is likely to happen to purchases of french fries and the price of french fries? (3) If bicycle tires become more expensive, what is likely to happen to purchases of bicycles and the price of bicycles?

EconomicsAmerica *Materials*

MCG 5-6, Lesson 6, "Demand Changes," pp. 25-28.

Content Statement

8.7 The level of competition among producers or buyers affects supply and demand and prices for different products.

Evidence of Student Learning

Students will *analyze* in a short essay what is likely to happen to the price of cars if either more sellers or more buyers enter the market.

EconomicsAmerica *Materials*

United States History, Eyes on the Economy, Vol. 1, Unit 6, Lesson 3, "Lowell Workers and Producers Respond to Incentives," pp. 102-108.

9. COMPETITION AND MARKET STRUCTURE

Same as for preceding grade level, and also:

Content Statement

9.2 The level of competition in a market is largely determined by the number of buyers and sellers in the market.

Evidence of Student Learning

Students will *survey* their community to find the number of fast-food restaurants and the number of bicycle shops present. Based on the results of the survey, they will *draw conclusions* about which market is more competitive.

EconomicsAmerica *Materials*

Entrepreneurship in the U.S. Economy, Lesson 27, "The Entrepreneur and Market Structure," pp. 118-121.

Content Statement

9.3 An industry is made up of all the producers of identical or very similar products in a market area.

Evidence of Student Learning

Using the economic definition of an industry, students will *identify* several industries in the local area and *state* whether these industries operate in international, nationwide, regional, or local markets.

Content Statement

9.4 Active competition among sellers results in lower prices and profit levels.

Evidence of Student Learning

After collecting data on community fast-food restaurants and the prices they charge for similar food items, students will *draw conclusions* about the relationship of the number of restaurants to the prices charged.

EconomicsAmerica *Materials*

Entrepreneurship in the U. S. Economy, Lesson 7, "Entrepreneurship in Our Market System," pp. 27-30; Lesson 27, "The Entrepreneur and Market Structure," pp. 118-121.

Content Statement

9.5 A monopoly exists when only one producer sells a product that has no close substitutes.

Evidence of Student Learning

Students will *identify* a monopoly in their local area and *explain* why it is, in fact, a monopoly.

EconomicsAmerica *Materials*

Entrepreneurship in the U. S. Economy, Lesson 27, "The Entrepreneur and Market Structure," pp. 118-121.

Content Statement

9.6 Competition among buyers of a product results in higher prices for the product

Evidence of Student Learning

Students will *predict* what would happen to the price of houses if a great many new people moved into their community.

Content Statement

9.7 Sellers engage in both price and nonprice competition.

Evidence of Student Learning

Students will *identify* several examples of newspaper *or* magazine advertisements showing competition on nonprice features and *analyze* whether the advertising claims are describing meaningful differences.

EconomicsAmerica *Materials*

Entrepreneurship in the U. S. Economy, Lesson 7, "Entrepreneurship in Our Market System," pp. 27-30; Lesson 27, "The Entrepreneur and Market Structure," pp. 118-121.

10. INCOME DISTRIBUTION

Content Statement

10.1 There are four basic categories of earned income: wages and salaries, rent, interest, and profit. Wages and salaries are payments for labor services; rent is the payment for the use of land (natural resources); interest is the payment for the use of capital, including financial capital (money); and profit is the return to business enterprise (entrepreneurship) when the value of sales exceeds the cost of the goods and services sold.

Evidence of Student Learning

Students will *define* the four basic categories of income and *give an example* for each category.

11. MARKET FAILURES

Content Statement

11.1 Governments provide public goods, due to the shared consumption and nonexclusion properties of these products.

Evidence of Student Learning

Students will *explain* why government instead of private industry usually provides police and fire protection and streets and roads.

EconomicsAmerica *Materials*

Entrepreneurship in the U. S. Economy, Lesson 31, "Government and the Entrepreneur," pp. 136-139.

Content Statement

11.2 Shared consumption (or nonrival) products are those that can be used simultaneously by more than one person without reducing the amount of the product available for others to consume.

Evidence of Student Learning

Students will identify examples of shared-consumption products in the following list and will *support the argument* that nobody loses anything when somebody uses a shared consumption product: a theatrical play; a book; a pizza; a movie; a shirt; information on jobs produced by the Bureau of Labor Statistics.

EconomicsAmerica *Materials*

Entrepreneurship in the U. S. Economy, Lesson 31, "Government and the Entrepreneur," pp. 136-139.

Content Statement

11.3 A nonexclusive product is one that, once produced, cannot be withheld even from those who do not pay for it.

Evidence of Student Learning

Students will *identify* examples of nonexclusive products in the following list and *provide justification* for each product selected: a movie; a fireworks display; national defense; a baseball game.

EconomicsAmerica *Materials*

Entrepreneurship in the U. S. Economy, Lesson 31, "Government and the Entrepreneur," pp. 136-139.

Content Statement

11.4 Externalities exist when some of the costs or benefits associated with the production or consumption of a product "spill over" to third parties other than the direct producers and consumers of the product. Positive externalities (external benefits) result in the underproduction or underconsumption of a product, since not all benefits are reflected in consumers' demand for the product. Negative externalities (external costs) result in the overproduction or overconsumption of a product, since not all costs are reflected in producers' supply of the product.

Evidence of Student Learning

Students will *identify* each of the following as an example of a positive or a negative externality and, in a short essay, will *justify* their responses: (1) A nearby high-rise apartment building blocks any sun from your back lawn for several hours each day; (2) Students who graduate from college are likely to get higher paying jobs and thus pay more taxes to the community; (3) A factory uses water from a nearby river and returns it to the river in a polluted condition.

EconomicsAmerica *Materials*

The Elementary Economist, "A Cleaner Environment," Vol. 10, No. 3.

11.5 A natural monopoly exists when one producer can supply total output in a market at a cost that is lower than if two or more producers divided the production of this output.

Evidence of Student Learning

Students will *name* examples of natural monopolies in their geographic area, such as local telephone services, water, natural gas, or sewage treatment, and *explain* why in each case it would raise costs if competitors were allowed to enter these industries at the local level.

EconomicsAmerica *Materials*

Entrepreneurship in the U. S. Economy, Lesson 27, "The Entrepreneur and Market Structure," pp. 118-121.

Content Statement

11.6 Because competition cannot serve to regulate the price, output, and quality of goods and services produced by natural monopolies, government regulatory agencies are generally established to perform these roles.

Evidence of Student Learning

Students will *predict* what would probably happen in the economy if there were no public service commission to regulate electric, telephone, or water companies.

EconomicsAmerica *Materials*

Entrepreneurship in the U. S. Economy, Lesson 27, "The Entrepreneur and Market Structure," pp. 118-121.

12. THE ROLE OF GOVERNMENT

Same as for preceding grade level, and also:

Content Statement

12.2 The government pays for the goods and services it provides through taxing and borrowing.

Evidence of Student Learning

Students will *apply* knowledge of the role of government in the economy in responding to the following question: Your community needs a new fire station. Who will pay for this building and how will they get the money?

EconomicsAmerica *Materials*

The Elementary Economist, "Taxes and Taxation," Vol. 9, No. 2.
The Elementary Economist, "Our Constitution," Vol. 9, No. 1.
United States History, Eyes on the Economy, Vol. 1, Unit 5, Lesson 1, "Problems Under the Articles of Confederation," pp. 68-71.

Content Statement

12.3 In a market economy, the government defines and enforces property rights and provides standard units of weights, measures and money.

Evidence of Student Learning

Students will *predict* what might happen if there were no legal way to settle boundary disputes or if every state had its own system of weights and measures.

EconomicsAmerica *Materials*

The Elementary Economist, "Our Constitution," Vol. 9, No. 1.
United States History, Eyes on the Economy, Vol. 1, Unit 5, Lesson 2, "The Constitution: Ground Rules for the Economy," pp. 74-78; Unit 5, Lesson 4, "Entrepreneurship Case Study: Adam Smith," pp. 79-85.

12.4 Operating government requires shifting scarce resources from the private sector of the economy to the public sector.

Evidence of Student Learning

Students will *answer* the following questions: If the national, state, and local governments had no power to tax, what goods and services would we have to do without? What goods and services might we have more of?

EconomicsAmerica *Materials*

The Elementary Economist, "Taxes and Taxation," Vol. 9, No. 2.
United States History, Eyes on the Economy, Vol. 1, Unit 5, Lesson 2, "The Constitution: Ground Rules for the Economy," pp. 74-78.

12.5 Other economic roles of government include providing public goods and services; correcting for externalities; maintaining competition; redistributing income; and promoting full employment, stable prices, and reasonable rates of economic growth.

Evidence of Student Learning

Students will *identify* at least three economic roles of our national government and *cite* a specific programmatic example of each.

EconomicsAmerica *Materials*

Entrepreneurship in the U. S. Economy, Lesson 31, "Government and the Entrepreneur," pp. 136-139.
United States History, Eyes on the Economy, Vol. 1, Unit 5, Lesson 2, "The Constitution: Ground Rules for the Economy," pp. 74-78; Unit 5, Lesson 4, "Entrepreneurship Case Study: Adam Smith," pp. 79-85.

13. GROSS DOMESTIC PRODUCT

13.1 When purchases are made, goods and services are transferred from businesses to households in exchange for money payments. The money is used by businesses to pay for factors of production: land, labor, capital, and entrepreneurship. This is often depicted in a circular flow diagram.

Evidence of Student Learning

Given an example of a familiar business, such as a candy store, students will *cite an* example of each factor of production involved in the business and *indicate* that each receives income.

EconomicsAmerica *Materials*

Entrepreneurship in the U. S. Economy, Lesson 9, "The Circular Flow Between Consumers and Entrepreneurs," pp. 36-39.

15. UNEMPLOYMENT

15.1 Unemployed people are those who are willing and able to work at current wage rates, but do not have jobs.

Evidence of Student Learning

Students will *apply* the standard definition of an unemployed person by explaining why a retired person is not considered unemployed.

15.2 People who are unemployed usually have less income to buy goods and services than those who have jobs.

Evidence of Student Learning

Students will *explain* in two or three sentences why an unemployed person is likely to have less income than a person who holds a job.

15.3 Governments provide income to some unemployed workers until they can find jobs.

Evidence of Student Learning

Students will *explain* why government payments are made to people who have lost their jobs.

EconomicsAmerica *Materials*

Entrepreneurship in the U.S. Economy, Lesson 33, "Changing Economic Conditions Affect Entrepreneurs," pp. 145-148.

15.4 The labor force is composed of people age 16 and over who are either employed or actively seeking work.

Evidence of Student Learning

Students will *apply* the standard definition of the labor force to decide whether each of the following would be a member of that category:(1) an elementary school student who has a paper route; (2) an army captain; (3) a retired butcher; (4) an insurance salesman; (5) a woman who has decided not to work outside the home until her children are in school.

15.5 The unemployment rate is the percentage of the labor force considered to be unemployed.

Evidence of Student Learning

Given the following problem, students will correctly *calculate* the unemployment rate: Jones County has 200,000 people. Of that population, 70,000 are full-time housewives, students, children, retired people or people not looking for work. Of the remaining residents of Jones County, 110,000 people have jobs. What is the unemployment rate of Jones County?

15.6 The unemployment rate rises during a recession.

Evidence of Student Learning

Students will *explain* why people lose jobs during a recession in terms of the decreased production of goods and services characteristic of recession.

16. INFLATION AND DEFLATION

16.1 Inflation is a sustained increase in the average price level of the entire economy; deflation is a sustained decrease in the average price level of the entire economy.

Evidence of Student Learning

Students will define inflation and deflation and *give at least two examples* of how the cost of living rises during an inflation and falls during a deflation.

EconomicsAmerica *Materials*

Entrepreneurship in the U.S. Economy, Lesson 33, "Changing Economic Conditions Affect Entrepreneurs," pp. 145-148.
United States History, Eyes on the Economy, Vol. 1, Unit 7, Lesson 3, "Boom and Bust in the 1830s," pp. 139-143.

Content Statement

16.2 The Consumer Price Index (CPI) is the most commonly used measure of price level changes. It compares prices in one year with some earlier period (a base period).

Evidence of Student Learning

Given data on the CPI for the past 30 years, students will *determine* during which time periods inflation was a serious problem.

18. FISCAL POLICY

Content Statement

18.1 Fiscal policy involves the use of national government spending and taxation programs to affect the level of economic activity in such a way as to promote price stability, maximum employment, and reasonable economic growth.

Evidence of Student Learning

Students will *describe* as "fiscal policy" changes in tax rates and in the amount of government spending for the purpose of managing the economy and *give at least two examples* of such changes in the last five years.

EconomicsAmerica *Materials*

Enterpreneurship in the U. S. Economy, Lesson 22, "Cash Flow and the Successful Entrepreneur," pp. 94-98.

19. ABSOLUTE AND COMPARATIVE ADVANTAGE AND BARRIERS TO TRADE

Content Statement

19.1 The quantity and quality of productive resources available in different nations vary widely.

Evidence of Student Learning

Using encyclopedias and textbooks, students will *identify* and *classify* the major productive resources in several countries and will *draw conclusions* about what kinds of resources are scarcer than others in those countries.

EconomicsAmerica *Materials*

The International News Journal, Lesson 2, "Characteristics of Countries," pp. 13-17; Lesson 3, "Similarities and Differences Around the World," pp. 18-21; Lesson 4, "Trading Partnerships Around the World," pp. 22-23; Lesson 5, "International Trade," pp. 24-28; Lesson 7, "Trade Among Businesses," pp. 31-34; Lesson 8, "Comparative Advantage," pp. 35-38; Lesson 9, "What the U. S. Imports," pp. 39-42.

Content Statement

19.2 International trade is the exchange of goods and services between people and institutions in different nations.

Evidence of Student Learning

Students will *answer* the following question: Because Japan lacks an abundance of the productive resource of land, what kinds of products must they purchase from other countries?,

EconomicsAmerica *Materials*

The International News Journal, Inc., Lesson 3, "Similarities and Differences Around the World," pp. 18-21; Lesson 4, "Trading Partnerships Around the World," pp. 22-23; Lesson 5, "International Trade," pp. 24-28; Lesson 9, "What the U. S. Imports," pp. 39-42.

Content Statement

19.3 Exports are goods and services produced in one nation but sold to buyers in another nation.

Evidence of Student Learning

Students will *determine* from information on their community or state what major products are produced for export and to what countries they are exported.

EconomicsAmerica *Materials*

The International News Journal, Inc., Lesson 3, "Similarities and Differences Around the World," pp. 18-21; Lesson 4, "Trading Partnerships Around the World," pp. 22-23; Lesson 9, "What the U.S. Imports," pp. 39-42; Lesson 10, "Japan and the U. S. are Trading Partners," pp. 43-47.

Content Statement

19.4 Imports are goods or services bought from sellers in another nation.

Evidence of Student Learning

Students will *examine* brand labels of products in their homes and *compile a* list of imported products and the countries from which they are imported.

EconomicsAmerica *Materials*

The International News Journal, Inc., Lesson 3, "Similarities and Differences Around the World," pp. 18-21; Lesson 4, Trading Partnerships Around the World," pp. 22-23; Lesson 9, "What the U.S. Imports," pp. 39-42; Lesson 10, "Japan and the U. S. are Trading Partners," pp. 43-47.

Content Statement

19.5 International trade promotes greater specialization, and specialization increases total world output.

Evidence of Student Learning

Students will *cite* the benefits of specialization in answering the following questions: The South American country of Ecuador could grow many agricultural products. However, the climate and terrain are best suited for the production of coffee and bananas, which can be grown in few other countries. Is it in the best economic interests of the farmers of Ecuador to attempt to grow many crops or to specialize in coffee and bananas? Why?

EconomicsAmerica *Materials*

The International News Journal, Inc., Lesson 5, "International Trade," pp. 24-28.

United States History, Eyes on the Economy, Vol. 1, Unit 5, Lesson 4, "Entrepreneurship Case Study: Adam Smith," pp. 81-85.

20. EXCHANGE RATES AND THE BALANCE OF PAYMENTS

Content Statement

20.1 Different currencies are used in different countries.

Evidence of Student Learning

Students will *calculate* the following: You are planning a trip to England for six days and will need to stay at a hotel, buy meals, take tours, and have some additional money. The British use pounds, not dollars, and each pound is worth $1.50. Your travel agent tells you that you will need about 700 pounds to cover all your costs. How many dollars will you need to spend to get the money for your trip?

EconomicsAmerica *Materials*

The International News Journal, Inc., Lesson 10, "Japan and the U. S. Are Trading Partners," pp. 43-47.

21. INTERNATIONAL ASPECTS OF GROWTH AND STABILITY

Content Statement

21.1 Economic growth is a sustained rise in the production of goods and services.

Evidence of Student Learning

Students will *define* economic growth and *give two examples* of countries experiencing economic growth.

EconomicsAmerica *Materials*

United States History, Eyes on the Economy, Vol. 1, Unit 3, Lesson 1, "Why Do Economies Grow?" pp. 40-44.

Content Statement

21.2 Technological change and improvements in a society's stock of productive resources promote economic growth.

Evidence of Student Learning

After reading about China's efforts toward economic growth in recent years, students will *cite* examples of at least three technological improvements that have contributed to China's growth.

EconomicsAmerica *Materials*

United States History, Eyes on the Economy, Vol. 1, Unit 3, Lesson 1, "Why Do Economies Grow?" pp. 40-44.

Chapter VII

Scope and Sequence Guidelines, 9-12

Because high school students are capable of a higher level of reasoning, it is possible to introduce many concepts and generalizations that cannot feasibly be taught at lower grade levels. An ideal place for many of these concepts and generalizations is in a course devoted specifically to economics. However, teachers know that most students cannot adequately grasp complex ideas after a single exposure. Students who enter an economics course with prior knowledge of the fundamentals of economic con-tent and reasoning will be able to develop a much more thorough and sophisticated understanding of how the economic world operates. Additionally, economic concepts can provide an organizing framework in many subjects for factual information that students might otherwise soon forget.

Teachers of most social studies subjects should be able to find economic concepts and topics that will enrich the courses that they teach. Teachers of geography and world studies will find that the concept categories concerning economic systems and institutions give them meaningful ways to compare and contrast societies. The section on productivity discusses the factors that have raised the living standards of many societies and to a large extent will determine the material advancement of societies in the future. The section on international economics outlines the fundamental relationships among countries that are increasingly important as the nations of the world become more interdependent.

Civics and government teachers can find in the microeconomics section of the scope and sequence guidelines an explanation of a privately operated market economy, modified where necessary by government intervention like that found in the United States. The role of the government in attempting to reduce unemployment and inflation and to promote economic growth can be found in the macroeconomics section of the guidelines.

American history teachers can use the conceptual categories of the scope and sequence guidelines as a framework for teaching many of the events of American history. The sections on productivity and on competition and market structure are useful in explaining the rise of big business in the late 1800s, and both the benefits and the problems resulting from this change in the economy. The money panics and depressions of the 19th and 20th centuries can better be understood with the aid of the sections on exchange, money and interdependence, and on monetary policy. The Great Depression of the 1930s and the policies of the New Deal, as well as subsequent government policies, can be taught effectively using the concepts and generalizations of the macroeconomics section.

Business education teachers can also use the guidelines to their advantage. The microeconomics section describes the processes by which basic economic decisions are made by consumers and business firms in a market economy. The effects of government on the economic climate in which business operates are discussed in the macroeconomics section, and the increasing influence of foreign trade upon our economy is covered in the section on international economics.

In many high schools, teachers of other subjects have also been able to introduce economic concepts into their classes. Mathematics teachers have found that students need to understand newspaper articles on the stock market, the GDP and the CPI. English teachers have employed economic concepts to explain human problems in novels such as *The Grapes of Wrath*. Science teachers have used the concepts of supply and demand to explain why the energy shortage of the 1970s gave way to the energy surplus of the 1980s. All these experiences show that economics is not just an abstract set of ideas to be studied in one isolated course, but a pervasive influence upon the lives of all American students and adults.

The content statements are presented in two different ways.

1. To provide the user a quick and comprehensive overview of the economic content recommended for grades 9–12, the content statements are organized according to the concept clusters discussed in Chapter II and are listed in the order in which they should be introduced in the curriculum.

2. In the second presentation, each concept statement is accompanied by a sample activity which suggests the kind of behavior that would indicate that students have mastered the content. The verb in each activity is highlighted to assist teachers in determining cognitive levels.

Also included is a list of materials from the National Council on Economic Education to use in teaching the content statements.

Evaluating Student Learning. The *Test of Economic Literacy* (Grades 11–12), published by the National Council on Economic Education, is a nationally normed test based on the content categories discussed in Chapter II. It is available in two equivalent forms for pretesting and posttesting upper elementary students. An examiner's manual is also available.

Content Statements, 9-12

1. SCARCITY AND CHOICE

Same as for preceding grade level.

2. OPPORTUNITY COST AND TRADE-OFFS

Same as for preceding grade level.

3. PRODUCTIVITY

Same as for preceding grade level, and also:

3.8 Although investments in capital goods and in human capital can increase productivity, such investments have significant opportunity costs and economic risks.

3.9 Technological change is a leading cause of long-run increases in productivity.

3.10 Technological change depends heavily on incentives to reward innovation and on investments in research and development and in capital goods.

3.11 Government expenditures, regulations, and tax policy influence productivity.

3.12 Technological change and investments in capital goods and human capital increase productivity.

3.13 Living standards are directly related to productivity.

4. ECONOMIC SYSTEMS

Same as for preceding grade level, and also:

4.7 Although wages and prices are found in all economic systems, they are determined in fundamentally different ways in traditional, command, and market economies.

4.8 Economic systems based on tradition do not adapt quickly to change or promote rapid economic growth.

4.9 Economic systems can be evaluated by their ability to achieve broad social goals such as freedom, efficiency, equity, security, and growth.

5. ECONOMIC INSTITUTIONS AND INCENTIVES

Same as for preceding grade level, and also:

5.10 An economic institution is an enduring organization, practice, or relationship established by people to cope with basic economic problems.

5.11 Economic institutions include such organizations as corporations, labor unions, banks, the stock market, cooperatives, and partnerships.

5.12 Private ownership of property is a basic institution in a market economy; property rights are defined, enforced, and limited through the process of government.

5.13 Specific financial and non-financial incentives often influence individuals differently.

5.14 In every economic system, consumers, producers, workers, savers, and investors seek to allocate their scarce resources to obtain the highest possible return, subject to the institutional constraints of their society.

6. EXCHANGE, MONEY AND INTERDEPENDENCE

Same as for preceding grade level, and also:

6.17 Transaction costs are those costs other than price associated with the purchase of a good or service (e.g., legal restrictions on trading, costs of gathering or disseminating information on products, transportation costs paid by the consumer). When transaction costs decrease, more exchanges will be made, thus enlarging the scope of markets.

7. MARKETS AND PRICES

Same as for preceding grade level, and also:

7.7 In a market system, prices provide information to consumers and producers, which encourages the efficient production and allocation of the goods and services consumers demand.

8. SUPPLY AND DEMAND

Same as for preceding grade level, and also:

8.8 The demand curve shows an inverse, or negative, relationship between price and quantity demanded.

8.9 Demand for a product will normally change (the demand curve will shift) if there is a change in consumers' incomes, tastes, and preferences, or the prices of related (complementary or substitute) products.

8.10 The short-run supply curve shows a direct, or positive, relationship between price and quantity supplied because of the law of diminishing returns.

8.11 The supply of a product will normally change (the supply curve will shift) if there is a change in technology or prices of inputs, or in the prices of other products that could be made and sold by producers.

8.12 In the long run, all factors of production are variable.

8.13 Prices set by supply and demand are measures of the relative scarcity of products.

8.14 Shortages or surpluses usually result in price changes for products in a market economy.

8.15 When price controls are enforced, shortages and surpluses occur and create long-run allocation problems in the economy.

*8.16 Economists describe the demand and supply schedules for various goods and services as elastic if the quantity responses to a change in price are relatively large compared to the change in price. If the quantity responses are relatively small, demand or supply is described as inelastic.

*8.17 Demand for products that have few close substitutes and that make up a small part of the consumer's budget tends to be inelastic, as does the demand for items that are regarded as necessities. Demand for large expenditure items, products with many close substitutes, and items regarded as luxuries tends to be elastic.

*8.18 Demand and supply are usually more elastic in the long run than in the short run.

---

* Indicates statements that would normally be covered in a one-semester Capstone course in economics.

9. COMPETITION AND MARKET STRUCTURE

Same as for preceding grade level, and also:

9.8 Collusion among buyers or sellers reduces the level of competition in a market. Collusion is more difficult in markets with large numbers of buyers and sellers.

9.9 Oligopoly exists when only a few relatively large producers sell a product that has no close substitutes.

9.10 Cartels are explicit forms of collusion concerning product price, output, service, or sales.

9.11 In the United States laws and government regulations have been adopted to maintain competition. However, many laws and regulations also have had the effect, often unanticipated, of reducing competition.

9.12 The level of competition in an industry is, in the long run, determined largely by how difficult and expensive it is for new firms to enter the market.

*9.13 Monopolistic competition exists when many sellers provide similar products that are differentiated to some extent by nonprice competition.

*9.14 A monopsony exists when there is only one buyer of a product in a market area; an oligopsony exists when there are only a few large buyers.

10. INCOME DISTRIBUTION

Same as for preceding grade level, and also:

10.2 Transfer payments are monetary payments or the direct provision of goods and services made by one party to another without receiving money, goods, or services in return.

10.3 The functional distribution of income classifies the income received by individuals and business firms according to the type of productive resources sold in resource markets.

10.4 The personal distribution of income classifies the population according to the amount of income they receive, including transfer payments.

10.5 The functional distribution of income has, over time, reflected changes in the occupational structure of the economy and changing economic conditions related to the business cycle.

10.6 The personal distribution of income has remained relatively stable in the United States over long periods of time.

10.7 Decisions about the distribution of income are made by individuals and firms making exchanges in resource markets, and also by governments through the political process.

10.8 Public policies that can be used to redistribute income include taxation (e.g., progressive or negative income taxes), spending and assistance programs targeted at particular income groups, and programs designed to provide training to workers or to encourage private investments in education or other kinds of human capital.

11. MARKET FAILURES

Same as for preceding grade level, and also:

*11.7 Government can correct for the over or underproduction/consumption of products affected by externalities through the use of tax policies, subsidies or regulations.

*11.8 Perfect competition does not eliminate the problem of market failures.

* Indicates statements that would normally be covered in a one-semester Capstone course in economics.

•11.9 Establishing and implementing government policies and programs to correct for market failures is itself a costly activity, and only when the expected benefits of such programs are greater than the costs involved are these actions economically justified. Economic analysis can help determine where market failures are important enough to justify corrective actions by government.

12. THE ROLE OF GOVERNMENT

Same as for preceding grade level, and also:

12.6 Different taxes affect different income groups differently. Progressive taxes levy higher tax rates on high-income groups; regressive taxes levy higher tax rates on low-income groups; and proportional taxes levy identical tax rates on all income groups.

12.7 The economic efficiency of a government policy is determined by comparing its costs and benefits.

12.8 Public policies involve economic and political choices and are influenced by both positive and normative concepts as well as by the actions of special interest groups.

12.9 Government policies often affect the well-being of people, businesses, and regions differently as a result of the impact of different kinds of taxes, transfer payments, laws, regulations, and the provision of goods and services that are not used equally by all groups.

12.10 The legal and economic incidence of a tax are often different.

12.11 Benefits of government spending programs are often shifted away from those who were initially intended to receive them.

13. GROSS DOMESTIC PRODUCT

Same as for preceding grade level, and also:

13.2 Gross Domestic Product (GDP) is a basic measure of economic output. It is used as an indicator of the state of the economy.

13.3 GDP is the total market value, expressed in dollars, of all final goods and services produced in an economy in a given year.

13.4 Nominal GDP is stated in current dollars; thus, an increase in GDP may reflect not only increases in the production of goods and services, but also increases in prices. GDP can be adjusted for price level changes; the resulting statistic is called "real GDP."

13.5 A country's potential GDP depends on the quantity and quality of natural resources available, the size and skills of the labor force, and the size and quality of its capital stock.

13.6 Measures of per capita real GDP (real GDP divided by population) are often compared across countries to evaluate the performance of economies and the well-being of their citizens. However, there are limitations to this approach. The measurement of GDP does not account for differences in the types of goods produced, nor for differences in the distribution of income.

13.7 In the United States and other industrialized economies, the rate of economic growth over long periods of time has been relatively steady. However, short-run fluctuations in business activity, called business cycles, are not smooth nor completely predictable.

13.8 A recession is said to occur when real GDP declines for a period of at least six months.

* Indicates statements that would normally be covered in a one-semester Capstone course in economics.

13.9 Government may attempt to reduce the fluctuations of the business cycle (stabilize economic activity) by implementing policies that can affect the level of real GDP.

•13.10 GDP is not a perfect measure of how well-off people are.

•13.11 GDP can be calculated by adding up all sales of final products. With minor adjustments, the same total is achieved by adding up all income paid to factors of production.

•13.12 Disposable income is the income available for use after taxes have been paid. It is either spent on consumption or saved.

14. AGGREGATE SUPPLY AND AGGREGATE DEMAND

Same as for preceding grade level, and also:

14.1 The relationship between potential aggregate supply and aggregate demand is an important determinant of the levels of unemployment and inflation in an economy.

14.2 Aggregate supply is the total quantity of goods and services produced in an economy in a given time period. Constraints on potential aggregate supply are the quantity and quality of productive resources and the level of available technology.

14.3 Aggregate demand equals consumption, investment, and government spending, plus net exports.

14.4 When aggregate demand is equal to aggregate supply at a level that just employs all available productive resources with no change in the overall price level, the economy is at a full-employment, noninflationary equilibrium.

14.5 When aggregate demand falls below the full-employment level of aggregate supply, production declines and some resources become unemployed in the short run. A reduction in aggregate demand below the full-employment level is the cause of cyclical unemployment.

14.6 When aggregate demand rises above the full-employment level of aggregate supply, competition for productive resources increases and costs and prices rise in the short run. An increase in aggregate demand above the full-employment level is the cause of demand-pull inflation.

•14.7 One person's spending becomes another person's income. This process eventually results in a multiple change in aggregate income whenever spending in any one sector of the economy changes.

•14.8 Aggregate demand changes when there are changes in consumer, investment or government spending, in net exports, or in price expectations.

•14.9 Aggregate supply changes when there are changes in the quantity or quality of resources, productivity, tax policies, or profit expectations.

15. UNEMPLOYMENT

Same as for preceding grade level, and also:

15.7 The standard measure of the unemployment rate is imperfect: it does not include discouraged workers, it does not weight part-time and full-time employment differently, nor does it account for differences in the intensity with which people look for jobs.

15.8 Because of regional economic differences and labor force immobility, unemployment rates differ across the country.

* Indicates statements that would normally be covered in a one-semester Capstone course in economics.

15.9 Unemployment rates differ for people of different ages, races, and sexes. This reflects differences in work experience, training, and skills, as well as discrimination.

15.10 There are four types of unemployment: frictional, seasonal, structural, and cyclical. Different policies may be required to reduce each.

15.11 The rate of unemployment is affected by the costs and benefits of searching for a job.

15.12 Currently full employment is considered to be the employment of about 93–95 percent of the labor force, allowing for frictional unemployment of about 5-7 percent.

15.13 Policies designed to deal with structural unemployment include education and training programs. Not increasing the minimum wage and reducing discrimination might also help.

15.14 Cyclical unemployment may be reduced through policies that stimulate demand (e.g., tax cuts, government spending for public works programs).

16. INFLATION AND DEFLATION

Same as for preceding grade level, and also:

16.3 The CPI is not a perfect measure of how inflation affects individual households.

16.4 Inflation creates uncertainty because it affects different groups differently.

16.5 There are two general types of inflation: demand-pull and cost-push. Demand-pull inflation occurs when total spending rises faster than total production. Cost-push inflation occurs when increases in the overall costs of making and selling goods and services raise the price level.

16.6 Demand-pull inflation may result from expansive monetary or fiscal policies, or from expectations of businesses and consumers that prices will rise in the future.

16.7 Cost-push inflation may result from the effects of monopolization in product or factor markets, or from supply shocks.

16.8 A variety of policy options is available to combat inflation;these include monetary and fiscal policies, wage and price controls, antitrust actions, and tax incentives. Alternatively, policy-makers may decide to rely upon automatic adjustment mechanisms.

16.9 Many economists believe that there is a trade-off between unemployment and inflation, at least in the short run. If the government stimulates demand to fight unemployment, inflation is likely to increase; if the government restrains demand to fight inflation, unemployment is likely to increase.

16.10 Stagflation is the combination of high unemployment (a stagnant economy) and high inflation in the same time period. It may result from reductions in aggregate supply.

16.11 People form expectations using both past experience and predictions about present and future government policies. This may have an impact upon the effectiveness of government policy actions.

17. MONETARY POLICY

17.1 Policies that change the size of the money supply can be used to promote price stability, maximum employment, and reasonable economic growth.

17.2 When the banking system makes loans, the money supply increases; when loans are paid off, the money supply decreases. Banks may lend the money deposited with them that is in excess of the reserves they are required to keep by the Federal

Reserve System, the central banking system of the United States.

17.3 Monetary policy refers to actions by the Federal Reserve System that lead to changes in the supply of money and availability of credit.

*17.4 One of the tools of monetary policy is raising or lowering the reserve requirement.

*17.5 A second tool of monetary policy is increasing or decreasing the discount rate.

*17.6 A third tool of monetary policy is open market purchase or sale of government securities.

*17.7 An initial increase or decrease in the money supply has a multiplier effect on the total money supply.

*17.8 The Federal Reserve's ability to control the total amount of money in the economy is not complete; the actions of individuals, firms, and foreign investors all influence the money supply.

17.9 Changes in the money supply may influence the levels of spending, employment, prices, and economic growth in the economy by leading to changes in interest rates and in individual and corporate spending.

*17.10 One of the limitations of monetary policy is that policies cannot be immediately determined, implemented, or evaluated. Instead there exist long and variable lags associated with each stage of the process.

17.11 Federal reserve policies can cause serious economic problems if they are inconsistent or inappropriate.

17.12 The conduct of monetary policy is influenced by political as well as economic conditions.

*17.13 Disagreements among economists about the effectiveness of monetary policy can be evaluated using the equation of exchange, which relates the money supply and its velocity (rate of turnover) to the nominal GDP.

18. FISCAL POLICY

Same as for preceding grade level, and also:

18.2 Tax reductions and increases in government spending increase aggregate demand and nominal income; tax increases and decreases in government spending reduce aggregate demand and nominal income.

18.3 The government budget is balanced when revenues equal expenditures. The government runs a budget deficit when its expenditures exceed its tax revenues. It must then borrow from individuals, corporations, or financial institutions to finance the excess of expenditures over tax revenues. When revenues exceed expenditures, the government has a budget surplus.

18.4 The national debt is the total amount of money the government owes; it is the accumulated annual deficits.

18.5 Foreigners and foreign governments may lend money to the United States government to finance its deficits. Repayment of loans from abroad results in a transfer of income from United States citizens to foreign economies.

18.6 Fiscal policies are often a result of political factors as well as economic factors.

18.7 Fiscal policy requires time to affect the economy.

18.8 Fiscal policies may be reinforced or offset by monetary policies.

* Indicates statements that would normally be covered in a one-semester Capstone course in economics.

*18.9 An expansionary fiscal policy may "crowd out" private spending if interest rates are raised by the increased government demand for credit.

*18.10 Fiscal policy can have a powerful impact on aggregate demand and national income if the government implements the proper policy, at the appropriate time, and at a level commensurate with needs and goals, and if crowding out effects are small.

19. ABSOLUTE AND COMPARATIVE ADVANTAGE AND BARRIERS TO TRADE

Same as for preceding grade level, and also:

19.6 International differences in factor endowments and relative prices are the basis for international trade.

19.7 A nation has an absolute advantage if it can produce more of a product with the same amount of resources than another nation can.

19.8 A nation has a comparative advantage when it can produce a product at a lower opportunity cost than another nation.

19.9 Despite the benefits of international trade, many nations restrict the free flow of goods and services through a variety of devices known as trade barriers, which include tariffs and quotas.

19.10 While free trade among nations will raise worldwide production levels and material standards of living, in the short run some groups are likely to be hurt by the effects of increased international competition.

20. EXCHANGE RATES AND THE BALANCE OF PAYMENTS

Same as for preceding grade level, and also:

20.2 Extensive international trade requires an organized system for exchanging money between nations.

20.3 An exchange rate is the price of one nation's currency in terms of another nation's currency.

20.4 A change in exchange rates can have a significant effect on the flow of trade between nations and on a nation's domestic economy. When the exchange rate between currencies changes, it changes the relative prices of goods and services traded by the two countries.

20.5 A nation's balance of payments is an accounting of all international transactions that involve the payment or receipt of foreign exchange.

*20.6 Exchange rates can be set in a free market, or established through controls imposed by national governments, or allowed to fluctuate within certain price ranges before triggering government action designed to stabilize the exchange rates between currencies.

*20.7 The balance of payments accounts are reported in three sections. These sections distinguish trade involving basic goods and services from trade involving capital resources and financial assets issued by businesses and government, and official transactions of reserve currencies and other assets.

*20.8 Countries often run surpluses or deficits in either their current or capital accounts, but the overall balance of payments account for a country must balance.

* Indicates statements that would normally be covered in a one-semester Capstone course in economics.

*20.9 The balance of trade figures regularly reported in the media include only the deficit or surplus position of merchandise exports. Therefore, this figure reflects only a small part of a nation's overall balance of payments account.

*20.10 Increasingly, we live in a global economy where what is done in this nation affects the rest of the world, and what is done there affects this nation. Economic issues associated with this trend must be analyzed by examining trends in trading levels, investments, foreign exchange values, and changes in public policies affecting these sectors.

21. INTERNATIONAL ASPECTS OF GROWTH AND STABILITY

Same as for preceding grade level, and also:

21.3 The level of real GDP per capita is frequently used to compare the level of economic development in different nations.

21.4 The international transfer of technology and the exchange of productive resources and finished goods and services have led to increased interdependence among nations.

21.5 Increasing international economic interdependence causes economic conditions and policies in one nation to affect economic conditions in many other nations.

21.6 Public policies affecting foreign trade impose costs and benefits on different groups of people; decisions on these policies reflect economic and political interests and forces.

* Indicates statements that would normally be covered in a one-semester Capstone course in economics.

Teaching Resources, 9-12

1. SCARCITY AND CHOICE

Same as content statements for preceding grade level.

Evidence of Student Learning

Using selected statistical data from government records students will *analyze* the relationship between earnings in several occupations and the relative scarcity of persons qualified for these occupations.

EconomicsAmerica *Materials*

Capstone, Unit 1, Lesson 3, "To Choose or Not to Choose: That is Not the Question," pp. 9-10; Unit 1, Lesson 6, "Survival Activity," pp. 18-19; Unit 1, Lesson 10, "Crime and Punishment," pp. 36-38.
Entrepreneurship in the U. S. Economy, Lesson 1, "What Is an Entrepreneur?", pp. 2-5; Lesson 5, "Making Things Entrepreneurs Sell," pp. 17-20; Lesson 26, "Human Resource Management: The Entrepreneur's Perspective," pp. 113-116; Lesson 34, "Successful Entrepreneurs Develop Their Own Human Capital," pp. 150-154.
MCG, Economics and Entrepreneurship, Lesson 1, "Entrepreneurs-Then and Now," pp. 3-5; Lesson 2, "Can I Be an Entrepreneur?" pp. 6-8; Lesson 7, "What Is an Entrepreneurial Innovation," pp. 23-25. *MCG, Economics and Entrepreneurship*, Lesson 14, "Borrowing Decisions and Expected Returns," pp. 49-52.
United States History, Eyes on the Economy, Vol. 1., Unit 2, Lesson 1, "The New World Was an Old World," pp. 36-32; Vol. 1, Unit 4, Lesson, "Understanding the Colonial Economy," pp. 52-59; Vol. 1, Unit 5, Lesson 3, "Entrepreneurship Case Study: George Mason," pp. 79-80; Vol. 1, Unit 6, Lesson 7, "Entrepreneurship Case Study: Samuel Slater," pp. 124-125; Vol. 2, Unit 2, Lesson 2, "Was Free Land a Good Deal?" pp. 30-34; Vol. 2, Unit 3, Lesson 3, "Entrepreneurship Case Study: Andrew Carnegie," pp. 64-66; Vol. 2, Unit 4, Lesson 1, "John D. Rockefeller: Nobody Loves a Competitor," pp. 70-76; Vol. 2, Unit 8, Lesson 3, "Entrepreneurship Case Study: Chuck Berry," pp. 201-205.

2. OPPORTUNITY COST AND TRADE-OFFS

Same as content statements for preceding grade level.

Evidence of Student Learning

Students will *draw and explain* production possibility curves that illustrate the difference between an economy in which productive resources are fully employed and one in which productive resources are underutilized.

EconomicsAmerica *Materials*

Capstone, Unit 1, Lesson 3, "To Choose or Not to Choose: That Is Not the Question," pp. 9-10; Unit 1, Lesson 4, "Individual Decision Making," pp. 11-14; Unit 1, Lesson 5, "Social Decision Making," pp. 15-17; Unit 1, Lesson 10, "Crime and Punishment," pp. 36-38; Unit 2 Lesson 1, "Is What I Like, What I Buy? Maybe," pp. 45-48; Unit 2, Lesson 6, "Marginal Analysis," pp. 65-66; Unit 3, Lesson 1, "Introduction to Consumers and Producers," p. 87; Unit 3, Lesson 2, "Consumers Make Marginal Decisions," p. 88; Unit 4, Lesson 10, "The Economics of Voting," pp. 133-138; Unit 4, Lesson 11, "Thinking Economically About the Environment," pp. 139-141; Unit 5, Lesson 5, "Macromysteries," pp. 164-167; Unit 7, Lesson 2, "Why Do People Trade?" pp. 203-204; Unit 7, Lesson 9, "Disagreements over World Trade," pp. 219-221.
Entrepreneurship in the U. S. Economy, Lesson 3, "Consumers, Businesses, Entrepreneurs, and Governments Face Opportunity Costs," pp. 10-12; Lesson 4,

"Successful Entrepreneurs Make Rational Choices," pp. 13-16; Lesson 22, "Cash Flow and the Successful Entrepreneur," pp. 94-98; Lesson 30, " The Costs and Benefits of Innovation," pp. 130-134; Lesson 35, "You and Entrepreneurial Skills," pp. 155-160.

MCG, Economics and Entrepreneurship, Lesson 3, "What Does the Entrepreneur Need to Know?" pp. 9-12; Lesson 4, "Have You Ever Had to Make Up Your Mind?" pp. 13-15.

United States History, Eyes on the Economy, Vols. 1 and 2, Unit 1, Lesson 1, "Solving Mysteries in United States History: A User's Guide," pp. 2-9; Vol. 1, Unit 4, Lesson 2, "The Costs and Benefits of Independence," pp. 60-66; Vol. 1, Unit 6, Lesson 1, "The Tale of the Corset and the Necktie," pp. 88-93; Vol. 1, Unit 8, Lesson 1, "Why Did the South Secede?" pp. 148-154; Vol. 1, Unit 8, Lesson 2, "The Economic Effects of the Civil War," pp. 154-157; Vol. 2, Unit 2, Lesson 1, "Free A Grades: The Consequences of Changing Allocation Plans," pp. 26-29; Vol. 2, Unit 2, Lesson 2, "Was Free Land a Good Deal?" pp. 30-34; Vol. 2, Unit 2, Lesson 3, "Why Give Away Land?" pp. 35-41; Vol. 2, Unit 5, Lesson 1, "What Does a Freed Slave Do?" pp. 98-103; Vol. 2, Unit 5, Lesson 2, "Jim Crow, Boycotts and Consumer Power," pp. 104-111.

3. PRODUCTIVITY

Content Statement

3.8 Although investments in capital goods and in human capital can increase productivity, such investments have significant opportunity costs and economic risks.

Evidence of Student Learning

Students will *analyze* the following: Jeanette is a junior high school teacher who decides she would like to become a physician. What are her opportunity costs and economic risks if she follows through on this decision?

EconomicsAmerica *Materials*

Capstone Unit 6, Lesson 3, "Making a Macro Model: Investment," pp. 182-184A.
Entrepreneurship in the U. S. Economy, Lesson 26, "Human Resource Management: The Entrepreneur's Perspective," pp. 113-116; Lesson 34, "Successful Entrepreneurs Develop Their Own Human Capital," pp. 150-154.
MCG, Economics and Entrepreneurship, Lesson 14, "Borrowing Decisions and Expected Returns," pp. 49-52.
United States History, Eyes on the Economy, Vol. 1, Unit 6, Lesson 6, "What is Investment?" pp. 120-123.

Content Statement

3.9 Technological change is a leading cause of long-run increases in productivity.

Evidence of Student Learning

Students will *explain,* citing differences in education and technology, why the United States is a more productive nation than India.

EconomicsAmerica *Materials*

United States History, Eyes on the Economy, Vol. 1, Unit 6, Lesson 4, "Cost Cutting Is Fashionable," pp. 109-114; Vol. 2, Unit 3, Lesson 3, "Entrepreneurship Case Study: Andrew Carnegie," pp. 64-66.

Content Statement

3.10 Technological change depends heavily on incentives to reward innovation and on investments in research and development and in capital goods.

Evidence of Student Learning

Using business magazines from recent years, students will identify examples of firms that have developed and capitalized on new technologies.

EconomicsAmerica *Materials*

MCG, Economics and Entrepreneurship, Lesson 14, "Borrowing Decisions and Expected Returns," pp. 49-52.

Content Statement

3.11 Government expenditures, regulations, and tax policy influence productivity.

Evidence of Student Learning

In a short essay, students will *analyze* the effects a government policy that raises taxes, reduces spending, or regulates an industry closely will have on productivity.

EconomicsAmerica *Materials*

Capstone, Unit 4, Lesson 9, "The Role of Government: Social Regulation of Business," pp. 130-132; Unit 6, Lesson 4, Making a Macro Model: Government," pp. 185-186.

Content Statement

3.12 Technological change and investments in capital and human capital increase productivity.

Evidence of Student Learning

Students will *evaluate* the following statement: If all Americans graduated from high school, as opposed to approximately 80 percent, there would be fewer poor people in the country. (Answer should consider other factors besides education that lead to productivity increases.)

EconomicsAmerica *Materials*

MCG, Economics and Entrepreneurship, Lesson 14, "Borrowing Decisions and Expected Returns," pp. 49-52.
United States History, Eyes on the Economy, Vol. 1, Unit 6, Lesson 4, "Cost Cutting Is Fashionable," pp. 109-114; Vol. 1, Unit 6, Lesson 5, "Improving Transportation," pp. 115-119.

Content Statement

3.13 Living standards are directly related to productivity.

Evidence of Student Learning

Students will *describe* how the living standards of their families would probably change if the productivity of every worker in the United States were to increase by 20 percent.

EconomicsAmerica *Materials*

United States History, Eyes on the Economy, Vol. 1, Unit 6, Lesson 2, "Productivity Raises Output," pp. 94-101.

4. ECONOMIC SYSTEMS

Same as for preceding grade level, and also:

Content Statement

4.7 Although wages and prices are found in all economic systems, they are determined in fundamentally different ways in traditional, command, and market economies.

Evidence of Student Learning

Students will *describe* how each of the following problems would be handled in a command economy and in a market economy: (1) Determining the mix between the production of machinery and the building of houses;(2) Setting relative pay for doctors and plumbers; (3) Deciding how much should be charged for a pair of shoes or a loaf of bread.

EconomicsAmerica *Materials*

Capstone, Unit 1, Lesson 8, "Rules Influence Economic Systems: Market, Command, and Traditional Economies," pp. 22-30.

Entrepreneurship in the U. S. Economy, Lesson 6 "Entrepreneurship in Different Economic Systems," pp. 22-26.

MCG, Economics and Entrepreneurship, Lesson 5, "The Role of Entrepreneurs in Our Economy, pp. 16-19.

Content Statement

4.8 Economic systems based on tradition do not adapt quickly to change or promote rapid economic growth.

Evidence of Student Learning

Students will *analyze* the importance of tradition in the economies of India, China, and Mexico as it has influenced their economic growth.

EconomicsAmerica *Materials*

Capstone, Unit 1, Lesson 8, "Rules Influence Economic Systems: Market, Command, and Traditional Economies," pp. 22-30.

Entrepreneurship in the U. S. Economy, Lesson 6 "Entrepreneurship in Different Economic Systems," pp. 22-26.

MCG, Economics and Entrepreneurship, Lesson 5, "The Role of Entrepreneurs in Our Economy, pp. 16-19.

Content Statement

4.9 Economic systems can be evaluated by their ability to achieve broad social goals such as freedom, efficiency, equity, security, and growth.

Evidence of Student Learning

Students will *construct* a matrix to show the relative achievements of the United States and China with respect to economic freedom, efficiency, equity, security and growth.

EconomicsAmerica *Materials*

Capstone, Unit 5, Lesson 2, "What Do We Want from Our Economy, " pp. 155-156A

5. ECONOMIC INSTITUTIONS AND INCENTIVES

Same as for preceding grade level, and also:

Content Statement

5.10 An economic institution is an enduring organization, practice, or relationship established by people to cope with basic economic problems.

Evidence of Student Learning

In a short essay students will *describe* at least three institutions that have affected economic decisions in the United States since its independence and will *analyze* their impact on United States history.

EconomicsAmerica *Materials*

United States History, Eyes on the Economy, Vol. 2, Unit 7, Lesson 6, "We Shall Not Be Moved," pp. 179-184.

Content Statement

5.11 Economic institutions include such organizations as corporations, labor unions, banks, the stock market, cooperatives, and partnerships.

Evidence of Student Learning

Students will *cite* and *explain* at least four advantages of a corporation, including raising money, limited liability, tax advantages, and risk spreading. After reading about conditions of labor and labor unrest during various American historical periods, students will *state* reasons for the development of the institution of collective bargaining.

EconomicsAmerica *Materials*

Entrepreneurship in the U. S. Economy, Lesson 18, "Entrepreneurs Choose Different Types of Business Organization," pp. 76-79.
United States History, Eyes on the Economy, Vol. 2, Unit 7, Lesson 6, "We Shall Not Be Moved," pp. 179-184.

Content Statement

5.12 Private ownership of property is a basic institution in a market economy; property rights are defined, enforced, and limited through the process of government.

Evidence of Student Learning

Students will *analyze* the following scenario and *predict* probable economic and social consequences: To save money, Congress has passed, and the President has signed into law, a bill that now makes it illegal for the federal government or any state or local government to settle any disputes or questions over property or property rights. From now on, property-related matters will be settled entirely in the private sector.

EconomicsAmerica *Materials*

Entrepreneurship in the U. S. Economy, Lesson 6, "Entrepreneurship in Different Economic Systems," pp. 22-26.
The Senior Economist, "The Economics of the Constitution," Vol. 2, No. 1.
United States History, Eyes on the Economy, Vol. 1, Unit 3, Lesson 1, "Why Do Economies Grow?" pp. 40-44; Vol. 1, Unit 3, Lesson 2, "Be a Planet Planner, " pp. 45-49; Vol. 2, Unit 3, Lesson 1, "The Changing U. S. Economy, " pp. 46-54.

Content Statement

5.13 Specific financial and nonfinancial incentives often influence individuals differently.

Evidence of Student Learning

After interviewing at least three people in different occupations and asking them to list and rank the reasons why they chose the occupation that they did, students will *draw conclusions* about the relative importance of various financial and nonfinancial incentives on occupational choice.

EconomicsAmerica *Materials*

Capstone, Unit 4, Lesson 5, "Why Do They Run?" pp. 117-118; Unit 4, Lesson 10, "The Economics of Voting," pp. 133-138.
United States History, Eyes on the Economy, Vol. 2, Unit 8, Lesson 2, "Why Live in 'Sin City' If You Are Not a Sinner," pp. 195-200; Vol. 2, Unit 9, Lesson 1, "Women in the Work Force: From Rosie the Riveter to Rosie the Loan Officer," pp. 210-219; Vol. 2, Unit 9, Lesson 2, "Why Does the Federal Government Overspend Its Budget?" pp. 220-225.

Content Statement

5.14 In every economic system, consumers, producers, workers, savers, and investors seek to allocate their scarce resources to obtain the highest possible return, subject to the institutional constraints of their society.

Evidence of Student Learning

Students will *evaluate* the following generalization, citing specific examples to support their arguments: Economic self-interest is the most powerful incentive influencing human behavior.

EconomicsAmerica *Materials*

Capstone, Unit 2, Lesson 2, "Markets Involve People, Too: A Market in Wheat," pp. 49-55; Unit 2, Lesson 3, "A Picture Is Worth A Thousand Words: Demand," pp. 56-58; Unit 5, Lesson 5, "Macromysteries," pp. 164-167.

6. EXCHANGE, MONEY AND INTERDEPENDENCE

Same as for preceding grade level, and also:

Content Statement

6.17 Transaction costs are those costs other than price associated with the purchase of a good or service (e.g., legal restrictions on trading, costs of gathering or disseminating information on products, transportation costs paid by the consumer). When transaction costs decrease, more exchanges will be made, thus enlarging markets.

Evidence of Student Learning

Students will *explain* why each of the following would tend to lower transaction costs and thereby encourage exchange: (1) Import taxes are removed from foreign cars; (2) A local TV station lowers the prices it charges to run commercials; (3) More efficiently engineered trucks can carry larger loads for the same fuel costs.

EconomicsAmerica *Materials*

Entrepreneurship in the U. S. Economy, Lesson 7, "Entrepreneurship in Our Market System," pp. 27-30.

7. MARKETS AND PRICES

Same as for preceding grade level, and also:

Content Statement

7.7 In a market system, prices provide information to consumers and producers, which encourages the efficient production and allocation of the goods and services consumers demand.

Evidence of Student Learning

Students will *describe* in a short essay how prices in a market economy reflect the answer to the basic economic questions of what will be produced, how it will be produced and for whom it will be produced. Students will also *describe* how prices measure relative scarcity of products and resources.

EconomicsAmerica *Materials*

United States History, Eyes on the Economy, Vols. 1 and 2, Unit 1, Lesson 3, "The Hula Hoop Market of 1958," pp. 17-22.

8. SUPPLY AND DEMAND

Same as for preceding grade level, and also:

Content Statement

8.8 The demand curve shows an inverse, or negative, relationship between price and quantity demanded.

Evidence of Student Learning

Students will *consider* both income and substitution effects in responding to the following: Michelle has an allowance of $7.00 a week. She likes to go to movies and usually goes to one each week. The ticket price at the local movie theater has been $3.50, but now it rises to $5.00. How might this change Michelle's movie-going habits over the period of a month?

EconomicsAmerica *Materials*

Capstone, Unit 2, Lesson 2, "Markets Involve People, Too: A Market in Wheat," pp. 49-55; Unit 2, Lesson 3, "A Picture Is Worth A Thousand Words: Demand," pp. 56-58; Unit 2, Lesson 9, "Become a 'Profit-Making Prophet' by Using the Market," pp. 76-78.
MCG, Economics and Entrepreneurship, Lesson 9, "How Much Are Consumers Willing to Pay?" pp. 29-32.

Content Statement

8.9 Demand for a product will normally change (the demand curve will shift) if there is a change in consumers' incomes, tastes, and preferences, or the prices of related (complementary or substitute) products.

Evidence of Student Learning

Students will *analyze* the following scenarios: (1) Michael Jones was so effective in his first year as a salesman for Acme Corporation that he received a raise from $25,000 to $30,000 a year. What changes are likely to occur in his demand for various kinds of goods? (2) Styles of clothing have changed in recent years, and students now wear more casual clothes to school. What has happened to students' demand for more formal clothing?(3) Peanut butter prices have been reduced because of major increases in the supply of peanuts. What change is likely to occur in the demand for jelly?

EconomicsAmerica *Materials*

Capstone, Unit 2, Lesson 7, "The Market Never Stands Still," pp. 67-70; Unit 2, Lesson 9, "Become a 'Profit-Making Prophet' by Using the Market," pp. 76-78.
Entrepreneurship in the U. S. Economy, Lesson 11, "What's the Right Price?" pp. 37-41; Lesson 15, "Competitive Markets," pp. 53-55.
MCG, Economics and Entrepreneurship, Lesson 9, "How Much are Consumers Willing to Pay?" pp. 29-32.
United States History, Eyes on the Economy, Vol. 2, Unit 7, Lesson 3, "When Greeting Cards Were Too Expensive to Buy and Milk Was Too Expensive to Sell," pp. 156-166.

Content Statement

8.10 The short-run supply curve shows a direct, or positive, relationship between price and quantity supplied because of the law of diminishing returns.

Evidence of Student Learning

Students will *explain* the following: A wheat farmer has fixed costs of $60,000 a year, including his land, buildings and equipment, depreciation on his buildings and equipment, interest on the borrowed money, and management input. His variable costs include seed, fertilizer, labor and irrigation water. The farmer finds that when he attempts to increase his output beyond 25,000 bushels of wheat, his variable costs per bushel begin to increase rapidly. Give some possible reasons for why this occurs.

EconomicsAmerica *Materials*

Capstone, Unit 2, Lesson 4, "A Picture Is Worth a Thousand Words: Supply," pp. 59-61; Unit 2, Lesson 9, "Become a 'Profit-Making Prophet' by Using the Market," pp. 76-78.
Entrepreneurship in the U. S. Economy, Lesson 12, "Entrepreneurs Supply Goods and Services," pp. 49-52; Lesson 21, "When Should an Entrepreneur Offer More Products for Sale?" pp. 90-93.
MCG, Economics and Entrepreneurship, Lesson 10, "How Much Should I Produce?" pp. 33-36.

8.11 The supply of a product will normally change (the supply curve will shift) if there is a change in technology or prices of inputs, or in the prices of other products that could be made and sold by producers.

Evidence of Student Learning

Students will *describe* how producers of automobile tires will change their supply if (1) new technology reduces the cost of making tires; (2) the price for rubber or other raw materials goes up; (3) the price of tractor tires increases sharply.

EconomicsAmerica *Materials*

Entrepreneurship in the U. S. Economy, Lesson 13, " What Type of Business Should I Start?" pp. 46-48; Lesson 15, "Competitive Markets," pp. 53-55.
MCG, Economics and Entrepreneurship, Lesson 10, "How Much Should I Produce?" pp. 33-36.
United States History, Eyes on the Economy, Vol. 2, Unit 7, Lesson 3, "When Greeting Cards Were Too Expensive to Buy and Milk Was Too Expensive to Sell," pp. 156-166.

Content Statement

8.12 In the long run, all factors of production are variable.

Evidence of Student Learning

Students will refer to the preceding problem of the wheat farmer (8.10) and *answer* the following questions: Under what circumstances might the farmer buy additional land, buildings or equipment in order to increase the maximum number of bushels of wheat he can produce? Under what circumstances might the farmer either grow a different crop or sell his land, buildings and equipment and cease to farm?

EconomicsAmerica *Materials*

Entrepreneurship in the U. S. Economy, Lesson 12, "Entrepreneurs Supply Goods and Services," pp. 43-57; Lesson 13, "What causes Entrepreneurs to Change the Quantity of Goods and Services offered for sale? pp. 53-57.

Content Statement

8.13 Prices set by supply and demand are measures of the relative scarcity of products.

Evidence of Student Learning

Students will *explain in* terms of relative scarcity why people are willing to pay higher prices for diamonds than for water, even though water is necessary for life and diamonds are not.

EconomicsAmerica *Materials*

Capstone, Unit 2, Lesson 7, "The Market Never Stands Still," pp. 67-69;
Entrepreneurship in the U. S. Economy, Lesson 14, "Entrepreneurs and Equilibrium," pp. 58-61; Lesson 15, "Entrepreneurs and Changing Prices," 62-65;
MCG, Economics and Entrepreneurship, Lesson 11, "What's the Right Price?" pp. 37-41.

Content Statement

8.14 Shortages or surpluses usually result in price changes for products in a market economy.

Evidence of Student Learning

Students will *predict* what will happen to market price in each of the following cases: (1) A crop disease destroys half of the Washington apple crop. (2) Department stores greatly overestimate the number of microwave ovens that will be sold before Mother's Day and have excess inventories on their shelves at the end of May.

EconomicsAmerica *Materials*

Entrepreneurship in the U. S. Economy, Lesson 14, "Entrepreneurs and Equilibrium," pp. 58-61.
MCG, Economics and Entrepreneurship, Lesson 11, What's the Right Price?" pp. 37-41.

Content Statement

8.15 When price controls are enforced, shortages and surpluses occur and create long-run allocation problems in the economy.

Evidence of Student Learning

Referring to the preceding problem, students will *describe* what events might occur if there were a price ceiling on Washington apples or a price floor on microwave ovens.

EconomicsAmerica *Materials*

Capstone, Unit 2, Lesson 8, "When There Are Floors and Ceilings," pp. 71-75.

Content Statement

8.16 Economists describe the demand and supply schedules for various goods and services as elastic if the quantity responses to a change in price are relatively large compared to the change in price. If the quantity responses are relatively small, demand or supply is described as inelastic.

Evidence of Student Learning

Students will identify demand or supply as being elastic or inelastic in each of the following cases: (1) The price of gasoline doubled in 1973, but consumers reduced their purchases of gasoline by only a small amount; (2) Airlines have found that when they lower airfares for vacation travelers, so many more people buy seats that airline revenues actually increase; (3) The price of oil doubled in 1973 because it takes time to find and drill for new sources of oil; (4) Demand for automobiles has risen and dealers are emptying their lots without giving price reductions. Automobile plants that have been running one shift call back their second shift workers and quickly increase the number of cars produced per day.

EconomicsAmerica *Materials*

Capstone, Unit 2, Lesson 5, "How Do Price Changes Influence My Behavior?" pp. 62-64; Unit 2, Lesson 9, "Become a 'Profit-Making Prophet' by Using the Market," pp. 76-78.

Content Statement

8.17 Demand for products that have few close substitutes and that make up a small part of the consumers budget tends to be inelastic, as is demand for items that are regarded as necessities. Demand for large expenditure items, products with many close substitutes and items regarded as luxuries tends to be elastic.

Evidence of Student Learning

Given a list of products that have inelastic or elastic demand, students will *state* reasons to explain the elasticity of each item. Examples of items with inelastic demand are coffee, medical services, salt, and textbooks. Examples of items with elastic demand are refrigerators, broccoli, fur coats and steak.

EconomicsAmerica *Materials*

Capstone, Unit 2, Lesson 5, "How Do Price Changes Influence My Behavior?" pp. 62-64; Unit 2, Lesson 9, "Become a 'Profit-Making Prophet' by Using the Market," pp. 76-78.

8.18 Demand and supply are more usually elastic in the long run than in the short-run.

Evidence of Student Learning

Students will *cite* examples of the adjustments that consumers made over a period of several years in order to reduce their demand for petroleum products after the 1973 oil price increases. Students will also *give examples* of how American oil producers were able to increase oil supplies substantially in the late 1970s as a response to higher prices.

EconomicsAmerica *Materials*

Capstone, Unit 2, Lesson 5, "How Do Price Changes Influence My Behavior?" pp. 62-64; Unit 2, Lesson 9, "Become a 'Profit-Making Prophet' by Using the Market," pp. 76-78.

9. COMPETITION AND MARKET STRUCTURE

Same as for preceding grade level, and also:

Content Statement

9.8 Collusion among buyers or sellers reduces the level of competition in a market. Collusion is more difficult in markets with large numbers of buyers and sellers.

Evidence of Student Learning

Students will *predict* the likely economic consequences of the following scenario: Suppose there were only three automobile manufacturers in the United States, and that the sale of all foreign cars were prohibited in this country. If the chief executives of these three companies were allowed to meet together to plan business strategy, what are some of the possible effects of such a meeting upon the American automobile market?

EconomicsAmerica *Materials*

United States History, Eyes on the Economy, Vol. 2, Unit 4, Lesson 3, "Regulation of Business," pp. 89-94.

Content Statement

9.9 Oligopoly exists when only a few relatively large producers sell a product that has no close substitutes.

Evidence of Student Learning

Given a list showing the market shares of the top four firms in several industries, students will *predict* and *explain* in which industries prices arc likely to be highest and output most restricted.

EconomicsAmerica *Materials*

Capstone, Unit 3, Lesson 7, "When There Isn't Pure Competition," pp. 98-100.

Content Statement

9.10 Cartels are explicit forms of collusion concerning product price, output, service, or sales.

Evidence of Student Learning

Students will *distinguish* between a cartel, such as OPEC, in which collusion is legally permitted, and an oligopoly, such as the American automobile industry, in which collusion is legally forbidden, although violations of the law may be difficult to detect.

EconomicsAmerica *Materials*

MCG, Teaching Strategies, International Trade, Lesson 19, "Organization of Petroleum Exporting Students and Teachers," pp. 123-131.

9.11 Laws and government regulations have been adopted to maintain competition. However, many laws and regulations also have had the effect, often unanticipated, of reducing competition.

Evidence of Student Learning

Students will *analyze* the effects of the following scenario: In order to become a lawyer in any state, a person must pass the bar examination of that state. Suppose that your state legislature passes a law allowing only those who score in the top 10 percent on the bar examination to become lawyers. Would this law restrict competition among lawyers? What are the possible economic effects of a law such as this one? Would there be any benefits to this legislation?

EconomicsAmerica *Materials*

United States History, Eyes on the Economy, Vol. 2, Unit 4, Lesson 3, "Regulation of Business," pp. 89-94.

9.12 The level of competition in an industry is, in the long run, determined largely by how difficult and expensive it is for new firms to enter the market.

Evidence of Student Learning

Students will *analyze the* relationship between entry into an industry and competition within that industry by answering the following questions: Which would be more difficult, to start a new automobile manufacturing firm or to open a new restaurant? Why? How might this relate to the prices charged for automobiles and the prices charged for hamburgers? Why?

EconomicsAmerica *Materials*

MCG, Economics and Entrepreneurship, "Competitive Markets," pp. 53-55.
United States History, Eyes on the Economy, Vol. 2, Unit 4, Lesson 2, "The Economic Effects of 19th Century Monopoly," pp. 77-88.

*9.13 Monopolistic competition exists when many sellers provide similar products that are differentiated to some extent by non-price competition.

Evidence of Student Learning

Students will *cite examples* of two or more monopolistically competitive industries and analyze the features of nonprice competition that are present.

EconomicsAmerica *Materials*

Capstone, Unit 3, Lesson 7, "When There Isn't Pure Competition," pp. 98-100.
Entrepreneurship in the U. S. Economy, Lesson 27, "The Entrepreneur and Market Structure," pp. 118-121.
MCG, Economics and Entrepreneurship, Lesson 15, "Competitive Markets," pp. 53-55.

*9.14 A monopsony exists when there is only one buyer of a product in a market area; an oligopsony exists when there are only a few large buyers.

Evidence of Student Learning

Students will correctly *identify* the following example of monopsony and *predict* the likely economic consequences of the situation: In a rural county in the South, catfish farming is a major form of agriculture. However, there is only one catfish processing plant in the county and, because of transportation costs, local catfish farmers cannot

---

* Indicates statements that would normally be covered in a one-semester Capstone course in economics.

afford to ship their produce 100 miles to the next nearest plant. This economic situation is called a _____. What are some likely economic effects of the situation described?*

10. INCOME DISTRIBUTION

Same as for preceding grade level, and also:

Content Statement

10.2 Transfer payments are monetary payments or the direct provision of goods and services made by one party to another without receiving money, goods, or services in return.

Evidence of Student Learning

Students will *differentiate* among the following examples and non-examples of transfer payments: (1) Government employee retirement benefits; (2) Wages for work in the local supermarket; (3) Commission for selling a house; (4) Unemployment compensation.

EconomicsAmerica *Materials*

Entrepreneurship in the U. S. Economy, Lesson 31, "Government and the Entrepreneur," pp. 136-139.

Content Statement

10.3 The functional distribution of income classifies the income received by individuals and business firms according to the type of productive resources sold in resource markets.

Evidence of Student Learning

Students will, after interviewing several family members or neighbors, *classify* their sources of income as wages and salaries, proprietor's income, rental income, interest payments, profits.

EconomicsAmerica *Materials*

See discussion page 23 and Exhibit 6, page 24.

Content Statement

10.4 The personal distribution of income classifies the population according to the amount of income they receive, including transfer payments.

Evidence of Student Learning

Given data on personal income distribution in the United States over the past fifty years, students will *analyze the* data to determine whether significant changes have occurred among income levels.

EconomicsAmerica *Materials*

See discussion page 23 and Exhibit 6, page 24.

Content Statement

10.5 The functional distribution of income has, over time, reflected changes in the occupational structure of the economy and changing economic conditions related to the business cycle.

Evidence of Student Learning

Using information from an American history textbook, students will *identify* the major differences in functional distribution of income in the United States in the 1780s and in the 1980s.

10.6 The personal distribution of income has remained relatively stable in the United States over long periods of time.

Evidence of Student Learning

Students will *collect* and *interpret* data on historical and contemporary personal income distribution for given years and, based on the data, will *present arguments to* support or reject the following statement: Personal distribution of income in the United States has remained relatively stable over time, although total income has increased.

Content Statement

10.7 Decisions about the distribution of income are made by individuals and firms making exchanges in resource markets, and also by governments through the political process.

Evidence of Student Learning

In a short essay students will *analyze* how distribution of income in the United States has been affected by (1) the Social Security Act of 1936; (2) increased opportunities for lower-income groups to get a college education since World War II; (3) the Tax Reform Act of 1986.

Content Statement

10.8 Public policies that can be used to redistribute income include taxation (e.g., progressive or negative income taxes), spending and assistance programs targeted at particular income groups, and programs designed to provide training to workers or to encourage private investments in education or other kinds of human capital.

Evidence of Student Learning

Students will *describe* three government assistance programs and *analyze* which groups in the economy benefit from them and which groups bear costs because of them.

EconomicsAmerica *Materials*

Entrepreneurship in the U. S. Economy, Lesson 31, "Government and the Entrepreneur," pp. 136-139.
The Senior Economist, "Federal Tax Reform," Vol. 2, No. 2, Spring, 1987.

11. MARKET FAILURES

Same as for preceding grade level, and also:

Content Statement

*11.7 Government can correct for the over- or under-production/consumption of products affected by externalities through the use of tax policies, subsidies or regulations.

Evidence of Student Learning

Students will *apply the* concept of externalities to explain why the government regulates industries to reduce air and water pollution, taxes alcoholic beverages, and provides low-cost loans for college students.

EconomicsAmerica *Materials*

Capstone, Unit 4, Lesson 11, "Thinking Economically About the Environment," pp. 139-141.

Content Statement

*11.8 Perfect competition does not eliminate the problem of market failures.

* Indicates statements that would normally be covered in a one-semester Capstone course in economics.

Evidence of Student Learning

In a short essay students will *defend or refute* the following statement: Our economy would be less efficient and we would have a lower standard of living if provision for all goods and services were left to the private sector.

EconomicsAmerica *Materials*

Capstone, Unit 3, Lesson 7, "When There Isn't Pure Competition," pp. 98-100.

Content Statement

*11.9 Establishing and implementing government policies and pro grams to correct for market failures is itself a costly activity, and only when the expected benefits of such programs are greater than the costs involved are these actions economically justified. Economic analysis can help determine where market failures are important enough to justify corrective actions by government.

Evidence of Student Learning

Given the following scenario, students will *state* the costs and benefits of each of the four possible government policies listed, *select* the policy they think provides the best solution to the problem, and *justify* their decision. Fletcher Iron Works is the largest business firm in Riverdale and employs 500 workers. The plant emits dangerously high levels of air pollution. The following are four possible actions the state pollution control board can take to deal with the problem:

- Close the plant and thereby eliminate all pollution.

- Require Fletcher Iron Works to buy pollution equipment that would eliminate 90 percent of pollution, but would also raise costs and thereby reduce sales. It is estimated that 100 workers would lose their jobs due to reduced output.

- Require Fletcher Iron Works to buy pollution equipment that would eliminate 70 percent of pollution and would raise costs somewhat less. It is estimated that 50 workers would lose their jobs due to reduced output.

- Do nothing about pollution, which would keep costs, sales, and jobs at the same level as before.

What are the costs and benefits of each solution? Which would you choose, and why?

EconomicsAmerica *Materials*

Capstone, Unit 3, Lesson 7, "When There Isn't Pure Competition," pp. 98-100.
MCG, Economics and Entrepreneurship, Lesson 17, "Entrepreneurs and Government Intervention," pp. 59-64.

12. THE ROLE OF GOVERNMENT

Same as for preceding grade level, and also:

Content Statement

12.6 Different taxes affect different income groups differently. Progressive taxes levy higher tax rates on high-income groups; regressive taxes levy higher tax rates on low-income groups; and proportional taxes levy identical tax rates on all income groups.

Evidence of Student Learning

Students will *apply* their knowledge of different categories of taxes by correctly labeling the following examples of taxes as progressive, regressive, or proportional: (1) A state income tax where all citizens pay the same percentage of earned income to the government; (2) A sales tax on food; (3) A state income tax where a family earning $50,000 a year pays a 10 percent income tax and a family earning $25,000 a year pays a five percent income tax.

* Indicates statements that would normally be covered in a one-semester Capstone course in economics.

EconomicsAmerica *Materials*

Capstone, Unit 4, Lesson 6, "What Is a Fair Tax?" pp. 119-123; Unit 4, Lesson 7, "Can Taxes Be Incentives?" pp. 124-125.

Content Statement

12.7 The economic efficiency of a government policy is determined by comparing its costs and benefits.

Evidence of Student Learning

In a short essay students will *analyze* the costs and benefits of a $1,000,000-a-year state government job training program to help adults without jobs.

EconomicsAmerica *Materials*

Capstone, Unit 4, Lesson 6, "What Is a Fair Tax?" pp. 119-123.

Content Statement

12.8 Public policies involve economic and political choices and are influenced by both positive and normative concepts as well as by the actions of special interest groups.

Evidence of Student Learning

Given a description of proposed legislation, students will *identify* the interest groups most likely to support the legislation and those most likely to oppose. Students will also *explain* how the values held by proponents and opponents of the bill influence their decisions.

EconomicsAmerica *Materials*

Capstone, Unit 4, Lesson 1, "Introduction to the Public Sector," p. 109.
United States History, Eyes on the Economy, Vol. 2, Unit 7, Lesson 5, "Can Higher Prices for Agricultural Products Help the Economy?" pp. 173-178.

Content Statement

12.9 Government policies often affect the well-being of people, businesses and regions differently as a result of the impact of different kinds of taxes, transfer payments, laws, regulations, and the provision of goods and services that are not used equally by all groups.

Evidence of Student Learning

Using the following scale, students will *evaluate* each of the following possible governmental actions in terms of the effect the policy would have on the economy of their own state and on one other state (preferably quite different from theirs): A = very positive; B = somewhat positive; C = neutral; D = somewhat negative; F = very negative.

(1) The federal government greatly increases military spending.

(2) The federal government increases aid to schools in large urban areas.

(3) The federal government cuts off wheat sales to communist countries.

(4) The federal government raises the tariff on imported beef.

(5) The federal government improves service and lowers fares on Conrail.

(6) The federal government begins extensive repairs all along Interstate Highways 40 and 80.

EconomicsAmerica *Materials*

Capstone, Unit 4, Lesson 1, "Introduction to the Public Sector," p. 109; Unit 4, Lesson 8, "The Economics of Special Interest Groups," pp. 126-129.
Entrepreneurship in the U. S. Economy, Lesson 31, "Government and the Entrepreneur," pp. 136-139.

12.10 The legal and economic incidence of a tax are often different.

Evidence of Student Learning

Students will identify from the following list those cases in which the tax can be shifted from the legal payer to someone else: (1) Mr. Smith paid $6,500 in income tax this year; (2) The Timbers Apartment Complex paid $100,000 in property tax to the city; (3) Hotels and motels pay a room tax that goes to the state tourism department; (4) Mrs. Caldwell paid $343 excise tax on her new car; (5) State corporation income tax is increased.

EconomicsAmerica *Materials*

Understanding Taxes, "Taxes...Can They Be Shifted?"

Content Statement

12.11 Benefits of government spending programs are often shifted away from those who were initially intended to receive them.

Evidence of Student Learning

Given an example of a government program such as the food stamp program, students will *identify* the group or groups the program was intended to help and will *name* other groups that also benefit from the program.

13. GROSS DOMESTIC PRODUCT

Same as for preceding grade level, and also:

Content Statement

13.2 Gross Domestic Product (GDP) is a basic measure of economic output. It is used as an indicator of the state of the economy.

Evidence of Student Learning

Students will *explain* what GDP is and how it can be used to compare economic growth rates for a country in different years.

EconomicsAmerica *Materials*

Capstone, Unit 6, Lesson 1, "How Does a Forecast Differ from a Guess?" pp. 173-178; Unit 6, Lesson 6, "Be a *Capstone* Fearless Forecaster," pp. 190-194.

Content Statement

13.3 GDP is the total market value, expressed in dollars, of all final goods and services produced in an economy in a given year.

Evidence of Student Learning

Students will *analyze* the following information and *determine* which is the final good: If a farmer grows cotton and sells it to a textile mill where cloth is made, and the cloth is sold to a shirt factory where a shirt is produced, and the shirt is sold to a clothing store and purchased by a consumer, what price(s) should be included in calculating the GDP? What prices should be counted as the prices of intermediate goods and therefore not counted as part of the GDP?

EconomicsAmerica *Materials*

Capstone, Unit 5, Lesson 2, "What Do We Want From Our Economy," pp. 155-156A; Unit 6, Lesson 1, "How Does a Forecast Differ from a Guess?" pp. 173-178.

Content Statement

13.4 Nominal GDP is stated in current dollars; thus, an increase in GDP may reflect not only increases in the production of goods and services, but also increases in prices. GDP can be adjusted for price level changes; the resulting statistic is called "real GDP."

Evidence of Student Learning

Students will *cite* examples illustrating how specific price changes would affect nominal GDP and *explain* why real GDP is a more accurate measure of economic growth than nominal GDP.

EconomicsAmerica *Materials*

Capstone, Unit 5, Lesson 2, "What Do We Want From Our Economy," pp. 155-156A.

Content Statement

13.5 A country's potential GDP depends on the quantity and quality of natural resources available, the size and skills of the labor force, and the size and quality of its capital stock.

Evidence of Student Learning

Given appropriate reference materials, students will *locate* and *analyze* relevant data to assess the validity of the following statement: It is extremely doubtful that the countries of Sub-Saharan Africa will ever have GDPs that approach the value of those of Western European countries.

Content Statement

13.6 Measures of per capita real GDP (real GDP divided by population) are often compared across countries to evaluate the performance of economies and the well-being of their citizens. However, there are limitations to this approach. The measurement of GDP does not account for differences in the types of goods produced, nor for differences in the distribution of income.

Evidence of Student Learning

Students will explain why it is necessary to know the income distribution patterns of a country as well as its real GDP per capita in order to make judgments about the economic well-being of the average citizen of that country.

EconomicsAmerica *Materials*

Capstone, Unit 5, Lesson 2, "What Do We Want From Our Economy," pp. 155-156A.

Content Statement

13.7 In the United States and other industrialized economies, the rate of economic growth over long periods of time has been relatively steady. However, short-run fluctuations in business activity, called business cycles, are not smooth nor completely predictable.

Evidence of Student Learning

Using information in an American history textbook, students will *identify* fluctuations in the business cycle since World War II and will *analyze* the causes of these fluctuations.

EconomicsAmerica *Materials*

Capstone, Unit 5, Lesson 3, "An Economy Never Sleeps," pp. 157-159.
Entrepreneurship in the U. S. Economy, Lesson 3, "Changing Economic Conditions Affect Entrepreneurs," pp. 145-148.

Content Statement

13.8 A recession is said to occur when real GDP declines for a period of at least six months.

Evidence of Student Learning

Students will *describe* characteristics of a recession and will *analyze* their impact by interviewing at least two local business persons about their experiences during the most recent recession.

EconomicsAmerica *Materials*

Capstone, Unit 5, Lesson 3, "An Economy Never Sleeps," pp. 157-159.

13.9 Government may attempt to reduce the fluctuations of the business cycle (stabilize economic activity) by implementing policies that can affect the level of real GDP.

Evidence of Student Learning

Using appropriate reference materials, students will *select* one post-World War II recession and *identify* policies used by the federal government to deal with the recession, and *evaluate* the impact of these policies.

EconomicsAmerica *Materials*

Capstone, Unit 5, Lesson 3, "An Economy Never Sleeps," pp. 157-159; Unit 5, Lesson 4, "If It Doesn't Work - Fix It," pp. 158-163; Unit 5, Lesson 5, "Macro-Mysteries," pp. 164-167A.

13.10 GDP is not a perfect measure of how well-off people are.

Evidence of Student Learning

Students will *write an essay* on the following topic: Although GDP is an important measure of the economic well-being of a society, it has several limitations. *Identify* these limitations and *explain* why a knowledge of each is important in judging economic well-being.

EconomicsAmerica *Materials*

Capstone, Unit 5, Lesson 2, "What Do We Want From Our Economy," pp. 155-156A.

*13.11 GDP can be calculated by adding up all sales of final products. With minor adjustments, the same total is achieved by adding up all income paid to factors of production.

Evidence of Student Learning

Given a product such as bread, students will *list* the factors of production needed for the production of a loaf and, based on research, estimate *the* cost of each factor.

EconomicsAmerica *Materials*

Capstone, Unit 5, Lesson 2, "What Do We Want From Our Economy," pp. 155-156A.

*13.12 Disposable income is the income available for use after taxes have been paid It is either spent on consumption or saved.

Evidence of Student Learning

Students will *calculate* the following problem: John Chang earned $30,000 last year working as an auto mechanic. He paid 20 percent of his income in taxes. What was his disposable income last year?

EconomicsAmerica *Materials*

Capstone, Unit 6, Lesson 2, "Making a Macro-Model: Consumers," pp. 179-181.

14. AGGREGATE SUPPLY AND AGGREGATE DEMAND

14.1 The relationship between potential aggregate supply and aggregate demand is an important determinant of the levels of unemployment and inflation in an economy.

Evidence of Student Learning

Students will *explain* why an imbalance of aggregate demand with respect to aggregate supply can lead to unemployment or inflation.

* Indicates statements that would normally be covered in a one-semester Capstone course in economics.

EconomicsAmerica *Materials*

United States History, Eyes on the Economy, Vol. 2, Unit 7, Lesson 2, "Where Did All the Income Go?" pp. 150-155.

Content Statement

14.2 Aggregate supply is the total quantity of goods and services produced in an economy in a given time period. Constraints on potential aggregate supply are the quantity and quality of productive resources and the level of available technology.

Evidence of Student Learning

Students will *describe* the major determinants of an economy's aggregate supply level and *give examples* of how changes in any of these determinants would change the level of aggregate supply.

EconomicsAmerica *Materials*

United States History, Eyes on the Economy, Vol. 2, Unit 7, Lesson 2, "Where Did All the Income Go?" pp. 150-155.

Content Statement

14.3 Aggregate demand equals consumption, investment, and government spending, plus net exports.

Evidence of Student Learning

Given a specific example of a country's demand for goods and services by consumers, business firms, government, and foreign buyers, students will *display* this information on a graph and *explain* why the aggregate demand curve slopes downward.

EconomicsAmerica *Materials*

United States History, Eyes on the Economy, Vol. 2, Unit 7, Lesson 2, "Where Did All the Income Go?" pp. 150-155; Vol. 2, Unit 7, Lesson 4, "The New Deal," pp. 167-172; Vol. 2, Unit 8, Lesson 1, "Growth After World War II," pp. 190-194.

Content Statement

14.4 When aggregate demand is equal to aggregate supply at a level that just employs all available productive resources with no change in the overall price level, the economy is at a full-employment, noninflationary equilibrium.

Evidence of Student Learning

Students will analyze the relationship between aggregate demand and aggregate supply in order for equilibrium in the economy to exist.

EconomicsAmerica *Materials*

United States History, Eyes on the Economy, Vol. 2, Unit 7, Lesson 4, "The New Deal," pp. 167-172.

Content Statement

14.5 When aggregate demand falls below the full-employment level of aggregate supply, production declines and some resources become unemployed in the short run. A reduction in aggregate demand below the full-employment level is the cause of cyclical unemployment

Evidence of Student Learning

Students will *describe* the effect on the economy when aggregate demand falls below the full use of the resources in the economy.

EconomicsAmerica *Materials*

United States History, Eyes on the Economy, Vol. 2, Unit 7, Lesson 4, "The New Deal," pp. 167-172.

14.6 When aggregate demand rises above the full-employment level of aggregate supply, competition for productive resources increases and costs and prices rise in the short run. An increase in aggregate demand above the full-employment level is the cause of demand-pull inflation.

Evidence of Student Learning

Students will *describe* the effect on the economy when aggregate demand rises above the full use of the resources in the economy.

EconomicsAmerica *Materials*

United States History, Eyes on the Economy, Vol. 2, Unit 7, Lesson 4, "The New Deal," pp. 167-172.

•14.7 One person's spending becomes another person's income. This process eventually results in a multiple change in aggregate income whenever spending in any one sector of the economy changes.

Evidence of Student Learning

Given the following scenario, students will *analyze* the effects on the economy: A visitor comes into a community and spends $100.00 on a single purchase at the video store. Although the video store's income is higher by $100, the store spends only $80 of the money to pay the telephone bill, which now becomes income to the telephone company, and so forth.

EconomicsAmerica *Materials*

United States History, Eyes on the Economy, Vol. 2, Unit 7, Lesson 2, "Where Did All the Income Go?" pp. 150-155.

•14.8 Aggregate demand changes when there are changes in consumer, investment, or government spending, in net exports, or in price expectations.

Evidence of Student Learning

Students will *analyze* and *depict graphically* the change in aggregate demand brought about by each of the following events: (1) Consumer spending is reduced because people are concerned about recession;(2) The government increases its spending; (3) Net exports increased last quarter; (4) Firms decide not to invest in new equipment; (5) The government raises taxes.

EconomicsAmerica *Materials*

United States History, Eyes on the Economy, Vol. 2, Unit 8, Lesson 1, "Growth After World War II," pp. 190-194.

•14.9 Aggregate supply changes when there are changes in the quantity or quality of resources, productivity, tax policies, or profit expectations.

Evidence of Student Learning

Students will *analyze* and *demonstrate graphically* the change in aggregate supply brought about by each of the following events: (1) New sources of easily recovered petroleum are found within the continental United States; (2) The expanded use of computers leads to greater output per worker in many industries; (3) Government increases corporate income taxes; (4) Consumer spending on goods and services appears to be dropping.

---

* Indicates statements that would normally be covered in a one-semester Capstone course in economics.

15. UNEMPLOYMENT

Same as for preceding grade level, and also:

Content Statement

15.7 The standard measure of the unemployment rate is imperfect: it does not include discouraged workers, it does not weight part-time and full-time employment differently, nor does it account for differences in the intensity with which people look for jobs.

Evidence of Student Learning

Students will *cite* examples to illustrate each of the flaws in the measurement of the unemployment rate, and will *describe* how these flaws affect our ability to know the real unemployment rate.

Content Statement

15.8 Because of regional economic differences and labor force immobility, unemployment rates differ across the country.

Evidence of Student Learning

Based on information obtained from reference books and other appropriate sources, students will *present arguments* to support or refute the following statement: Unemployment has historically been higher in the Southeastern region of the United States than in the Northeastern region. Some economists believe the reason for this is that it is more difficult for poor people to be geographically mobile than non-poor people, and this has negative effects upon the former group's chances for finding jobs.

Content Statement

15.9 Unemployment rates differ for people of different ages, races, and sexes. This reflects differences in work experience, training, and skills, as well as discrimination.

Evidence of Student Learning

Using reference books and other appropriate print materials, students will *locate* data pertaining to the unemployment rates of young people and minorities, and will *assess* the arguments generally used to explain the differences between the unemployment rates for these groups and the unemployment rates for other groups in the economy.

Content Statement

15.10 There are four types of unemployment: frictional, seasonal, structural, and cyclical. Different policies may be required to reduce each.

Evidence of Student Learning

Students will *define* and *give examples* of each of the four types of unemployment and *analyze* their differences.

Content Statement

15.11 The rate of unemployment is affected by the costs and benefits of searching for a job.

Evidence of Student Learning

Students will *analyze* the following scenario and *state* the economic and social costs and benefits the individual must weigh in deciding to look for a job and what kind of employment to seek: Jane Smith is a 40-year old full-time housewife who has a daughter in college and a son in junior high school. Jane graduated from college with a degree in elementary education but, since she married and became pregnant shortly after completing school, she has never taught. Teachers in Jane's state now have a beginning average salary of $25,000. Jane's husband is a civil engineer who earns

$60,000 after taxes each year. Should Jane accept a position as a teacher? Should she look for other work? Should she remain a full-time housewife? Make a list of the economic and social costs and benefits of each choice.

15.12 Currently full employment is considered to be the employment of about 93–97 percent of the labor force, allowing for frictional unemployment of about 5 to 7 percent.

Evidence of Student Learning

Students will *analyze* and *state* arguments for or against the following statement: Full employment is more a political than an economic concept.

Content Statement

15.13 Policies designed to deal with structural unemployment include education and training programs. Decreases in the minimum wage and in the degree of discrimination might also help.

Evidence of Student Learning

After conducting research on a current government policy to relieve structural unemployment, students, in a brief oral or written report, will *assess* the costs and benefits of the policy. Based on their assessment, students will *decide* what position they will take regarding continuation of the policy.

Content Statement

15.14 Cyclical unemployment may be reduced through policies that stimulate demand (e.g., tax cuts, government spending for public works programs).

Evidence of Student Learning

Students will *decide* in which of the following cases a policy for increasing aggregate demand would be most effective and will *justify* their choice: (1) Inexpensive clothes imported from Asia have caused a high unemployment rate among garment workers; (2) Consumer spending is down, and the decreased demand for goods and services has led to increasing unemployment in many sectors of the economy;(3) Workers who have dropped out of high school have difficulty in finding employment.

16. INFLATION AND DEFLATION

Same as for preceding grade level, and also:

Content Statement

16.3 The CPI is not a perfect measure of how inflation affects individual households.

Evidence of Student Learning
Students will *explain* several common flaws in the OPI and give an example of each.

EconomicsAmerica *Materials*
Capstone, Unit 5, Lesson 2, "What Do We Want From Our Economy," pp. 155-156A.

Content Statement

16.4 Inflation creates uncertainty because it affects different groups differently.

Evidence of Student Learning

Students will *state* which of the following people would be harmed by a 10 percent inflation rate and which would be benefited: (1) Joe's income depends primarily on a private retirement pension; (2) Susan borrowed $5,000 last year and must pay it back at the end of this year; (3) John lent the $5,000 to Susan last year and will be paid back at the end of this year; (4) Ralph and Mary Larson bought several houses as an investment 10 years ago, and now they plan to sell them.

EconomicsAmerica *Materials*

Capstone, Unit 5, Lesson 3, "An Economy Never Sleeps," pp. 157-159.
United States History, Eyes on the Economy, Vol. 2, Unit 6, Lesson 1, "Raising Inflation on the Farm," pp. 116-122; Vol. 2, Unit 6, Lesson 2, "Free Silver or a Cross of Gold," pp. 123-130.

Content Statement

16.5 There are two general types of inflation: demand-pull and cost-push Demand-pull inflation occurs when total spending rises faster than total production. Cost-push inflation occurs when increases in the overall costs of making and selling goods and services raise the price level.

Evidence of Student Learning

Students will *distinguish between* the following examples of demand-pull and cost-push inflation: (1) Shortages of labor in many areas force employers to raise wages to get the labor they need (cost-push); (2)Creditors make it easier to borrow and consumers respond by borrowing and spending more (demand-pull).

Content Statement

16.6 Demand-pull inflation may result from expansive monetary or fiscal policies, or from expectations of businesses and consumers that prices will rise in the future.

Evidence of Student Learning

Students will *explain* why each of the following events could contribute to demand-pull inflation: (1) The federal government enacts a massive tax cut; (2) The inflation rate has risen every month over the last few months and people fear that it will continue to do so.

Content Statement

16.7 Cost-push inflation may result from the effects of monopolization in product or factor markets, or from supply shocks.

Evidence of Student Learning

Students will *analyze* the following scenarios and *predict* what is likely to occur in each case: (1) Currently most office workers are not unionized. Suppose that this situation changes and 75 percent of all secretaries join one major union. What effect might this have on the inflation rate? Why? (2) What would you expect to happen to the inflation rate if a new crop disease destroyed half of this year's wheat harvest?

Content Statement

16.8 A variety of policy options is available to combat inflation; these include monetary and fiscal policies, wage and price controls, antitrust actions, and tax incentives. Alternatively, policy-makers may decide to rely upon automatic adjustment mechanisms.

Evidence of Student Learning

After selecting one of the policy options used to combat inflation in the past, students will *collect data* on the results of that policy, both intended and unintended, and *state* their conclusion on whether the benefits of that policy outweighed its costs.

EconomicsAmerica *Materials*

Capstone, Unit 5, Lesson 3, "An Economy Never Sleeps," pp. 157-159; Unit 5, Lesson 4, "If It Doesn't Work—Fit It," pp. 160-163.

16.9 Many economists believe that there is a trade-off between unemployment and inflation, at least in the short run. If the government stimulates demand to fight unemployment, inflation is likely to increase; if the government restrains demand to fight inflation, unemployment is likely to increase.

Evidence of Student Learning

Students will *demonstrate* an understanding of the theoretical trade-off between unemployment and inflation by *constructing a curve* on a graph that shows a relationship between the unemployment rate and the inflation rate.

Content Statement

16.10 Stagflation is the combination of high unemployment (a stagnant economy) and high inflation in the same time period. It may result from reductions in aggregate supply.

Evidence of Student Learning

Students will *explain* the term "stagflation" and *describe* how stagflation differs from the traditional business cycle.

Content Statement

16.11 People form expectations using both past experience and predictions about present and future government policies. This may have an impact upon the effectiveness of government policy actions.

Evidence of Student Learning

Given a scenario in which, in an effort to control rising prices, the federal government announces a policy of wage and price controls in the oil industry to take effect in six weeks, students will *predict* probable economic actions of consumers, producers, retailers, and distributors of oil.

EconomicsAmerica *Materials*

Capstone, Unit 5, Lesson 4, "If It Doesn't Work—Fix It," pp. 160-163.

17. MONETARY POLICY

Content Statement

17.1 Policies that change the size of the money supply can be used to promote price stability, maximum employment, and reasonable economic growth

Evidence of Student Learning

Given information about a hypothetical unemployment problem or inflation problem, students will *analyze* the data and *decide* whether it would be better to increase or decrease the money supply to solve that problem.

EconomicsAmerica *Materials*

Capstone, Unit 5, Lesson 4, "If It Doesn't Work - Fix It," pp. 158-163.
United States History, Eyes on the Economy, Vol. 2, Unit 6, Lesson 2, "Free Silver or a Cross of Gold," pp. 122-131.

Content Statement

17.2 When the banking system makes loans, the money supply increases; when loans are paid off, the money supply decreases. Banks may lend the money deposited with them that is in excess of the reserves they are required to keep by the Federal Reserve System, the central banking system of the United States.

Evidence of Student Learning

Students will *state* which of the following cases results in new money being created and will *explain* their answers: (1) John Smith lends $100 to Mary Jones; (2) Margaret Burns deposits $100 in her account at the First National Bank; (3) Edward Robinson borrows $100 from the First National Bank.

EconomicsAmerica *Materials*

Capstone, Unit 5, Lesson 4, "If It Doesn't Work - Fix It," pp. 158-163.
Entrepreneurship in the U. S. Economy, Lesson 19, "Financing the Entrepreneurial Enterprise," pp. 80-84.
United States History, Eyes on the Economy, Vol. 2, Unit 6, Lesson 3, "The Federal Reserve System is Established," pp. 133-138; Vol. 2, Unit 7, Lesson 1, "Whatdunit? The Great Depression Mystery," pp. 142-149.

Content Statement

17.3 Monetary policy refers to actions by the Federal Reserve System that lead to changes in the supply of money and availability of credit.

Evidence of Student Learning

Students will *describe* and *explain* the major responsibilities of the Federal Reserve System, including its responsibility for determining the size of the money supply and how it performs that function.

EconomicsAmerica *Materials*

Capstone, Unit 5, Lesson 1, "Can Higher Prices for Agricultural Products Help the Economy?" pp. 173-178.
Entrepreneurship in the U. S. Economy, Lesson 19, "Financing the Entrepreneurial Enterprise," pp. 80-84.
United States History, Eyes on the Economy, Vol. 2, Unit 7, Lesson 1, "Whatdunit? The Great Depression Mystery," pp. 142-149.

Content Statement

*17.4 One of the tools of monetary policy is raising or lowering the reserve requirement.

Evidence of Student Learning

Students will *apply* their knowledge of the effects of varying actions by the Federal Reserve to answer the following questions: Bank A has not loaned all the money it is allowed to lend; it is required to have $1 million in reserve, but actually has $1.2 million, or excess reserves of $200,000. If the Federal Reserve raises the reserve requirement from 10% to 12%, what effect will this have on the bank's ability to lend money? What effect will this have on the money supply of the country?

EconomicsAmerica *Materials*

Capstone, Unit 5, Lesson 4, "If It Doesn't Work—Fix It," pp. 158-163; Lesson 5, "Macro-Mysteries," pp. 164-167A.
United States History, Eyes on the Economy, Vol. 2, Unit 6, Lesson 3, "The Federal Reserve System Is Established," pp. 132-138.

Content Statement

*17.5 A second tool of monetary policy is increasing or decreasing the discount rate.

Evidence of Student Learning

Students will *describe* and *analyze* the effect on the money supply when the Federal Reserve raises and lowers the discount rate.

EconomicsAmerica *Materials*

Capstone, Unit 5, Lesson 4, "If It Doesn't Work - Fix It," pp. 160-163; Lesson 5, "Macro-Mysteries," pp. 164-167A.

* Indicates statements that would normally be covered in a one-semester Capstone course in economics.

*17.6 A third tool of monetary policy is open market purchase or sale of government securities.

Evidence of Student Learning

Students will *describe* and *analyze* the effect on the money supply when the Federal Reserve purchases or sells government securities on the open market.

EconomicsAmerica *Materials*

Capstone, Unit 5, Lesson 4, "If It Doesn't Work–Fix It," pp. 160-163; Lesson 5, "Macro-Mysteries," pp. 164-167A.

*17.7 An initial increase or decrease in the money supply has a multiplier effect on the total money supply.

Evidence of Student Learning

Students will *apply* their knowledge of the "multiplier effect" to solve the following problems: (1) Bank A loans Mr. Rivera $1,000 to buy a new console TV. Mr. Rivera purchases his TV from an appliance dealer, who deposits the check in his account at Bank B. Assuming a reserve requirement ratio of 20 percent, how much can Bank B now lend? (2) If a $5,000 loan is repaid, assuming a 20 percent reserve ratio requirement, by how much will the money supply decrease?

EconomicsAmerica *Materials*

United States History, Eyes on the Economy, Vol. 2, Unit 7, Lesson 1, "Whatdunit? The Great Depression Mystery," pp. 142-149.

*17.8 The Federal Reserve's ability to control the total amount of money in the economy is not complete; the actions of individuals, firms, and foreign investors all influence the money supply.

Evidence of Student Learning

Students will *explain* why each of the following limits the ability of the Federal Reserve to control the money supply: (1) individual and corporate decisions to hold cash balances; (2) depository institutions' decisions to hold reserves; (3) the strength of the United States dollar in exchange markets; (4) the United States balance of payments account.

EconomicsAmerica *Materials*

Capstone, Unit 5, Lesson 4, "If It Doesn't Work–Fix It," pp. 158-163.

*17.9 Changes in the money supply may influence the levels of spending, employment, prices, and economic growth in the economy by leading to changes in interest rates and in individual and corporate spending.

Evidence of Student Learning

Students will *explain* how an increase in the money supply could influence individual and business total spending and how that, in turn, would influence levels of unemployment, prices, and economic growth.

EconomicsAmerica *Materials*

United States History, Eyes on the Economy, Unit 6, Lesson 2, "Free Silver or a Cross of Gold," pp. 122-131.

---

* Indicates statements that would normally be covered in a one-semester Capstone course in economics.

17.10 One of the limitations of monetary policy is that policies cannot be immediately determined, implemented, or evaluated. Instead there exist long and variable lags associated with each stage of the process.

Evidence of Student Learning

Students will *analyze* a hypothetical change in monetary policy and the processes that must occur before it becomes fully effective.

EconomicsAmerica *Materials*

Capstone, Unit 5, Lesson 4, "If It Doesn't Work - Fix It," pp. 158-163; Lesson 5, "Macro-Mysteries," pp. 164-167A.

17.11 Federal Reserve policies can cause serious economic problems if they are inconsistent or inappropriate.

Evidence of Student Learning

With the aid of an American history textbook or other print resources, students will *describe* changes in the United States money supply in the 20th century and *analyze* the effects of those Federal Reserve policies upon the money supply.

EconomicsAmerica *Materials*

United States History, Eyes on the Economy, Vol. 2, Unit 7, Lesson 4, "The New Deal," pp. 167-172.

17.12 The conduct of monetary policy is influenced by political as well as economic conditions.

Evidence of Student Learning

Using appropriate reference materials, students will *analyze* selected actions of the Federal Reserve since 1975 with regard to the money supply, *state* which actions have appeared to be political in nature, and *explain* their choices.

EconomicsAmerica *Materials*

Capstone, Unit 5, Lesson 4, "If It Doesn't Work - Fix It," pp. 158-163.

•17.13 Disagreements among economists about the effectiveness of monetary policy can be evaluated using the equation of exchange, which relates the money supply and its velocity (rate of turnover) to the nominal GDP.

Evidence of Student Learning

Students will *use* the equation of exchange to solve the following problem: There is an economy whose total supply of money (M) is $80.00. The output (Q) of this economy is 60 units of a good and the average price (P) of the output is $4.00 per unit. what is the velocity?

18. FISCAL POLICY

Same as for preceding grade level, and also:

18.2 Tax reductions and increases in government spending increase **aggregate demand** and nominal income; tax increases and decreases in government spending reduce aggregate demand and nominal income.

---

* Indicates statements that would normally be covered in a one-semester Capstone course in economics.

Evidence of Student Learning

Given the following examples of policy actions, students will *state* which is expansionary and which is contractionary, and will *predict* the likely effects each type of policy will have on the economy: (1) The federal government cuts business and personal income taxes and increases its own spending; (2) The federal government reduces salaries of government employees and raises taxes on consumers and businesses.

EconomicsAmerica *Materials*

Capstone, Unit 5, Lesson 4, "If It Doesn't Work–Fix It," pp. 158-163.

Content Statement

18.3 The government budget is balanced when revenues equal expenditures. The government runs a budget deficit when its expenditures exceed its tax revenues. It must then borrow from individuals, corporations, or financial institutions to finance the excess of expenditures over tax revenues. When revenues exceed expenditures, the government has a budget surplus.

Evidence of Student Learning

Given the statement, "'this year the government received $800 billion in taxes," students will *state* whether the budget is in surplus, in deficit, or is balanced, and whether the effect upon the economy will be contractionary, expansionary or neutral, in each of the following cases: (1) Government spending is $800 billion; (2) Government spending is $900 billion; (3) Government spending is $700 billion.

EconomicsAmerica *Materials*

The Senior Economist, "The Federal Deficit," Vol. 1, No. 1.
United States History, Eyes on the Economy, Vol. 2, Unit 9, Lesson 2, "Why Does the Federal Government Overspend Its Budget?" pp. 220-225.

Content Statement

18.4 The national debt is the total amount of money the government owes; it is the accumulated annual deficits.

Evidence of Student Learning

Students will *explain* the difference between the terms "budget deficit" and "national debt."

EconomicsAmerica *Materials*

United States History, Eyes on the Economy, Vol. 2, Unit 9, Lesson 2, "Why Does the Federal Government Overspend Its Budget?" pp. 220-225.

Content Statement

18.5 Foreigners and foreign governments may lend money to the United States government to finance its deficits. Repayment of loans from abroad results in a transfer of income from United States citizens to foreign economies.

Evidence of Student Learning

Students will *analyze* both the short-run and the long-run impact of a foreign loan to finance a United States government deficit budget on the foreign economy and on the United States economy.

EconomicsAmerica *Materials*

The Senior Economist, "The Federal Deficit," Vol. 1, No. 1.

Content Statement

18.6 Fiscal policies are often a result of political as well as economic factors.

Evidence of Student Learning

Students will *analyze* the political factors involved in the following scenario: Imagine that you are a member of the House of Representatives. As part of a contractionary fiscal policy, the President has requested that Congress reject a bill to construct several veterans' hospitals. One hospital was to have been located in your district, which has suffered from high unemployment rates lately. How do you think you will vote? why?

EconomicsAmerica *Materials*

Capstone, Unit 5, Lesson 4, "If It Doesn't Work–Fix It," pp. 160-163.

Content Statement

18.7 Fiscal policy requires time to affect the economy.

Evidence of Student Learning

In a short essay students will *describe* the problems that exist in forecasting the need for and in timing of changes in fiscal policy and will *analyze* causes for time lags.

EconomicsAmerica *Materials*

Capstone, Unit 5, Lesson 4, "If It Doesn't Work–Fix It," pp. 160-163.

Content Statement

18.8 Fiscal policies may be reinforced or offset by monetary policies.

Evidence of Student Learning

Students will *analyze* the effects on the economy if the government reduces taxes and increases spending, while at the same time the Federal Reserve sells securities in the open market.

EconomicsAmerica *Materials*

Capstone, Unit 5, Lesson 4, "If It Doesn't Work–Fix It," pp. 160-163.

Content Statement

*18.9 An expansionary fiscal policy may "crowd out" private spending if interest rates are raised by the increased government demand for credit.

Evidence of Student Learning

Students will *describe* the "crowding out effect" of expansionary fiscal policy and *analyze* its effects on economic growth.

EconomicsAmerica *Materials*

Capstone, Unit 5, Lesson 4, "If It Doesn't Work–Fix It," pp. 160-163.

Content Statement

*18.10 Fiscal policy can have a powerful and effective impact on aggregate demand and national income if the government implements the proper policy, at the appropriate time, and at a level commensurate with needs and goals, and if crowding out effects are small.

Evidence of Student Learning

Students will *explain* how the multiplier effect increases the impact of changes in fiscal policy.

EconomicsAmerica *Materials*

Capstone, Unit 5, Lesson 4, "If It Doesn't Work - Fix It," pp. 160-163.
United States History, Eyes on the Economy, Vol. 2, Unit 7, Lesson 4, "The New Deal," pp. 167-172.

---

* Indicates statements that would normally be covered in a one-semester Capstone course in economics.

19. ABSOLUTE AND COMPARATIVE ADVANTAGE AND BARRIERS TO TRADE

Same as for preceding grade level, and also:

Content Statement

19.6 International differences in factor endowments and relative prices are the basis for international trade.

Evidence of Student Learning

Students will *name* three things, such as bananas, coffee and other goods, that could be produced in the continental United States, although production would be very costly, and *explain* in terms of opportunity costs why the United States is probably better off to import such goods.

EconomicsAmerica *Materials*

MCG, Teaching Strategies, International Trade, Lesson 2, "Why Do People Trade?" pp. 17-18; Lesson 3, "Why Do People and Nations Trade," pp. 19-23.
The Senior Economist, "International Competition," Vol. 3, No. 1.
United States History, Eyes on the Economy, Vols. 1 and 2, Lesson 1, "The New World Was the Old World," pp. 26-32.

Content Statement

19.7 A nation has an absolute advantage if it can produce more of a product with the same amount of resources than another nation can.

Evidence of Student Learning

Using textbooks and other materials, students will *compile* a list of products for which the United States has an absolute advantage in comparison to some of its trading partners and *explain* why the United States may not specialize in all of these products.

EconomicsAmerica *Materials*

Capstone, Unit 7, Lesson 3, "Why People Trade: Comparative Advantage," pp. 205-206.
MCG, Teaching Strategies, International Trade, Lesson 3, "Why People and Nations Trade," pp. 19-23.

Content Statement

19.8 A nation has a comparative advantage when It can produce a product at a lower opportunity cost than another nation.

Evidence of Student Learning

Students will *apply* the concepts of opportunity cost and comparative advantage to answer the following: Using the same amount of resources, the Netherlands can produce in one day either four drill presses or eight embroidered tablecloths. Using the same amount of resources, Portugal can produce either two drill presses or seven embroidered tablecloths. Which country has an absolute advantage in drill presses? Which has an absolute advantage in tablecloths? Which country has a comparative advantage in drill presses? Which has a comparative advantage in tablecloths? Which country should specialize in drill presses and import tablecloths? Which country should specialize in tablecloths and import drill presses?

EconomicsAmerica *Materials*

Capstone, Unit 7, Lesson 3, "Why People Trade: Comparative Advantage," pp. 205-206.
MCG, Teaching Strategies, International Trade, Lesson 3, "Why People and Nations Trade," pp. 19-23; Lesson 4, "Trade and Specialization," pp. 25-28.
The Senior Economist, "International Competition," Vol. 3, No. 1.

19.9 Despite the benefits of international trade, many nations restrict the free flow of goods and services through a variety of devices known as trade barriers which include tariffs and quotas.

Evidence of Student Learning

Based on data provided on supply and demand graphs students will *analyze* the effects upon price and quantity in the American market if a tariff is levied on imported automobiles and if a quota is placed on imported shirts.

EconomicsAmerica *Materials*

Capstone, Unit 7, Lesson 4, "Trade Barriers," pp. 207-209; Unit 7, Lesson 6, "Ripples," pp. 212-213.
MCG, Teaching Strategies, International Trade, Lesson 10, "Trade Barriers," pp. 57-64; Lesson 21, "The U. S.-Japan Trade Relationship," pp. 143-150.
The Senior Economist, "International Competition," Vol. 3, No. 1.
United States History, Eyes on the Economy, Vol. 1, Unit 5, Lesson 1, "Problems Under the Articles of Confederation," pp. 68-73; Vol. 1, Unit 6, Lesson 3, "Lowell Workers and Producers Respond to Incentives," pp. 102-108; Vol. 2, Unit 9, Lesson 5, "Why Does the U. S. Government Discourage World Trade?" pp. 231-239.

Content Statement

19.10 While free trade among nations will raise worldwide production levels and material standards of living for some, in the short run some groups are likely to be hurt by the effects of increased international competition.

Evidence of Student Learning

Students will *analyze* the following scenario: The United States allows Taiwan to export shirts to this country without placing a tariff on imports from Taiwan. The Taiwanese can produce shirts at one half the cost per shirt, on average, as can American manufacturers. What groups in the United States and in Taiwan will be helped, and what groups will be hurt, if the United States continues the present free-trade policy toward Taiwan?

EconomicsAmerica *Materials*

Capstone, Unit 7, Lesson 4, "Trade Barriers," pp. 207-209; Unit 7, Lesson 9, "Disagreements Over World Trade," pp. 219-221.
The Senior Economist, "International Competition," Vol. 3, No. 1.
United States History, Eyes on the Economy, Vol. 2, Unit 9, Lesson 5, "Why Does the U. S. Government Discourage World Trade?" pp. 231-239.

20. EXCHANGE RATE AND THE BALANCE OF PAYMENTS

Same as for preceding grade level, and also:

Content Statement

20.2 Extensive international trade requires an organized system for exchanging money between nations.

Evidence of Student Learning

Students will *explain* why there is a foreign exchange market and *give three examples* of the need for foreign exchange.

EconomicsAmerica *Materials*

Capstone, Unit 7, Lesson 7, "Foreign Currencies and Foreign Exchange," pp. 214-216B.
MCG, Teaching Strategies, International Trade, Lesson 16, "Foreign Currencies and Foreign Exchange," pp. 103-108; Lesson 17, "Rubles and Dollars," pp. 109-113;

Lesson 18, "Exchange Rates," pp. 115-121.

Content Statement

20.3 An exchange rate is the price of one nation's currency in terms of another nation's currency.

Evidence of Student Learning

Students will *calculate* the following: (1) The British pound is worth $1.42. How much would you have to pay in England for a record that is worth the same as $8.00? (2) The Canadian dollar is equal to $.72 in American money. What is the amount in Canadian money of $15.00? (3) It takes 1,372 Italian lira to buy $1.00. If you purchased an Italian sweater for 27,000 lira, what is it worth in American dollars? (teachers should use the financial section of a newspaper to find current exchange rates.)

EconomicsAmerica *Materials*

Capstone, Unit 7, Lesson 7, "Foreign Currencies and Foreign Exchange," pp. 214-216B.

Content Statement

20.4 A change in exchange rates can have a significant effect on the flow of trade between nations and on a nation's domestic economy. When the exchange rate between currencies changes, it changes the relative prices of goods and services traded by the two countries.

Evidence of Student Learning

Using the following scenario, students will *analyze* the effects on trade of a change in exchange rates: In one year, the American dollar equaled 250 Japanese yen; in the following year, the American dollar equaled 150 yen; and in the third year, it equaled 200 yen. A Nikon camera costs 75,000 yen and a Sony Walkman radio costs 25,000 yen.(1) What will be the price in dollars of these two products in each year for an American? (2) Will an American want to buy more or less in year one, year two and year three? Why?

EconomicsAmerica *Materials*

Capstone, Unit 7, Lesson 5, "Balance of Payments," pp. 210-211.
MCG, Teaching Strategies, International Trade, Lesson 13, "Balance of Payments," pp. 77-83.

Content Statement

20.5 Other economic roles of government include providing public goods and services; correcting for externalities; maintaining competition; redistributing income; and promoting full employment, stable prices and reasonable rates of economic growth.

Evidence of Student Learning

Students will *identify* at least three economic roles of our national government and *cite a* specific programmatic example of each.

EconomicsAmerica *Materials*

Capstone, Unit 7, Lesson 7, "Foreign Currencies and Foreign Exchange," pp. 214-216B.
MCG, Teaching Strategies, International Trade, Lesson 16, "Foreign Currencies and Foreign Exchange," pp. 103-108; Lesson 17, "Rubles and Dollars," pp. 109-113; Lesson 18, "Exchange Rates," pp. 115-121.

Content Statement

*20.6 Different taxes affect different income groups differently. Progressive taxes levy higher tax rates on high-income groups; regressive taxes levy higher tax rates on low-income groups; and proportional taxes levy identical tax rates on all income groups.

Evidence of Student Learning

Students will *apply* their knowledge of different categories of taxes by correctly labeling the following examples of taxes as progressive, regressive or proportional: (1) A state income tax where all citizens pay the same percentage of earned income to the government; (2) A sales tax on food; (3) A state income tax where a family earning $50,000 a year pays a 10 percent income tax and a family earning $25,000 a year pays a five percent income tax.

EconomicsAmerica *Materials*

Capstone, Unit 7, Lesson 5, "Balance of Payments," pp. 210-211.
MCG, Teaching Strategies, International Trade, Lesson 16, "Foreign Currencies and Foreign Exchange, : pp. 103-108; Lesson 17, "Ruples and Dollars: The Tale of Two Currencies," pp. 109-114; Lesson 18, "Exchange Rates," pp. 115-122.

Content Statement

*20.7 The balance of payments accounts are reported in three sections. These sections distinguish trade involving basic goods and services from that involving capital resources and financial assets issued by businesses and government, and official transactions of reserve currencies and other assets.

Evidence of Student Learning

From a study of the U.S. Balance of Payments in recent years, students will *locate, explain,* and *record* entries in the current "accounts" and the "capital" accounts, describing the trends that appear.

EconomicsAmerica *Materials*

Capstone, Unit 7, Lesson 5, "Balance of Payments," pp. 210-211.
MCG, Teaching Strategies, International Trade, Lesson 13, "Balance of Payments," pp. 77-82.

Content Statement

*20.8 Countries often run surpluses or deficits in either their current or capital accounts, but the overall balance of payments account for a country must balance.

Evidence of Student Learning

In a short essay, students will *explain* why the overall balance of payments always sums to zero, even if a country such as the United States has an unfavorable balance of trade with another country.

EconomicsAmerica *Materials*

Capstone, Unit 7, Lesson 5, "Balance of Payments," pp. 210-211.
MCG, Teaching Strategies, International Trade, Lesson 13, "Balance of Payments," pp. 77-82.

Content Statement

*20.9 The balance of trade figures regularly reported in the media include only the deficit or surplus position of merchandise exports. Therefore, this figure reflects only a small part of a nation's overall balance of payments account.

Evidence of Student Learning

After studying United States Department of Commerce data on U.S. imports and exports for recent years, students will *analyze* the current balance of trade position of the United States with Japan, Canada, the Soviet Union, Great Britain, and Saudi Arabia.

EconomicsAmerica *Materials*

Capstone, Unit 7, Lesson 5, "Balance of Payments," pp. 210-211.

* Indicates statements that would normally be covered in a one-semester Capstone course in economics.

MCG, Teaching Strategies, International Trade, Lesson 13, "Balance of Payments," pp. 77-82.

Content Statement

•20.10 Increasingly, we live in a global economy where what is done in this nation affects the rest of the world, and what is done there affects this nation. Economic issues associated with this trend must be analyzed by examining trends in trading levels, investments, foreign exchange values, and changes in public policies affecting these sectors.

Evidence of Student Learning

Students will *explain* how a country can have a surplus in its balance of trade and at the same time have a deficit in its balance of payments. Students will also *describe* the kind of information provided by a study of changes in the value of one country's currency compared to currencies of other nations.

EconomicsAmerica *Materials*

Capstone, Unit 7, Lesson 6, "Ripples," pp. 212-213; Unit 7, Lesson 9, "Disagreements over World Trade," pp. 219-221.
MCG, Teaching Strategies, International Trade, Lesson 21, "The U.S.-Japan Trade Relationship: How Fair Is It?" pp. 143-150; Lesson 22, "Disagreements over World Trade," pp. 151-160; Lesson 23, "World Trade and Developing Countries: What to Do?" pp. 161-168.

21. INTERNATIONAL ASPECTS OF GROWTH AND STABILITY

Same as for preceding grade level, and also:

Content Statement

21.3 The level of real GDP per capita is frequently used to compare the level of economic development in different nations.

Evidence of Student Learning

Students will *analyze* data on real GDP per capita for each of the following countries and will *draw conclusions* pertaining to each country's level of economic development: China, India, Mexico, Canada, Japan and the United States.

EconomicsAmerica *Materials*

The Senior Economist, "Economic Reform in China," Vol. 9, No. 2; "Reforming the Economies of Eastern Europe," Vol. 6, No. 4.

Content Statement

21.4 The international transfer of technology and the exchange of productive resources and finished goods and services have led to increased interdependence among nations.

Evidence of Student Learning

Students will *explain* in a short essay how international trade among countries has led to increased interdependence and will *give several examples*.

EconomicsAmerica *Materials*

MCG, Teaching Strategies, International Trade, Lesson 4, "Trade and Specialization," pp. 24-29; Lesson 3, "Trade Around the World," pp. 51-53.

Content Statement

21.5 Increasing international economic interdependence causes economic conditions and policies in one nation to affect economic conditions in many other nations.

Evidence of Student Learning

Students will *analyze* data on the kinds and value of goods that Japan, Canada, Mexico, and Germany export to the United States and will *predict* the likely effect a recession in the United States would have on the economies of these countries.

EconomicsAmerica *Materials*

Capstone, Unit 7, Lesson 6, "Ripples," pp. 212-213.
MCG, Teaching Strategies, International Trade, Lesson 12, "Laws Influence Trade," pp. 71-75.
The Senior Economist, "International Competition," Vol. 3, No. 1.

Content Statement

21.6 Public policies affecting foreign trade impose costs and benefits on different groups of people; decisions on these policies reflect economic and political interests and forces.

Evidence of Student Learning

In an essay on the value of trade, students will *state* the costs and/or the benefits of three current trade policies of the United States.

EconomicsAmerica *Materials*

Capstone, Unit 7, Lesson 9, "Disagreements over World Trade," pp. 219-221.
MCG, Teaching Strategies, International Trade, Lesson 22, "Disagreements over World Trade," pp. 151-159.
The Senior Economist, "International Competition," Vol. 3, No. 1.

Index of Terms

Numbers in parentheses ( ) are content statement numbers.